Praise for *One If b*

One If by Land is a well-researched book that explores our border issues with unflinching integrity. It provides a depth of understanding for those who want a comprehensive understanding that goes well beyond the talking points of the political and entertainment media. In the process it provides Border Patrol agents a voice that is seldom heard by the public.

Border Patrol agents are patriotic, hardworking men and women dedicated to protecting our country. Exposing the obstacles agents face every day will make us more effective in accomplishing our mission. On behalf of the nearly 3,500 rank-and-file men and women of the US Border Patrol in the Tucson, Arizona sector, it is my pleasure to endorse *One If by Land* and declare it a must-read for all who want an insight into our nation's border issues.

> *Brandon Judd, President, National Border*
> *Patrol Council, Local 2544 (AFL-CIO)*

Often when one of the major networks does a story about illegal aliens, they show a couple of small children with a poor woman who plaintively tells a tale of poverty and victimization that has forced her into a dangerous trek across the desert in the hopes of finding a better life for her children and herself. You will never see the faces of the dangerous thugs who now terrorize American ranchers and communities all along the border. You won't see the faces of the family members who have seen their loved ones murdered by drug-dealing border crossers. No, you will not see life as it really is on our southern border. You will, instead, see Janet Napolitano declaring the border "safe," and anyone who suggests anything to the contrary being portrayed as racist xenophobes.

One If by Land shines a spotlight on the gritty truth that is the chaos and terror ripping apart our southern border and the lives of those who, for generations, have made a home near it.

> *Tom Tancredo, United States House of Representatives, 1999–2009*

As with the previous two books that I have worked with Bill Daniel on, he has done a remarkable job of "separating the wheat from the chaff" with this excellent piece of research. It has been clear for a long time that political agendas as well as a certain degree of personal protectionism of career status have been at the root of the continued failure to achieve meaningful progress in the battle for our border. At stake here is the safety and welfare of all of America, not just border ranchers. Sadly, the duplicitous approach to policy by so many of those who should be leading the fight has failed all who live in and legally visit this great nation.

Larry A. Dever, Sheriff of Cochise County

One If by Land

Also by William R. Daniel

Shootout at Miracle Valley
Shootout at Miracle Valley: The Search for Justice

Next book

Conspiracy: Big Oil and the Memo That Changed the World

One If by Land

What every American needs to know about
our border

William R. Daniel

One If by Land: What every American needs to know about our border

Published by Wheatmark®
1760 East River Road, Suite 145
Tucson, Arizona 85718 U.S.A.
www.wheatmark.com

ISBN: 978-1-60494-820-2
LCCN: 2012938872

ONE IF BY LAND is dedicated to the ranchers and citizens living along the border with Mexico, as well as law enforcement personnel who protect our borders. This book is the result of conversations with ranchers, citizens, members of law enforcement, government agencies, intelligence personnel, and others who spoke out with considerable candor, knowing that livelihoods, careers, and sometimes personal safety would be at risk. Despite the possibility of reprisal, scores of people related their experiences and gave their testimonies about not only the border, but also about the governmental dysfunction that threatens the well-being of the country.

It is especially important to note the ultimate sacrifice rancher Rob Krentz and Border Patrol agent Brian Terry made—simply by doing their jobs and living their lives.

And finally, *One If by Land* is dedicated to all Americans who want to move beyond sound bites and agenda-driven misinformation, which distort and conceal the truth about our borders. Welcome to the border and what has been hidden from you.

Contents

Foreword

IF YOU DO NOT appreciate how your vote in any democratic election directly impacts your trust in government then Bill Daniel's *One If by Land* will show you how your vote matters.

In the United States, we live on the precipice of anarchy when our elected representatives choose not to lead the people and manage government programs. When appointed leaders in the executive branch fail to uphold the duties and responsibilities of their offices, we often see many ambitious, lower-level executives attempting to fill that vacuum, largely for their own promotion.

When this happens, America's domestic and foreign policy becomes the agenda of the non-elected bureaucratic government official. This shadow government, led by these "blue-flamers," then designs and publicly announces the policies of our government.

This leaves the elected part of our government with a choice: Representatives can play catch-up with a virtually unknown bureaucracy's already-implemented program, assuming the policy and programs as their own, or they can admit that they have no control over their agencies and programs. The first choice is a dangerous gamble with the public's trust. The latter choice almost always becomes a political dagger, especially in the run-up to a national election.

The ironic reality is that ambitious unelected and non-appointed US government senior managers are not evil. They are often well-intentioned individuals who have dedicated a lifetime of service to the people of the United States, the Constitution, and the government, but get lost along the way in the elixir of power and notoriety. They are less than one percent of the hard-working and honest law enforcement men and women of our country. When our elected and appointed officials fail to lead and manage their agencies, the risk of catastrophic mistakes increases un-proportionally to any expected beneficial outcome. In the case of Fast and Furious, poor leadership, ambition, bad assumptions, and poor judgment cost the lives of US citizens, US law enforcement officers, and Mexican citizens, including the bad guys.

This book also peels back the layers of deception and misdirection with our "war on drugs" and our relationship to our narco-state neighbor, Mexico. Bill Daniel looks at how our government officials willingly ignore the fact that Chapo Guzman and an oligarchy of wealthy families control Mexico.

Our government leaders continue to proclaim that our border is much safer than it has ever been. But the government's own facts show that there are more drugs available on the streets of America than in the history of this country's addiction crisis. "We the People," fail to recognize that our survival as a society depends on investments in fixing those in the throes of addiction and providing jobs to those in recovery.

We need to tell the truth about Mexico: It is a failed state, lost in corruption and void of integrity. The next PRI president, Nieto, has already been bought and paid for by the cartels. It is time we decertify Mexico as a cooperating country in reducing the drugs that are produced in, and transit from, Mexico. Decertification allowed honest Colombians to regain control of their country. Decertification will allow honest Mexicans to regain control of theirs. A difficult pill to swallow? Certainly. Eliminating trade with Mexico will be hard on Americans and tougher on Mexicans. But how else can we get the attention of Mexico's oligarchy? It is better to face up to protecting Americans now than to have that crash at the end of 2012 when Mexican cartels amp up their war on rivals, the thousands of Mexican factories arrayed along their northern border, and popular tourist destinations.

One If by Land examines how "We the People" should be the authors of what defines us as an American society. What are our values, ethics, and character? Coupled with the power struggles of political groups, how do those values, ethics, and character interact with our decision to protect, defend, and provide law enforcement services to our people? How do they play in terms of integrity and public trust?

Bill Daniel also examines how fundamental truths get buried for political power and money. He explores how the losers are the people of the US and our international neighbors. President Obama's "Medvedev moment" is too often the values by which our government functions. Unfortunately, it is not exclusive to just one party or administration. How do you feel when your president cannot tell you the truth because there is a risk of backlash? Is the political party more important than transparency to the electorate? I do not think our founding fathers envisioned that paradigm.

As you read this book you will be angry. Think about who these government officials are accountable to and then examine how you vote. When you enjoy that constitutionally guaranteed privilege in the next election, how do you decide which person deserves that vote? Do TV and radio personalities determine how you vote? I hope not.

Anthony Coulson, ASAC (ret.) of the DEA's Tucson District Office. Coulson, a twenty-eight year veteran of the DEA, directed the federal government's drug enforcement strategy in Southern Arizona from November 2003 to August 2010.

Preface

"A nation that is afraid to let its people judge the truth and false-
hood in an open market is a nation that is afraid of its people."
                                        President John F. Kennedy

IN THE VAST EXPANSE between Washington, D.C., and the West
Coast, Americans labor every day to put food on the table, raise their
families, and leave behind a country that allows for their children a
life filled with more opportunity and liberty than they experienced.
To millions of Americans, these simple desires reflect the American
dream and are a gift from our founding fathers.

In the process they wish to live lives unabused by outside forces.
Oddly enough, this is both the strength and weakness of America.
The average American leaves others alone and expects the same. What
they get are terrorists flying into the Twin Towers, an out-of-control
national debt, and the border situation.

American citizens are unique. Their tolerance and forgiveness is
often labeled as ignorance. But when pushed too far, they have been
willing to give their lives on the beaches of France fighting fascists,
or in the fields of Mississippi standing against racists. And so it is in
twenty-first century America.

Oppression through fear is the same, whether it originates from
the cartels in Mexico or the political establishment in Washington,
D.C. This is what one should keep in mind when judging the credibility of those who shared their stories to make this book possible.
None of these people had anything to gain personally by coming
forward. None of these people had an axe to grind. But every one of
them had something to fear.

Many who gave accounts jeopardized their careers; others
recorded in this volume put their lives at risk. They were pushed too

far and loved their country too much to remain silent. They simply wanted to be heard.

One If by Land began as a simple project, to tell the stories of some ranchers on the Arizona border and their experiences with drug smugglers and illegal immigrants. As those stories unfolded, it became much more. It became a vehicle to give those without a voice a voice. Including people within government agencies who strive every day to ensure our safety.

It gave those who didn't share the establishment's official view on what was occurring on our borders a chance to speak out. It provided a few hundred pages to counter the millions of words that have come from Republican and Democratic administrations alike, government agencies, and powerful special interest groups. It is a small book and in a small way shows the other side of the issue. And hopefully, it proves that what average Americans think and say is important—if others are willing to listen.

Acknowledgements

SPECIAL RECOGNITION NEEDS TO be extended to Larry Dempster, whose tireless energy, counsel, and dedication helped bring this book to the public. Without his partnership and resolve to see that the border ranchers' stories were told, this project would not have been possible.

Previously, Larry Dempster fulfilled the dying wish of Cochise County sheriff Jimmy Judd to make the true story of the shootout at Miracle Valley public. The result was a two-volume set (*Shootout at Miracle Valley* and *Shootout at Miracle Valley: The Search for Justice*) that chronicled the bravery and restraint of the citizens of Cochise County and Sheriff Judd's deputies when confronted by a militant and radical cult that came from the south side of Chicago and settled in Miracle Valley, Arizona. Larry Dempster is a true friend.

The tremendous help given to this book by people who have lost loved ones is forever appreciated. There is no way to adequately express appreciation for their selfless contributions.

It is also important to single out and thank Alberto Moore whose generous and principled advice was greatly appreciated. Moore was especially valuable in providing access to experts from differing perspectives concerning border issues and added greatly to *One If by Land*. Alberto Moore is truly an honorable man.

A book is a cooperative effort and without the help and contributions of people like Sheriff Larry Dever, Raul Castro, Bill Breen, Anthony Coulson, Ed Ashurst, John Ladd, Carolyn Terry, Don Barnett, Sue Krentz, Ed Pyeatt, Rod Rothrock, Gary Thrasher, Wendy and Warner Glenn, George Monzingo, Walt Kolbe, Hamdy Singury, Mike Detty, Jim Runyon, Seth Nadel, and countless others, *One If by Land* would not have been written.

It is also impotant to acknowledge those who shared so much, but could not be identified. You know who you are, and thank you.

One If by Land

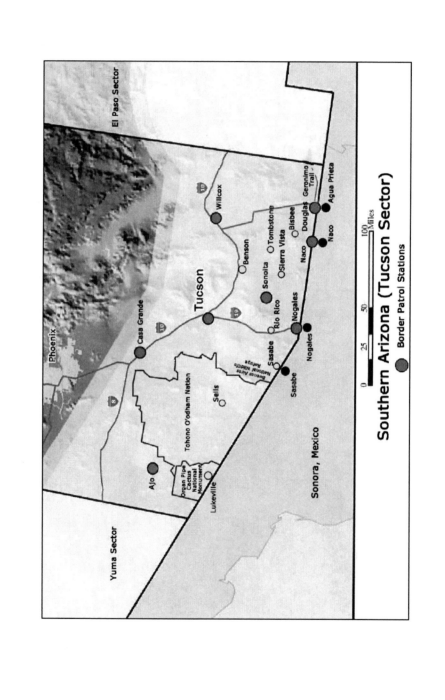

Southern Arizona (Tucson Sector)

● Border Patrol Stations

Chapter One

The Smugglers' Light

"We used to be very bold and now we're bold in our message, but we are smarter in our approach. We realize we're dealing with the cartel and they don't play fair."

American rancher, 2011[1]

A HUNDRED AND FORTY years ago the southern border of the United States was a dangerous place. No place was more dangerous than the border country of the Arizona Territory. Settlers were kidnapped, shot, mutilated, and robbed. Ranches were raided and buildings burned. Cattle and horses were rustled. Citizens lived with fear and a gun within easy reach.

And yet the federal government told them that it was safe. After all, the violence in Sonora and Chihuahua was much worse. In fact, the Mexican government was fearful Sonora would be depopulated. All of this made little difference, however, to an American citizen being murdered in Guadalupe Canyon or on the road to Tucson. It was the age of the "Indian Wars."

Apaches were raiding from their strongholds in the Sierra Madres across the border into Arizona Territory. But the government reported there was progress being made. The great Apache leader Victoria was slain in the Mexican State of Chihuahua, and the Mexican government started to regain control of that area.[2]

As a result of a unique border protocol, United States general George Crook crossed the border and headed into the Sierra Madres. He succeeded in killing or capturing most Apache leaders, with the exception of Geronimo.[3]

General Nelson Miles replaced General Crook, and with the help of five thousand soldiers and high-tech heliographs chased Geronimo to ground. Facing death at the hands of overwhelming Mexican forces or surrendering to Miles, Geronimo chose the latter. On September 4, 1886, Geronimo surrendered in Skeleton Canyon, Arizona Territory.[4]

Geronimo surrendered but the violence continued.

With much fanfare and a flurry of self-congratulation, the Army announced victory over the "Indians" in the Southwest. A fawning press picked up the story and America breathed a sigh of relief. Historians and newspapers remarked, "The border was an administrative problem and not a military one."[5] This was not a popular view if you lived along the Arizona-Mexico border, because it wasn't true.

Among the local papers that disagreed with the national press was the *Tombstone Epitaph*. The paper charged the military with "willful blindness." It continued, "... not a month has passed in two years without at least two murders along the border between the U.S. and Mexico. The Indians have constantly raided back and forth ..."[6] The *Tombstone Epitaph* noted that the Army headquarters were in Los Angeles and were out of touch with the realities of the border.

The newspaper was correct. In fact, 1890 was a banner year for violence from Apache raids. A May 3 article reports a surveying crew being attacked and besieged by ten Apaches. Several days later, a man was killed and another wounded when a freight wagon was attacked with Apaches armed with United States Army Springfield rifles. Violence continued unabated throughout the year.

President Benjamin Harrison's response to appeals for help was uninspiring. Harrison answered with "generalities about maintaining law and order but did nothing."[7] Inspired by the lack of leadership from Washington, D.C., the Army responded with all the ineffectiveness they could muster.

The Tombstone Epitaph was unrelenting. "Still the military insist that there are not any Indians out." The newspaper reported the cavalry was camped in a "safe place" thirty miles away from the Apaches' trail "where the officers can issue bulletins that there are no signs of Indians."[8] In fact, the Army had a policy to hunt for raiders in areas where they were sure not to be found. It helped them to maintain the position that the border was safe and secure. But the last Apache raid took place well into the twentieth century.[9]

In those early days of border violence, there were often no conspicuous good guys. At one time or another, all participants, be they Native American, Mexican, or American, were sometimes victims of the other groups' agendas.

All of which demonstrates that border issues were as complicated in the nineteenth century as they are today, and the American government's response remarkably similar. Now, like then, no politician is taking care of it.

Fast-Forward

In the shadows of the mountains in one of the remote areas of the Arizona borderlands, a rancher stands in front of his one hundred-

year-old stone house. In the darkening twilight he gazes across the
sweeping landscapes and sees lights, like his great grandfather had.
However, the lights are not from Apache campfires but from drug
smugglers. And despite assurances from Washington, D.C. about
safety on the border, he knows the cartels are here. And it affects his
life and the lives of his family. He looks toward the mountains where
his daughter and son-in-law live. No lights there. They have learned
to turn their lights off early so the smugglers moving past their home
won't know where they are in the house.

Virginia looks south toward her father's house and closes the
shade. She picks up her revolver and moves to the kitchen table where
a box sits. It is full of documents, articles, letters, clippings, and pho-
tographs. It belonged to her mother. There was a time ranchers were
more vocal. There was a time when it was safer. The spring of 2011
is not one of those times. Nonetheless, she has decided to speak out.
She picks up the box and walks to her car. After a long drive she sits
down to tell her story.

"We used to be very bold and now we're bold in our message,
but we are smarter in our approach. We realize we're dealing with
the cartel and they don't play fair. We've had close brushings with the
cartels," she says.[10]

This observation is echoed across the borderlands. One rancher
tells of walking out on his porch one morning and being greeted by
several cartel members who indicated that he should leave his gates
unlocked because "locked gates slow us down."[11] Another rancher was
told not to put up several miles of fence because it impeded moving
loads north.[12]

On a regular basis smugglers heading back to Mexico for another
load of dope will pass Virginia and her husband's ranch house and
toss rocks on the roof, turn on a drinker for cattle, or leave some other
sign that they are still present. If they want a ride, they will place
rocks across the road in order to intimidate drivers into giving them
one, or they will simply steal vehicles.

On one occasion, a rancher was driving along the Geronimo trail
and saw a man walking along the road. He carried a sack of groceries,
had a coat slung over his arm, and was accompanied by a dog. The
man stepped in front of a rancher's pickup to stop it, then approached

the driver. He asked for a ride. The armed rancher said, "I reckon so, but first I'd like my coat, groceries, and dog back."[13] The man was an illegal immigrant and had burglarized the rancher's home.

Changing Times

"It wasn't always like this. When I was growing up we had Mexican men that came across the line to work for us," relates Virginia. "We basically adopted them into our family. We loved these men. They were here for the right reasons. They were here to work, but they took what they earned back to their families in Mexico. Their homes were in Mexico. They were precious."

When the border situation started to ramp up, "One of the older gentlemen who we hadn't seen in years came back to give us a message. He told us, 'Be careful. Do not trust anyone. I do not travel in groups. When I come through, I come through alone, because the cartel is controlling everything and they will kill you. Be careful.' He added, 'I probably will never see you again, but I love you and want you to know that.'"

They had been aware that things were changing, but his message emphasized it. They took his warning seriously. They started to see a lot of families fleeing Mexico. "I don't blame them. If I were stuck down there in that mess, I'd probably be trying to work my way up here too," notes Virginia. She remembers a husband and wife who walked down the road with four children and a baby. "We gave them water and the Border Patrol was called." They were among the first of hundreds of illegal immigrants Virginia and her family would have personal contact with.

By the time Virginia grew up, married, and had a family of her

Collateral Damage

Virginia and her husband, Jay, have found at least five bodies of illegal immigrants or smugglers on their ranch. One of the dead stands out in Virginia's mind. Jay found him next to a stock-watering tank four or five days after the man died. "We know not to go near dead bodies, or handle them in any way," says Virginia. "But this situation was odd because there was a mountain lion working the area, crows and other animals. But not critter one touched this man. We thought there was something seriously wrong with this man before he died."

A month later Jay came home with a 104-degree temperature and was hardly able to stand. Virginia took him to the hospital where his temperature shot up to 106 and then plummeted to 92 degrees. He was transferred to a Tucson hospital and the first thing the doctor treating Jay asked was, "Have you had any contact with illegals?" Jay answered, "Yeah, a dead one." It was three months before Jay regained his health. His ailment was never diagnosed, which illustrates one of the problems with people who come into the United States illegally from third-world countries.

There is a rise in diseases that had been eradicated in the United States. Hepatitis B, TB, and malaria are making comebacks. But there may be an even greater threat from diseases that we have little experience with—so little experience, in fact, that they are grossly misdiagnosed in our country. One of these is Chagas disease. It is a parasitic illness that once claimed more than five thousand lives a year in Brazil.

Once Chagas passes into the chronic stage there is no cure. Eventually about 20 percent of people in the chronic stage will die, often from damage caused to the heart. It is transmitted from blood-sucking insects (called the "kissing bug" in the United States) that carry the parasite. The kissing bugs become carriers after biting an infected person or animal.

It is estimated that at least ten million Latin Americans, usually from rural areas, carry the parasite. The World Health Organization map showing endemic countries indicates that it is prevalent throughout Mexico, Central America, and South America. The same WHO map indicates that it has not crossed into the United States.

However, "approximately three hundred thousand infected people live in the United States, which is likely the result of immigration from Latin American countries."[14] Chagas is but one disease immigrating with some of the undocumented immigrants.

own, the world had totally changed. Huge groups of people were coming across the isolated ranch they operate with her parents. "My husband and I had individuals come into our house. The coyotes do terrible things to these people, and sometimes the women are raped." In one week she had two women come to her seeking help.

Their groups had left them. One had heart problems and the other had hurt her leg. One of the women who had traveled from Mexico City was highly educated and a paralegal. She spoke excellent English.

Her husband had left three years earlier for New Jersey. She hadn't heard from him for a year and had decided to come to the United States to find him. She had finally saved enough money to pay a coyote to bring her north, but her journey was over. "We sat on the porch and talked. She cried, and I cried. She said, 'I'll never see my husband.'" Virginia knew she was right.

Virginia has great compassion for the individuals, but not for what they are doing. Her attitude toward the drug and human smugglers is something else. "Those cartel and those bad guys are a whole other breed." As politicians and Americans turned a blind eye, the Arizona border was being turned upside down.

Chasing Liberty

The cartels have been scouting the border for years. Cartel lookouts are stationed throughout the American side of the borderlands. They roam the back roads and supply intelligence. They use radios and phones to relay information about where the Border Patrol is and isn't. They keep track of ranchers' whereabouts—who is home and who is not. Their presence is not only intimidating, but also dangerous.

Virginia and Jay's daughter Liberty got her first pistol when she was nine years old, although she had been shooting for several years. All of their children learned to shoot at an early age. It is one of the skills children need to know on the border for their own protection. In the wild country near the international line, for a citizen of any age to be without a gun is a dangerous proposition. This is a truth Liberty and her grandmother found out the hard way.

Virginia and Jay had left their children with her parents. A beautiful Arizona blue sky hung over the picturesque landscape as Grandpa, Grandma, and three children bailed out of two pickups. They had driven fifteen or twenty minutes up a ranch road, through a gate, and into a large pasture that contained some heifers. The grandchildren, including eleven-year-old Liberty, were "whooping it up and having a good time."

Liberty's grandpa declared they needed some hay, so the young girl and grandma climbed into the ranch pickup. Most ranch children learn to drive on their property at an early age, and Liberty was no exception. As soon as her feet could touch the pedals, she was qualified to learn how to drive on the ranch. She confidently slid in behind the wheel of the ranch pickup and shifted gears easily as they drove out of the pasture.

They laughed and made small talk as they drove to the stone ranch house and pulled up by a large barn. In a few minutes, the pickup was headed back toward the pasture loaded with hay. In the distance, approaching at a high rate of speed, was another pickup. The ranch road narrowed ahead because of a cattle guard and the young girl slowed, as did the approaching three-quarter-ton Chevy truck with two men in it. The men motioned for Liberty and her grandmother to pass over the cattle guard.

As Liberty started "putting along," her grandma realized the men in the Chevy were "part of the illegal network." As they passed, the driver stuck his head out of the window and made "some extremely obscene hand gestures and laughed at them." Liberty gripped the wheel, eyes forward, as the man yelled in border Spanish, "We want you, and we will get you!"

The young girl shifted and glanced into the rearview mirror. The Chevy was turning around behind them. Liberty heard her grandmother shout, "Let's go! We don't have time to switch drivers." Rocks sprayed as the young girl hit the gas and shifted up.

Liberty's grandmother realized she didn't have her phone, and neither of them had brought their guns. "If you have to, bust through the barb wire," she told her granddaughter. She looked frantically through the cab for a weapon and found only a lug wrench and a pair of pliers as she yelled, "Go! Go! Go!"

Liberty pressed the gas and stayed ahead of their pursuers. She was getting every bit of speed she could out of the old pickup. "Grandma, you know what they are going to do if they catch us. I know in the Bible it says 'Thou shall not kill,' but it's got to say someplace that God will understand if you need to protect someone you love."

But Grandma was thinking, "If I had a gun I would blow their despicable, nasty heads off." She looked back at the truck behind them and prayed, "Dear God, please keep your arms around this child."

The Chevy that had almost caught them was falling behind. It had a flat, and the "scouts" were driving on a rim. After several bends in the road Grandma told Liberty to turn onto a hidden road. Hearts pounding, they looked behind them. The Chevy limped past the turn. They waited. A few minutes later the Chevy drove past the hidden road again—going south. Liberty slipped back onto the ranch road and delivered the load of hay.

Cartel members, forty miles north of the border, had chased them, and they had narrowly escaped being assaulted or killed. Grandpa called the Border Patrol, but despite it having been a slow day (there were only four abandoned vehicles in the area and two groups of illegal immigrants spotted) the Border Patrol couldn't find the pair that chased Liberty and her grandmother.

A Border Patrol agent advised, "If those wackos had been able to catch you, they would have definitely carried out their threats."

America's Most Unwanted

At the time, the border was being flooded with over a million illegal immigrants a year. America's love affair with drugs was sky-rocketing, and the Arizona border with Mexico was being erased. In fact, David Aguilar, the future chief of the Border Patrol, who was once the Tucson Sector chief, would come to describe the border as "a third country that joins Mexico and the United States."[15]

The border was certainly a no-man's-land. It was a time citizens on the border suffered in silence and their children grew up in a world that no American should have to endure. But they did. They persevered. They became stronger, trying to blend a life of normality with the totally abnormal.

At times, life almost seemed normal for Virginia and Jay's family. It was summer, and school was out. It had been a day without illegal immigrants and without drug smugglers. Virginia and Jay had gone for a couple of hours, leaving their daughter Liberty (now twelve) and their youngest son (fourteen) home alone to watch the place.

Everything was fine until the dog barked. Inside their house Liberty and her brother exchanged knowing looks.

He opened the front door to see a tall man, probably an illegal immigrant or smuggler, walking toward the house. The teenager told him to stop when he tried to enter the yard. The man asked for water and started to move toward the yard again. Liberty's brother stepped forward and told him again to stop in a very determined voice. He told the man that he could have a drink from the water hose, but he couldn't come any closer. The man was persistent and aggressive, testing the boy's will—which did not bend. He noticed the holstered gun on the boy's hip.

Liberty called her grandfather, who notified the Border Patrol. She stepped from the house beside her brother. She also was armed. They watched the man drink from the hose and walk away. He crossed by the corral that contained half a dozen horses and disappeared from view—blocked by the barn. Both children knew the man was up to no good. They ran to the water tower and climbed up to the top for a better view. They knew that illegal immigrants usually sent one person ahead with others hidden to see if the coast was clear.

They saw the unwanted man sneaking toward the corral. He slipped into the corral toward the horses. It was easier to ride than walk, and people had tried to steal their horses before. The boy called out from the tower and ordered the man off the property. The man retreated and a small group of illegal immigrants stepped into view and then hurried off.

America's Most Wanted

On a Friday night, Virginia and her family gathered around the television watching *America's Most Wanted*. It was a segment highlighting the possible crossing of the border by terrorists. It focused on Agua Prieta, which is immediately across the border from Douglas, Arizona. Agua Prieta was then and still is today dominated by Chapo Guzman's Sinaloa Cartel. It is a prime center for human smuggling and drug smuggling.

At that time there were reports that individuals from Yemen were looking for passage into the United States. They were staying in a hotel in Agua Prieta looking for a coyote to bring them across the border. The program was interviewing local coyotes, who were charging up to $30,000 each to bring Arabs into the United States. As one of the coyotes in the TV segment turned around, Liberty and her brother yelled, "That's him!" It was the man who had crossed their property earlier in the week and asked for water.

Groups coming across the border illegally are made up of people willing to break the law to enter the country and continue to break the law by working in the United States. Some are people who regularly break the law whether in their homelands or the United States. Border Patrol agents have notified Virginia and her husband of murderers, rapists, thieves, and child molesters who have been apprehended crossing their property.

You Won't Shoot Me

Liberty and her brothers were raised in an environment reminiscent of pioneer families, where guns were always handy and you thought before you did something. In recent years, their house has been broken into; they have been watched and even taunted by the cartels.

When they come home to an "empty house," Jay always goes through the house while the rest of the family waits in the car. He clears the house one room at a time until it's confirmed it's safe for the others to come in. This routine is something many ranchers along the border are familiar with.

Despite their vigilance there are incidents. One night, Liberty, now a senior in high school, was taking a shower while her father talked on the phone to her oldest brother, who was attending college in Texas. Virginia was making supper, and their other son was doing homework. Outside the two family dogs weren't thinking about Texas, supper, schoolwork, or a shower; their ears perked up at a noise and they started barking.

Virginia heard the dogs and thought, "They've heard an illegal or smuggler. It's pitch dark. What are we going to do? Maybe ignore it?" Virginia thought better of it, picked up her pistol, and stuck her head out the door.

With the light coming from the house, she couldn't see much, but she did see the barking dog wasn't looking at her. She heard a noise and saw a young Mexican man by the side of the house. She was scared and enraged. "Who are you and how dare you come near my house?" she demanded.

The man spoke very good English. "You know, miss, it's not my problem you didn't know I was here." He mistakenly added, "You know I've been watching you in the shower for twenty minutes."

Her husband came out and asked, "Who do you think you are?"

The man was full of bravado. He told how he was a member of MS-13 and lived in Los Angeles. He had been down in Mexico and was headed back. Virginia didn't know if he was telling the truth, but she did know that "He was a jackass—a cocky little sucker." Virginia becomes more livid in her telling of the story. "We've called the Border Patrol, but we feel helpless." The man turned and walked into the night announcing, "You won't shoot me."

No Protection

In a sense the March 27, 2010, murder of fellow rancher Rob Krentz was not a surprise. "It was a shock—but not a surprise," Virginia says. Even before the murder, area ranchers talked about safety concerns. They would ask, "Who will be the first to be killed?" "We knew that one or more of us was going to be killed," she explains.

Virginia observes that what is going on along the border is progressive. It occurs in phases. The murder of their friend and fellow rancher Rob Krentz was another step in the ladder. "We knew full well that that was going to happen, but when it does it is very sobering.

"You learn to live with it and it becomes normal, but you never forget the danger. You don't leave children out in a yard. You are always there, and you are always armed. Little things change, like you put locks on the inside of closets."

She stops. There is so much to say. Her drive back to the ranch is long, and it is getting late. There isn't time to go through the dozens of photos spread out before her. Collectively, they provide a snapshot of the American borderlands. She sifts through photos, putting them back in the box. She can't resist telling about some of them.

The Border Patrol told them they were not allowed to take pictures. This refrain is heard again and again. "But we're documenters and some of the guys in our area have given up on us." She shows a picture of a group of illegal immigrants sitting on the ground in front of a Border Patrol vehicle. One of the men is making a gang sign for MS-13. Another picture shows a Chinese illegal. He spoke perfect English and tried to avoid having his picture taken. She stops. There are too many pictures and too many stories.

Pictures boxed—time to go and a parting thought. In the end she doesn't think the government will protect us. As the tsunami of smugglers and illegal immigrants smashes across the border from the south, to Virginia and others living on the border, the government appears to be AWOL. And nothing has changed. In late summer of 2011 her house was broken into again.

Endnotes

1. Virginia (rancher), interview, April 20, 2011.

2. Douglas V. Meed, *They Never Surrendered: Bronco Apaches of the Sierra Madres, 1890–1935.* (Tucson: Western Lore Press, 1993).

3. Meed, *They Never Surrendered.*

4. Meed, *They Never Surrendered.*

5. Odie B Clark, *Crimson Desert: Indian Wars of the American Southwest* (New York: Oxford University Press, 1974).

6. Meed, *They Never Surrendered.*

7. Meed, *They Never Surrendered.*

8. Meed, *They Never surrendered.*

9. Meed, *They Never Surrendered.*

10. Virginia, interview.

11. Rancher, interview, 2011.

12. Rancher, interview.

13. Sheriff Larry Dever, interview, October 14, 2010.

14. "Chagas disease," last modified April 19,2012.http://www.nlm.nih.gov/ medlineplus /ency /article/001372.htm.

15. Dennis Wagner, "Up on Arizona Border,"*Arizona Republic*, May 2, 2010.

Chapter Two

Terrorism in America

"They are all around us here ... "

Rancher, autumn of 2011

THE LAND SOUTH OF Arivaca to the boundary that divides the United States and Mexico is some of the roughest terrain in Arizona. It is a wild country, at the same time austere and imposing. It is mixture of ravines, canyons, hills, oaks, and Arizona dry. It is a country made for tough, no-nonsense people. But as tough and independent as ranchers are on the borderlands, sometimes the cartels are tougher. No place is this more true than in Santa Cruz County, Arizona.

The rugged terrain of this county provides a major gateway for drugs pouring into the United States. The question of who controls the countryside is sometimes in dispute. As in Mexico, control is often a matter of proximity to the border. And in this equation, choices of citizens are often made not because of the "security" provided by the Border Patrol and Homeland Security, but because of the heavy hand of the cartels. On the border rhetoric and reality are two different things.

A rancher who was very forthright in his opinions two years ago is now fearful of talking. He is in a bind. His government tells him he is safe, but armed cartel lookouts are almost constantly present on the hills of his ranch. He urgently says, "They are all around us here." He continues, "I know the Border Patrol isn't much help, but they're all we got. I can't piss them off. I don't have anybody else." His behavior is being controlled by the cartels and his safety ignored by our government. He is but one victim of narco-terrorism in the United States.

In the summer of 2010 Homeland Security director and former Arizona governor Janet Napolitano visited Texas and assured America that the "border has never been more secure."[1] In an interview with the media, Napolitano added that she is not sure what "secure" means. She may not understand what secure means, but many ranchers on the border clearly understand the meaning of "unsecured." They live it.

The Cartels Seize Control of the Border

In 2002 the Border Patrol closed the fence between Nogales (USA) and Nogales, Sonora (Mexico). The Border Patrol built the fence, extending approximately four to five miles east and west from Nogales, with the intention of pushing smugglers and illegal aliens into the desert. It was a partial success.

Many ranchers of Santa Cruz County witnessed the "success" of the closing of Nogales fence firsthand. Streams of trucks crossed their ranches at all hours of the day and night on roads that were rough to begin with. Many ranch roads became "international highways." As one rancher recalls, "One night I was surrounded by sixteen to seventeen truckloads of people with twenty or twenty-five people in each truck."

The rancher continues, "The next night this happened again, and we were run off the road. Our road. They were moving so fast they had their arms wrapped around each other so they wouldn't fall out—men, women, children, and babies."

The years 2003 and 2004 were really bad. Ranchers were getting thousands of illegal immigrants across their land every day. Smugglers were cutting barbed wire fence and bringing loads of drugs over using horses and human mules. The Border Patrol had little effect on the intruders—though they made some attempts.

In Santa Cruz County, the government positioned vehicle obstacles along the border, often putting them in washes. Despite being asked to position the obstacles on the south side of the barbed wire fences they were often positioned on the north side. When the monsoon rains arrived, the obstacles were washed south, cutting huge gaps in ranch fences.

The Army Corps of Engineers in Cochise County addressed this problem. There are border areas in Cochise County with very substantial fencing. In washes, however, huge gates were built and are opened in the fence during the monsoons. The gates are so large and cumbersome, they remain open throughout the monsoon season, which generally starts around the first of July and ends in the middle of September.

During the monsoon season border gates are opened in the washes and are often unguarded. Photo by William Daniel.

As a result of washed-out or cut fences, cattle wander south of the border while illegal immigrants and drugs pass north. At one time ranchers could go south and get their cattle. "The stakes are much higher now," notes a rancher. It is unsafe to travel without a gun, but "if you go south into Mexico with a gun, you are gone."

Several years ago there was a major change in the area—things became much more dangerous. The local smugglers disappeared. They were not bought out. They were encouraged to either leave or die.

The ranchers of southern Arizona didn't know what was happening, but they were feeling the first effects of a startling fact. The great cartels had to all intents and purposes seized control of the Mexican side of the border.

Power abhors a vacuum. In the absence of any meaningful federal law enforcement efforts to stop drug smuggling into the United States, the cartels started moving north—in force. Territories were being carved out and a new order took root.

Along the borderlands and into Arizona itself corridors were established, responsibilities delegated, and the hell engulfing Mexico was on its way north. If you walk these lands today with Border Patrol agents, they can tell who and which cartel controls the canyons and corridors that extend into America. These corridors supply a large proportion of the drugs and illegal immigrants that feed the insatiable appetite of some Americans for drugs and cheap labor.

Rape Trees

The times were changing and with it the attitudes of illegal immigrants. "Once they asked for help, now they demand help," a rancher observes. More than one rancher has faced illegal immigrants who will not take no for an answer. They will not leave the ranchers' property.

The rancher continues, "The character of stuff started changing. That's when we started seeing the 'rape trees.'" It is a common practice for coyotes who lead groups of illegal immigrants across the border to rape any female they want—including children. The coyotes often will encourage other men to participate and force husbands to watch.

Rape tree on the border.

The coyotes hang the women's bras and underwear in trees. "That's how these disgusting animals mark where they have raped women," notes the rancher. Today, rape trees are present on many ranches in southern Arizona.

People unfamiliar with the border are astounded at stories of the rape trees. Some believe they are urban legends. Confirming the stories are ranchers, Border Patrol agents, supervisors, intelligence experts, and others in authority. One agent admitted the existence of rape trees and explained that some women will buy contraceptives, anticipating the possibility of being raped on the way north. After a long pause the agent added, "If I ever come on someone doing that I'll kill him."[2]

Before the cartels took over "you had moral smugglers," observed another rancher. "If the Border Patrol caught a smuggler they might say, 'Oh, you got me.' The agent would reply 'Yeah,' and they would walk out. They don't do that any longer. An agent doesn't know when they'll be accused of a civil rights violation or be killed."

The National Guard vs. the Federales

In 2010, President Obama agreed to send 1,200 National Guard troops to the southern border of the United States to silence demands coming from Arizona governor Jan Brewer and a rising tide of public sentiment that he secure the border. To many observers, it was a reluctant, halfhearted, insincere gesture.

In 2007, President George Bush was equally reluctant when he was pressured into the same position of sending National Guard troops to Arizona. In what was also to prove to be an empty gesture, Bush sent six thousand troops.

While a large number of the six thousand National Guard troops deployed by President Bush were billeted in Tucson resort hotels and served only in support roles to the Border Patrol, a few almost ended up on the border.[3] Of these troops it has been reported that each of the soldiers were issued ten bullets.

"There were guys from Louisiana, New York, and New Jersey," recalls a Santa Cruz County rancher. " They were in awe of what was happening on the border." The small contingent of National Guard troops took up positions on a hill near the border.

South of the border the Mexican Federal Judicial Police (aka Federales) learned of the presence of the Guard troops on the hill. They promptly crossed the border and penetrated several miles into the United States. The Federales, equipped with bandoliers and assault weapons, confronted the National Guard Unit. The Federales demanded the American troops be removed. The commander checked with his superiors, and the Guard Unit withdrew to Tucson. Control over America territory was being abdicated. An old time rancher remembers the day of the retreat. "Some of these guys were back from Iraq—do you know how mad they were?"

The Not-So-Judicial Police

The senior law enforcement agency in Mexico is the Federal Judicial Police. The Office of the Attorney General heads it. The Federal Judicial Police has power and duties very similar to the Federal Bureau of Investigation and Drug Enforcement Agency. Their jurisdiction covers the entire country of Mexico, and as will be noted without any sense of hyperbole, parts of the United States. It also has a well-deserved reputation as an untrustworthy and corrupt organization. The personnel of the Federal Judicial Police are known for their attitudes and arrogance. They bow to no one except the cartels.

Each of Mexico's thirty-one states also has State Judicial Police, which are under the control of the governor of each state. The low wages of the Federal and State Judicial police make it easy for the cartels to infiltrate them.

Every state in Mexico also has municipal police. These forces enforce minor laws and traffic infractions. It is estimated that along the border, 90 percent of these law enforcement personnel are on the payrolls of the cartels.[4] In addition, there are police forces for towns and cities. Finally, there is a highway patrol in Mexico that is equally susceptible to graft.

It should be noted that the Mexican Army is no less corrupt than the other government organizations in Mexico. On the contrary, as will be explained later, the Mexican Army is arguably the most corrupt organization in the Mexican government.

In July of 2008, the National Guard troops were pulled out of Arizona as planned. The level of violence, smuggling, and influence of the great cartels continued unchecked—in fact the cartels were emboldened.

Unscheduled Landing

The fragility of American sovereignty over the borderlands is further illustrated by the landing of a Mexican military helicopter on the Tres Bellotas Ranch in 2005. The Tres Bellotas ranch belongs to Lyle Robinson. His ranch has limited phone service and he generates his own electricity.[5] Despite the remote location, the ranch can be busy—with traffic from the south.

A "fuel guy" who was making a delivery to the Tres Bellotas ranch discovered the intrusion of the Mexican Military helicopter. He was about ready to pump some diesel in a tank and stopped. He watched in disbelief as the helicopter landed and discharged Mexican troops.

"He said he didn't know what they wanted, but he thinks they were demanding fuel," relates a rancher. According to the rancher the fuel guy said, "If I had thought about it, I would have given them some. The helicopter would have gone up about three feet and crashed."

Also present at the unscheduled landing was R. D. Ayers, who had driven to Tres Bellotas to check up on his injured dog (the owner of the ranch is also a veterinarian.) Ayers claimed he saw the helicopter circle and land. When he approached the Huey-type helicopter, "Six men in black commando-type uniforms stepped out." He relates, "Five had ski-type masks over their faces, and they wore body armor and carried automatic rifles." On their sleeves, Ayers saw the word "Mexico."[6]

According to a rancher, "R. D. starts yelling at the men to get out of his country. He confronts Federales jumping out of a helicopter to get the hell out of his country, and they did." The FBI later approached R. D. and told him to keep his mouth shut.

Apparently not only does the American government not want pictures taken of illegal immigrants, but citizens are not to speak of incursions. At the same time the media often appears uninterested in reporting incursions by Mexican authorities or armed cartel units. However, ignoring reality doesn't change it.

As recently as January 22, 2011, "Five armed members from

the Mexican Army chased a vehicle into the northbound inspection lane" inside the U.S. Port of Entry at Naco, Arizona. They forcibly attempted to remove a driver from a pickup and take him back into Mexico. The Border Patrol interrupted them, and the Mexican troops "pointed their weapons at the CBP (Customs Border Protection) staff." After a brief standoff the Mexican troops retreated without the American driver of the pickup.[7]

Open Borders

On the border ranches the unusual is the common. More than one border rancher has looked across the international line and watched Mexican Army troops or Federales supervise the crossing of illegal immigrants into the United States. A rancher recalls, "We would look down into the wash and see Federales and vehicles with the people lined up waiting to cross into the US. Now with the vehicle barriers, they often wait until the monsoons. The barriers wash out, and since it takes three or four months for the barriers to be replaced, the Federales and illegals reappear."

But vehicle traffic has not stopped because of the barriers. The smugglers (human and drug) will breach the wire fences on the border ranches at will and drive north. The barbed wire fence on one ranch is cut two or three times a week.

A local ranchers says, "Once they get past the border there is nothing to stop them." There was a road being built along the border to improve lateral movement of the Border Patrol agents—the intention was a twenty-minute response time. For some unexplained reason, "The administration stopped construction when they found out about it."

The agents on the ground are trying—but the contradictory mission they are being asked to perform frustrates them. They are mandated to protect and secure the border, but at the same time often expected to be victim advocates for illegal immigrants.

Border Control

There is a fight to control the border. Sometimes, however, it is a fight between rival cartels. A rancher and one of his hands witnessed this firsthand. As they crouched behind some rocks they watched "A running gunfight. These guys shooting automatic weapons at each other—and when they'd go through the gates, they would stop and shut the gates. That's the old smuggler ways. Back in those days they didn't want the rancher to be mad at them. Now they don't care. Now the ranchers don't want the smugglers mad at them."

Much of the border in Santa Cruz County is under the watchful eye of the cartels. There always are six to twelve observers on the peaks of border ranches. "We're always under surveillance," notes a rancher. The extensive cartel observer network is not limited to border ranches. It runs north up to Interstate 8. Not only does it facilitate drug trafficking, but also it is intimidating to citizens living in rural areas.

The Border Patrol will occasionally run them off, but as soon as the agents leave the observers return. If the Border Patrol actually picks up any of the lookouts, they have "ditched their weapons and are just illegals looking for a better life."

In the early days the observers were equipped with standard radios and the Border Patrol would often listen in on their conversations. Recently, the smugglers upgraded to more sophisticated equipment that encrypts their conversations. A rancher asked, "Why don't you de-encrypt it." The answer was, "We aren't allowed to." They explained it was an invasion of the spies' "privacy."

Privacy appears to be a one-way street, however. Because cell phone reception is so poor in rural Santa Cruz County, one rancher bought a satellite phone so he would always be able to contact the Border Patrol if needed. He used the expensive satellite phone for several weeks. At first the phone worked well, then started to drop calls. Finally, all of his calls began mysteriously routing through a Mexican operator in Hermosillo. Even Verizon's technical people couldn't explain it.[8] A Border Patrol agent confirmed what the rancher suspected—the cartels were rerouting his calls and listening in.

Federal Corridors

An especially troublesome issue in the borderlands is the establishment of wilderness areas by Congress. An example of such an area is the Buenos Aires National Wildlife Refuge. The federal refuge is located near the western edge of Santa Cruz County and shares the international border with Mexico. It stretches ten miles north into Pima County. Smugglers often use areas like the Buenos Aires National Wildlife Refuge as smuggling corridors into the United States.

In 2006, an eighty-mile stretch of the Buenos Aires National Wildlife Refuge southern boundary was closed to the public "due to human safety concerns." In 2010 some other areas were closed and more signs were erected, warning that "smuggling and illegal immigration may be encountered in this area."[9] A rancher whose property borders the refuge declares, "Whoever runs the refuge has declared that no one is to drive or go on certain parts of the refuge. This is a wildlife refuge that no one can go to, because we are giving it to Mexico."

The problem is that "wilderness areas" on the border often end up not protecting the environment, but protecting smugglers. Critics argue rules established in the refuges handcuff the Border Patrol and Immigration and Customs Enforcement (ICE). Wilderness areas typically do not permit, or at least inhibit:

1. Use of any mechanized equipment (including helicopters or bicycles)
2. Evidence of the hand of man.
3. Placement of sensors or cameras.
4. Structures.
5. Setting up FOBs (forward operating bases), including but not limited to mobile radar units (subject to extensive regulation).

Despite concerns from many in law enforcement, the Congressional House Subcommittee on National Parks, Forests, and Public Lands is considering creation of a Tumacacori Wilderness area west of the Buenos Aires National Wildlife Refuge, as well as border areas in New Mexico.

The Tumacacori Mountains extend into Mexico. Human traffickers and drug smugglers have already trashed the rugged mountain area. The practical effect of a Tumacacori Wilderness would be to facilitate the smuggling of drugs and illegal immigrants into the United States.

A local area rancher criticized a prominent Congressman supporting the creation of a Tumacacori Wilderness area. "This is his baby—he wants that place really bad. Imagine that, his legacy would be a drug corridor."

MOU

It is argued that memorandums of understanding (MOU) between the Border Patrol and Federal land managers take care of any possible enforcement concerns on refuges or designated wilderness areas.

Even the GAO (General Accounting Office) recognizes that federal land managers hinder securing the border. Anu K. Mittal from the GAO testified before the US House of Representatives "that it has routinely taken several months to obtain permission from land managers to move mobile surveillance systems. The patrol agent-in-charge told us that before permission can be granted, land managers generally must complete environmental and historic property assessments—as required by the National Environmental Policy and National Historic Preservation acts."[10] It is a process that can take months, during which the need of equipment at that particular location has changed.

Beyond the environmental issues and operational consideration there are safety concerns. The Organ Pipe Cactus National Monument, for example, is a dangerous place. On August 2, 2002, twenty-eight-year-old park ranger Kris Eggle was shot to death while helping Border Patrol agents catch two men suspected by Mexican officials in a drug-related quadruple murder.[11] The Monument can still be a dangerous place. A recent GAO report indicates, "Drug smugglers frequently used the parking lot of the Visitor Center on the Organ Pipe Cactus National Monument as a staging area."[12]

Even as some politicians in Washington, D.C., appear to work to make the world safer for drug smugglers and human traffickers, many ranchers feel betrayed and alone on the border. Ranchers are threatened by drug smugglers, are sued by American courts, and are having their land invaded by illegal immigrants, bandits, and heavily armed drug smugglers. Murdered rancher Rob Krentz paid the ultimate price of an unsecured border.

Ranchers are outnumbered, outvoted, and ignored—unless they fight back against the cartels. And then God help them.

Endnotes

1. Janet Napolitano (speech, University of Texas, El Paso, January 31, 2011).

2. Border Patrol agent, interview, 2010.

3. Arizona State Senator Al Melvin, interview, 2010.

4. Intelligence analyst, interview, 2011.

5. Leo Banks, "Images From the Battleground," *Tucson Weekly*, August 11, 2005.

6. Banks, "Images From the Battleground."

7. Cochise County Sheriff's Department Incident Report, April 4, 2011.

8. Banks, "Images From the Battleground."

9. "Uptick in Violence Forces Closing of Parkland Along Mexico Border to Americans," June 16, 2010, http://www.foxnews.com/us/2010/06/16/closes-park-land-mexico-border-americans/.

10. Anu K. Mittal, General Accounting Office, testimony before U.S. House of Representatives, April 15, 2011.

11. Tom Clynes, "Arizona Park 'Most Dangerous' in U.S.," *National Geographic News*, January 13, 2003.

12. GAO, "Additional Actions Needed to Better Ensure a Coordinated Federal Response to Illegal Activity on Federal Lands," November 18, 2010, http://www.gao.gov/products/GAO-11-177.

Chapter Three

Standing Alone

"If an illegal immigrant crosses the border and the Border Patrol sees him, but doesn't count him, has he crossed the border?"

Anonymous ICE Agent

WITH THE GREAT CARTELS extending their power and influence into once sovereign areas of the United States, the Barnett brothers were among the first to fight back. As with other border ranchers, drug smugglers and illegal immigrants poured across Roger Barnett's ranch, located in the extreme southern portion of Cochise County. Barnett was faced with disabled water pumps, killed calves, destroyed fences and gates, and stolen trucks. His home was broken into. Trails the illegal immigrants followed across his ranch were covered "with trash ten inches deep, including human feces, used toilet paper, soiled diapers, cigarette packs, clothes, backpacks, and empty one-gallon water bottles."[1] It could not go on.

Roger Barnett and his brother Don, both with a background in law enforcement, decided they would help the Border Patrol whether or not the Border Patrol wanted any help. The brothers started placing sensors on Roger's ranch—and responding to them.

No Volunteers

Don Barnett recalls when it all started—a sensor went off in the middle of the night, and he acted. He did not wake his brother. "I grabbed a group of twenty-five or thirty illegal immigrants and called the Border Patrol. They were all mad because they had to write all these guys up." When his brother woke up the next morning, Don told him that sensor six had gone off and he had captured thirty illegal immigrants. Roger complained, "Why didn't you wake me up?" Don answered that it was no big deal, and he didn't want to bother him. However, this modest beginning was going to turn into a big deal.[2]

The brothers started to pick up more illegal immigrants. The Border Patrol's response continued to be lukewarm. Don relates how he and Roger picked up a bunch of illegal immigrants and phoned the Border Patrol, telling them, "We got a group out here." The Border Patrol complained, "We don't have anyone to pick them up."[3]

Roger Barnett is a pilot, and would sometimes patrol his ranch by plane. "We'd spot them (illegal immigrants) from the plane," relates Don. "They'd be hiding in the bush and of course we can't land the plane, so we'd call the Border Patrol." According to Don, on more than one occasion the Border Patrol replied, ""We don't have anyone that can come out right now.' So, we'd ask them for the phone number for ICE or the customs guys, because we think those are bundles of marijuana down there with them."

They answered, "No we won't give you their phone number!" Don laughs, "Boom—there they were. They were disappointed when the bundles ended up not being dope, just their little tricky bags"[4] (bags often worn around the waist to carry essential items).

The issues that surround the responsiveness of the Border Patrol are not a thing of the past with Roger Barnett. Don explains that his brother has sensors on his land just like the Border Patrol uses. With the sensors, it's possible to tell the number of illegal immigrants and their direction of travel across the Barnett ranch. It is also easy to determine if people or animals set off the sensors.

On one occasion, Roger alerted the Border Patrol that a sizable group of illegal immigrants were headed across his land and their direction of movement. He knew when the Border Patrol arrived, a certain sensor would be tripped—he waited and waited. Finally, he phoned the Border Patrol and asked them, "What's going on? What are you doing?"

The Border Patrol commander said he "didn't have the volunteers to respond." A shocked Barnett thought, "Volunteers? They're getting paid good money and they have to volunteer to do their jobs?"[5]

Recount Until You Get the Number They Want

It was during this period of exploding drug and human trafficking that some people started to become suspicious of the counts supplied by the authorities regarding the number of illegal immigrants captured and the amount of dope and drugs confiscated. Their suspicions were well founded. According to a reliable source, in one case a Border Patrol helicopter pilot out of Tucson picked up an agent on the border. Their mission was to "cut the line" (determine foot traffic and vehicle traffic by tracks left in the desert) on the border between Douglas and New Mexico.

The helicopter would hover, the agent estimated traffic, and then the aircraft would move ahead. The process was repeated until the helicopter reached the New Mexico line. After finishing, the helicopter returned to the station, and the agent gave the estimate of the number of crossers to the station chief. The station chief was supposed to forward the data to Washington, D.C.

The problem was, the agent estimated the number of crossers to be in the thousands. An unhappy station chief sent the agent and helicopter out to do a recount. Upon returning, the agent had a total about the same as the number he had initially estimated, which did not satisfy his superiors. The agent responded, "That's what I see." The second number was an estimated 2,430 crossers. The estimate was forwarded to Washington, D.C., and courtesy of a convenient typo was reported at 430.

If there were questions, the figure could be defended as an "honest mistake." The truth is, in the days when the Barnett brothers were trying to defend Roger's ranch, not only did politicians in Washington not want to hear about the flood of drugs and humans, neither did the Border Patrol. The numbers were so staggering, the Border Patrol leadership was in a "hear no, see no, speak no evil" operating mode. The political heat that accurate counts could bring to people that were supposed to be in charge of the border was unacceptable.[6]

The Border Patrol leadership concluded that they might not be able to control the border, but by God they could control the count.[7] As will become apparent later in this book, "rigging the numbers" has been raised to an art form and will conveniently help administration after administration maintain an unofficial policy of "open borders."

The Dividing Line

The Barnetts did not start doing the Border Patrol's job for them out of any vigilante mind-set. They did it in self-defense.

Around 2000 the Border Patrol started having monthly meetings with concerned citizens along the border. An FOS (Border Patrol Field Office Supervisor) talked to Don Barnett before a meeting. He told Don that his brother Roger was really going to be 'hot' in a little bit. He explained that the "people of Douglas are sick of it [illegal immigrants and drug smugglers] and we're going to have to stop it." In those days illegal immigrants would be running across Douglas residents' yards all night long as they headed north.

"Roger is going to be really unhappy," another agent told Don. "We're going to put so many men in Douglas it's going to funnel the illegal immigrants and drug smugglers toward and across your brother's ranch." They weren't going to catch them—they were going to funnel them. "You think your brother is pissed now with what's coming through, wait until we stop them in Douglas."[8]

The Border Patrol began funneling illegal immigrants across the Barnett Ranch. Photo courtesy of Donald Barnett.

Airport Road was essentially the last road on the east side of Douglas. A Border Patrol agent told Don that he was stationed on Airport Road. He said, "If I see an illegal on this side [west] of the road I'm allowed to take action. If I'm sitting here and a hundred illegal immigrants are ten feet on the other side [east] of the road I can't 'see' them—I'm not allowed to do anything."[9]

New Math: Honest Counts

It was early 2001 that Don Barnett decided, "We should start counting some of these groups. In fact, I thought, why don't I count them all? Keep track." The two men began stopping large numbers from crossing the ranch—and turning them into the Border Patrol. The biggest group they caught was ninety-three.[10]

In those days, most illegal immigrants that the Barnetts stopped understood they were doing something wrong, and when they were told to stop and sit down, they complied.

While most people were submissive, sometimes they would come up on people "that looked like they were going to take your guns away and kill you. They just had that look about them and we were extra careful."[11] Once when the Border Patrol arrived to pick a group up, they told the Barnetts, "These guys are Sinaloan Cowboys. They would kill you if they had the chance."[12]

In his first year of keeping count of the illegal immigrants they caught, Don recorded the following numbers:

Illegal immigrants caught by the Barnetts crossing Roger's ranch—2001:[13]

January	229
February	407
March	356
April	216
May	450
June	103
July	65
August	20
September	47

October	47
November	74
December	27
Total	**2,041**

The Barnetts also were stopping drug smugglers. Early one morning Don was driving north of Roger's ranch and saw a Border Patrol agent. He stopped and asked what was going on. The agent said he had lots of tracks, but couldn't figure out where they went. The agent left, but Don kept on looking. On Roger's ranch, about half a mile from where he had stopped to talk with the Border Patrol agent, Don spotted fifteen smugglers.

The Border Patrol agent was nowhere to be found, so Don radioed his brother. Roger called the Border Patrol, but the brothers were alone when they stopped the fifteen smugglers. The smugglers dropped their load and scattered, but Roger took off on his ATV and sent the smugglers back toward Don in groups of two or three. By the time the Border Patrol arrived they had captured a dozen smugglers.[14]

A Warning

The persistence of the Barnett brothers had startling results. The numbers of illegal immigrants crossing Roger's ranch plummeted. In 2001 they captured 2,041 illegal immigrants, but by 2006 the total was 688. In that period they did not release a single illegal they captured—all of them were handed over to the Border Patrol. One time the Border Patrol was busy so Don loaded a group into the back of his pickup and drove them to a Border Patrol station. On the way a Border Patrol helicopter saw him and pursued him all the way to the Border Patrol headquarters in Douglas.[15]

Illegal immigrants caught by the Barnetts crossing Roger's ranch, 2001–2007:[16]

2001	2,041
2002	2,369
2003	1,248
2004	2,431

Smugglers dropped their load of dope after being stopped by the Barnetts.
Photo courtesy of Donald Barnett.

The seized dope is loaded in Border Patrol vehicles.
Photo courtesy of Donald Barnett.

2005	1,294
2006	688
2007	203
Total	**10,274**

Dope Confiscated by the Barnetts on Roger's ranch, 2001–2007:[17]

2003	155 lb
2004	748 lb
2005	523 lb
2006	961 lb
Total	**2,387 lb (plus 1,100 lb with Border Patrol assistance)**

It's interesting that these statistics record counts made by Don Barnett from the years 2001–2007 only on weekends. Don was only able to help his brother on Saturdays and Sundays.

The effect of the efforts is clear. As the brothers persisted the amount of traffic declined. In essence, coyotes and smugglers learned and adapted. It wasn't so easy to cross Roger Barnett's ranch, so traffic started to move a canyon or two east. They would cross the ranches of Phil Krentz, Rob Krentz, and others along the isolated corridors of southeast Arizona.

A lesson learned from the Barnetts is, consistent and determined effort, even by two individuals, can make a difference. But their success caused pushback. The Barnetts and other ranchers noticed that smugglers and illegal immigrants were becoming increasingly aggressive and hostile.

It was not just Roger's house being broken into, a pickup truck stolen, or a water truck stolen. On more than one occasion, the FBI advised Roger that he shouldn't be home on certain weekends.[18] The Barnetts were making powerful enemies, and the illegal immigrants and smugglers were about to get help.

It was a time the amnesty/immigrant lobby was beginning to flex its muscles and look for a cause to use to push its agenda. It was not a good time to be a Barnett.

The Set Up

Roger Barnett was not doing anything other ranchers in the area had not done to some degree. Ranchers helped law enforcement stop drug smugglers, tried to defend their livelihoods by keeping their property from being trashed and overrun by illegal immigrants, and attempted to discourage theft and worse. However, three factors came together to make Roger Barnett a target.

First, his ranch east of Douglas, Arizona, was located on one of the busiest drug and illegal immigrant smuggling corridors in Arizona. Second, Roger Barnett appeared to have substantial financial resources. And finally, with the help of his brother Don, Roger was extremely effective in disrupting drug trafficking and illegal entrants.

Money was being lost. Cartel bosses were not happy. Coyotes and their bosses weren't happy. Powerful border politicians were not happy. Just as important, the illegal immigration lobby was displeased. It was time to get rid of the impediment to their profits and their agendas. Roger Barnett was sued.

A group of fifteen illegal immigrants (four women and eleven men) gathered near Agua Prieta, Sonora, on the night of March 6, 2004. An informant reports that one of the women was told by their coyote that bandits would probably rob them before they crossed the border. They were advised not to resist and everything would be fine.

As if upon cue the illegal immigrants were confronted by men brandishing guns. The thieves were never caught, punished, or sued. No issues of mental anguish after being robbed at gunpoint ever arose. The now penniless immigrants bravely continued toward the United States where they were warned they might meet a "bad man," in contrast presumably to the men that had held them at gunpoint and robbed them.[19]

The group illegally crossed the border east of Douglas, Arizona, and like thousands before them started across Roger Barnett's Cross Rail Ranch. The afternoon of March 7, Roger was patrolling his ranch when his dog alerted him that something was up.

The group of fifteen illegal immigrants was concealed in an indentation in the ground, surrounded by brush.[20] The rancher pulled his gun, circled the group to make sure they didn't have any weapons (which drug smugglers commonly do), and determined they weren't a threat.

"Since drug smugglers are frequently armed, I drew my handgun," Roger Barnett said in an April 18, 2007, deposition. "I holstered it after assuring myself they were not armed."

The sixty-two-year-old rancher called the Border Patrol and ordered the trespassers into the open. They responded with the exception of one of the women, "who was unresponsive." He tapped her foot, and she joined the others.[21] The Border Patrol arrived and took the illegal immigrants into custody.

But that wasn't the end of the encounter. With the help of nine lawyers, Roger Barnett was sued for $32 million.[22] It was claimed Barnett violated the civil rights of fifteen people who had illegally snuck into the country and who were trespassing on his ranch. No one expressed concern that Barnett's rights might have been violated.

The lawsuit threw a wide net—Roger Barnett was not the only target of the fifteen illegal immigrants. They also sued Barnett's wife, Barbara, his brother Don, and Cochise County sheriff Larry Dever. This came as a surprise to Don Barnett, who wasn't present the day his brother ran into the uninvited guests. Sheriff Dever was included in the suit because the Sheriff's Office had allegedly knowingly allowed Roger to detain illegal immigrants and turn them over to the Border Patrol.[23]

The suit charged the Barnetts "engaged in a private campaign and conspired with each other and others to 'hunt' and detain against their will, and at gunpoint, migrants."

Never Kick a Plastic Jesus

The Chief Judge of the US District Court for Arizona, John Roll, heard the case. Judge Roll is best remembered now for being killed by a madman on January 8, 2011, while attending a "Congress on Your Corner" meeting held by United States Representative Gabrielle Giffords.

Judge Roll dismissed the claims of ten of the illegal immigrants because they did not testify. Since they had apparently violated immigration laws, they were either back in Mexico or had disappeared into the United States.

Judge Roll threw out conspiracy charges against Barbara and Don Barnett. Roll also concluded that illegal immigrants had no constitutionally protected right to travel in the United States. He further decided the Barnetts could reasonably assume that smugglers were aiding people crossing their land. The Judge noted that the illegal immigrants were subject to a citizen's arrest under Arizona law.

The case finally came down to six plaintiffs with nine lawyers. Claims against Sheriff Dever and Don Barnett had been dismissed. It was the word of allegedly illegal immigrants versus the word of an United States rancher. The only real impartial witness was God, which is where Jesus entered the picture—in this case a plastic Jesus. It was a tearjerker.

Don Barnett watched as a female plaintiff testified that Roger Barnett had terrified her. Her story was full of tears, but the eight-person jury had remained dry-eyed. Don remembers that she then held up a plastic Jesus and wailed that her "dying mother" had given it to her. She testified that when Roger Barnett "kicked her," he broke her plastic Jesus. Don laughs and says, "Heck, by then even I was ready to convict him."[24]

The jury ruled that the six remaining plaintiffs did not have their civil rights violated. It also ruled that Roger Barnett was not guilty of false imprisonment, battery, or conspiracy.

But the plastic Jesus had taken its toll. The verdict came back on April 29, 2009. The jury awarded money to the plaintiffs for emotional distress and claims of assault. In addition, $60,000 in punitive damages was awarded to the six plaintiffs. The $32 million lawsuit had dwindled to an award of $77,802. Avoiding the obvious, lawyers for the plaintiffs claimed success.

Barnett's defense lawyer, David Hardy, commented, "When the conspiracy case was thrown out, they lost all claims for attorney fees. They were going to stack them up on Roger. There were nine attorneys, for a little case in Tucson, Arizona. They brought in three high-priced attorneys from New York. They were going to run up lawyer bills to $500,000, maybe a million dollars and stick Roger with that."[25] Hardy added, "He feels he got screwed. I have some sympathy for that view."[26]

In response to the Barnett affair, the Arizona Legislature began consideration of a law that would prohibit any punitive damages being paid to an illegal alien after winning a lawsuit. The voters approved a state constitutional amendment to that effect in 2006. The proposed bill in the legislature would make the constitutional amendment retroactive to 2004 and save Roger Barnett $60,000.

Get Roger Barnett

The attempt to crush Roger Barnett, thereby discouraging border ranchers from defending their property against illegal immigrants and drug smugglers, also played out behind the scenes. Western ranches are successful because they are combinations of private land as well as leases of state and/or federal public lands. As early as 2006 it was reported that some so-called humanitarian groups were working to put Roger Barnett out of business.

The special interest groups and powerful border politicians attempted to have state land leases held by Roger Barnett cancelled. Normally, a rancher's leases are secure as long as the land is managed responsibly and he fulfills the provisions of his contract. Roger Barnett was meticulous about his stewardship of the land whether leased or private. These efforts to get Barnett failed.

If the efforts had succeeded, the illegal immigration lobby would have made it easier for thousands of illegal immigrants to flood across not only his ranch but other private property. In addition, the profitable drug smuggling routes of southeastern Arizona would have become even more profitable.

In October of 2011 the Supreme Court upheld the ruling by the Ninth US Circuit Court of Appeals that Roger Barnett must pay four of the illegal immigrants who brought suit against him in 2004 $87,000 for emotional distress.[27] The ruling of the Ninth Circuit that Barnett was innocent of violating the trespassers' civil rights, inflicting battery, or false imprisonment was not affected.

While the Barnetts, Virginia and her family, and dozens of other ranchers faced an unprecedented wave of lawlessness, there were several important trends beginning to appear.

As illustrated, among those trends were the growing influence of amnesty/humanitarian groups, the power of border politicians, and the loss of sovereignty in some areas to the cartels.

However, what was especially significant were two questions that began to emerge. Was the poor performance of the Border Patrol in protecting the border a result of incompetence or intent? And if you couldn't depend on the Border Patrol for protection, who did you call? One rancher would answer the last question in an unorthodox manner.

Endnotes

1. Jerry Seper, "16 illegals sue Arizona Rancher," *The Washington Times*, February 9, 2009, http://www.washingtontimes.com/news/2009/feb/09/16-illegals-sue-arizona-rancher/?page=all.

2. Don Barnett, interview, July 14, 2010.

3. Don Barnett, interview.

4. Don Barnett, interview.

5. Don Barnett, interview.

6. Border Patrol agent, 2010.

7. Border Patrol agent, 2010.

8. Don Barnett, interview.

9. Don Barnett, interview.

10. Don Barnett, interview.

11. Don Barnett, interview.

12. Don Barnett, interview.

13. Records courtesy of Don Barnett.

14. Don Barnett, interview.

15. Don Barnett, interview.

16. Records courtesy of Don Barnett.

17. Records courtesy of Don Barnett.

18. Don Barnett, interview.

19. Protected source, 2010.

20. Roger Barnett, interview by Glenn Beck, *Fox News*, February 17, 2009.

21. Roger Barnett, interview.

22. Jerry Seper, "16 illegals sue Arizona Rancher."

23. Sheriff Larry Dever, interview, October 14, 2010.

24. Don Barnett, interview.

25. Roger Barnett and David Hardy, interview by Glenn Beck, *Fox News*, February 17, 2009.

26. Roger Barnett and David Hardy, interview.

27. Nicholas Riccardi, "Court upholds verdict against Arizona rancher who detained illegal immigrants on his land," *Los Angeles Times*, February 4, 2011, http://articles.latimes.com/2011 /feb/04/nation/ la-na-arizona-rancher-20110205.

Chapter Four

Who Do You Call?

"Here I am in Mexico with someone I turned into the Border Patrol..."

George Monzingo, rancher

LIGHTNING PULSES THROUGH A billowing thunderhead miles to the south—across the border in Mexico. It is the monsoon season in southern Arizona. The heavy air settles in. The moon will soon be up, replacing the twilight. Cars, vans, and pickups litter the yard surrounding the Running N Bar ranch house. The large ranch is located along the San Pedro River north of Tombstone.

Kit Monzingo stands at the door to the ranch house, backlit by a pale yellow light. Despite the latest border rumor, she and her husband are willing to talk. The rumor has silenced many voices along the border. It is said that there is going to be something big happening within the next thirty days. Rumor or not, one of their neighbors whispered over the phone, "The cartel is here. I can't talk."

But the cartel isn't at the Running N Bar Ranch—not tonight. A tall, white-bearded George Monzingo mutes the television and settles into his chair. He and Kit are not afraid to talk. "I think they [the cartel] know where everybody lives. But they know what they can get away with and what they can't get away with. These guys [ranchers] better wake up to the fact that they [the cartel] are here and sooner or later they are going to be in the way." But he has more than cartels to worry about.

Never More Secure

Monzingo stopped a group of illegal immigrants crossing the Running N Bar Ranch a few weeks earlier. There were eight or nine of them led by a well-dressed man. The apparent leader could speak fluent English without an accent. He admitted being illegal—in fact laughed about it. He said he had a wife and child in Mexico and was coming north to work a construction job. When he was two years old, his parents "sneaked" him into the United States. He went to school in San Angelo, Texas, and graduated from San Angelo High School.

He travels to Phoenix on a regular basis to work. He is paid cash every night at a rate of $17 an hour. "I pay no FICA, no taxes, no nothing," he boasts. "I send all my money home. I'm bilingual, so I am the lead man of this group. I am as illegal as any of these guys. I don't have to pay anything like you do—I take all my pay."

"The border is as secure as it's ever been," a phrase used by Janet Napolitano, has become infamous on the border. No other comment made by the head of DHS has done so much to strip her of credibility among ranchers, especially since as former governor of Arizona, she claimed the border was not secure and pushed for additional manpower to secure it.

Secretary Napolitano's boast usually gives rise to reactions of disgust, disbelief, and anger. But not with Monzingo—just hearing the comment produces a huge laugh. He is a big man with a big sense of humor. He moves on with his stories.

"They were here last night. The illegals were running around here—big time. They got separated and were hollering at one another trying to get back together. I got the Border Patrol in here to chase them." He called the agent to see how many were caught. The agent said they couldn't get them all because they separated. This occurs almost every day regardless of how secure Washington claims the border to be.

Redrawing the Map

There have been some changes, but not for the good. The illegal crossers and smugglers are becoming much better organized. "In the last four or five weeks the traffic is different than it has been before. Instead of walking in a line and following a trail, they're spreading out military style—about fifty yards wide. When they are in a line following each other they are separated from each other by about twenty yards."[1]

He explains that another thing the illegal immigrants or drug smugglers do is to come down the San Pedro River in groups of ten or twelve. Four or five will leave the main group and move away from the river. They circle back and join the rear of the column. They repeat these loops over and over to throw the Border Patrol off.

As noted by every rancher interviewed, there has also been a definite difference in the type of people encountered. George and Kit are no exception. "The people today are more aggressive and pushy. They think you owe them something, and we don't have the right to be where we are at today. They say this is their country—that this is part of their country."

Despite being caught on his land, illegal immigrants tell George, "The Gadsden Purchase was stolen. We stole that piece of ground. If you look at the school books in Mexico today, California, New Mexico, Arizona, Texas, and Nevada are darker than any of areas of the United States map—showing they should belong to Mexico."

"It wasn't that way five years ago. They were courteous, respectful. They asked for water, they didn't demand it. But what do you expect. We're teaching the same thing here in our schools."

Response Time

George notes that he calls the Border Patrol almost every time he sees illegal immigrants or drug smugglers. He adds that they respond quickly to his calls. "That's because of me," says Kit.

George chuckles. "I left here one afternoon and got back just after dark. There were red lights everywhere. It had me spooked out, because I thought something real serious had happened."

Kit explained she had a large group of illegal immigrants pounding at the front door and windows wanting to get into the house. She called a Border Patrol highway checkpoint, and they told her they couldn't respond because they didn't have time.

Kit answered, "Well, OK." She had a .357 handgun with her. She held the phone, barged outside with the .357, and emptied it in the air. She raised the phone and said, "You don't have to come now. It's all taken care of." They responded immediately and have responded well since.

In truth, the Monzingos have a great respect for the Border Patrol agents. "They just get run ragged," comments George. "I've had good response from the Willcox group [of Border Patrol agents].

George laughs about the incident. But even though he takes most hardships inflicted by the flood of illegal immigrants and smugglers in stride, he is deeply concerned about Kit's safety .

Sky High

George has found drugs on his property as well as illegal immigrants, but drugs also come by air. One night George was at a watering hole. It was around 9:30 at night. He heard it first—the sound of an engine. Then an ultralight aircraft flew over him without lights. He turned to Kit and said, "That guy's got a death wish flying out here in the dark."

The next morning he ran into a couple of Border Patrol agents and asked if they were flying ultralights now. They asked where he heard that, and George replied that one "flew right over me last night."

The agents told George they were following two ultralights. One flew north over I-10, made a circle, and headed back toward Mexico. The other one kept going all the way to Colossal Cave. The pilot dropped a three hundred-pound load of marijuana near the cave and headed south. The Border Patrol caught two men when they came to pick up the load.

The first ultralight dropped a 270-pound load on a ranch belonging to George's brother. The Border Patrol found the load, but not the people who were to pick it up.

One of the Border Patrol agents told Monzingo that they have had flights of ten ultralights at a time fly through the San Rafael Valley (carrying 2,500 to 3,000 pounds of marijuana).[2] "They just flood us, and we can't do a thing about it," remarked one of the agents.

What amazes Monzingo about the over flights is that there's a virtual news blackout. "It's all hush-hush," he says. "They got to keep their numbers down and say we aren't getting very many. How many times have you heard the numbers are really down? That they've really shut things down? The reasons the numbers are down is because we aren't trying to catch them like we did. The only people that don't know what's going on are the average Americans."

Smugglers carry dope north in ultralights and drop their loads. This ultralight crashed near Tucson. U.S. Customs and Immigration Enforcement photo.

Back Roads and Heavy Traffic

"The smugglers know how the Border Patrol operates," notes Kit. George nods, "If you got a rainstorm or it gets too windy, the Border Patrol shuts down their highway checkpoints and go into their offices." He laughs. "They don't think the illegal immigrants travel in the rain or wind, but they whiz right past the closed checkpoints." Kit has heard them say, "There's none going through, it's raining."

George got tired of the heavy vehicle traffic across his ranch. He devised a plan "so they don't make it too far." He takes a piece of rebar and sharpens one end. He pounds the rebar into his ranch roads at specific intervals. "Tires don't last long on those roads. The thing is, if I put up a sign saying 'Stay off the road,' I mean it," George says, laughing.

So far he has collected over sixty vehicles, mostly with flat tires. The Border Patrol says he can keep the vehicles and sell them, but the state of Arizona says he can't sell them because he needs a dealer license. The vehicles George doesn't donate to charities sit in his yard.

In reality, this is serious business for the Monzingos. One of the trucks crossing their land crashed through three gates, causing almost a thousand dollars in damage. The damage is not confined to gates. Recently illegal immigrants filled a well casing on their land with plastic bottles ... the price tag for that vandalism was over $1,400 dollars. Their land is being trashed, cattle are being killed, and worse things can happen. Kit and George never know when an encounter with illegal immigrants or drug smugglers will go bad.

Negotiations

Despite the Border Patrol's efforts, things were not getting better. An old friend of the Monzingos who lived in Mexico had heard about their troubles. He called George to see if he could be of any help. Monzingo traveled across the border and had lunch with him. His friend also took the liberty of inviting eight coyotes to lunch. George, who speaks fluent Spanish, explained what was happening to his ranch. "I told them where my ranch was and about all the trash and so on." The well-dressed coyotes were courteous, listened, and agreed, "It was bad."

One of the coyotes sitting straight across the table looked at George and said, "Now that I know where your ranch is, I know you. I've seen you before."

"I don't know how you would know me," answered George.

"You turned me into the Border Patrol."

George's mind raced. He thought, "Here I am in Mexico with someone I turned into the Border Patrol ... "

However, the other coyotes came to George's defense: "What were you doing on his ranch?" At that point the complaining coyote stood and excused himself, explaining he had to leave and get some people across the line. One of the guys asked, "What's up?" The coyote answered that they (ICE) picked up a crew working an Olive Garden Restaurant in Chicago and they needed replacements.

The outcome of the meeting was that traffic was reduced across his ranch by two-thirds. Despite this improvement, the Monzingos estimate that more than six thousand illegal immigrants have crossed their ranch in the past few years. In truth, this estimate is probably low.

Coyotes: The Basics

George remarks that the numbers of crossers don't change a lot. When the Border Patrol hits one area, the crossers and smugglers just adjust. Two things are constant however. Coyotes always guide the crossers, and the smugglers are well-organized.

George notes, "I could get on the telephone and find someone to bring people through right now—no problem."

Kit adds, "And they are good. They watch. They can tell you what time the Border Patrol has shift changes, the areas being patrolled. They have it all down pat."

"They are very well organized," observes George. "A friend of mine has a ranch down here at the end of the Huachucas (Mountains), and there's a cave or old mine up there. It's fully stocked with food, water, and cots for the smugglers. My friend says he doesn't go up into that area of his ranch any more—he doesn't ride near it."

George gives a quick overview of how the coyote business is run. The boss stays in Mexico and has guides he assigns to bring the illegal immigrants across the line. Usually the illegal immigrants are in groups of twenty or thirty. A guide or coyote may get $100 per illegal immigrant to get them to some ranch or drop area like Sierra Vista.

At that point a vehicle picks them up and takes them to a drop house in Phoenix. The driver will also get $100 per illegal. The illegal immigrants are held in the drop house until someone uses Western Union to wire the boss in Mexico the fee for transporting them north.

The amount the boss gets per illegal usually depends on nationality. A Mexican might cost $1,500 or $2,000 while somebody from China or Iran would cost considerably more. Once the boss gets his money, he pays off the hired help downstream.

If an illegal wants to go to Chicago or Boston or Brooklyn, they pay extra and transportation is arranged. George recalls a woman who was eight months pregnant. She had an Oregon driver's license, and her goal was to fly to Oregon for the birth of her baby.

Denial

The moon is up as George and Kit exit their ranch house and walk into the yard. George looks at the moon. "They'll be running tonight. It's perfect for them. I knew this one coyote—a woman. She could cover a mile real fast." There is a long silence. For a moment the beauty of the Arizona night surrounds and blots out reality—but only for a moment. George is reflective.

"People have been asleep for a long time," observes Monzingo. He recalls a meeting six or seven years earlier in Bisbee with some ranchers and government officials. A US representative, a US attorney, and other officials gathered to listen to the concerns of the ranchers about illegal immigrants. Among the ranchers present at the meeting were Rob and Susan Krentz.

"What it amounted to," recalls Monzingo, "is they thought we were renegade ranchers. Every one of those guys sat there and said, 'We don't have a problem.'"

Monzingo told the politicians how he had been in Phoenix and had seen 150 illegal immigrants outside of a hotel with signs. The signs told what they could do for work. Monzingo related he was upset and called David Aguilar (head of the Border Patrol Tucson Sector at the time). Aguilar told him that he could not do anything past Casa Grande.

The officials at the Bisbee meeting were surprised that Monzingo thought it was an issue. "Well, it's a free zone," one of them replied. An astounded Monzingo replied, "This is the United States. We shouldn't have any cotton picking free zones."

The meeting headed south as Monzingo noted they had a free zone in South Phoenix, a free zone in Mesa, a free zone in Chandler. "It isn't right," says Monzingo. "They all sat right there and said we don't have a problem—it was interesting that those people were all sitting there with their heads in the sand. That was when it was really starting and nothing's changed since."

He comments, "The last time we saw Rob and Sue Krentz was at a meeting a week before he was shot." The Krentzes and Monzingos would attend almost any meeting trying to bring attention to the border situation.

The truth is that for a long time the Arizona political establishment was in as much denial about the tidal wave of drugs and illegal
immigrants pouring across the border as Washington, D.C. While
the politicians in Phoenix could not come to believe the unbelievable,
the danger of the situation was becoming all too real.

Endnotes

1. In an interview with a military intelligence expert, he noted that the Border Patrol often uses old sensors with a range of fifteen or twenty feet. Since the illegal immigrants are widely separated, the sensor will signal that only a single subject has passed. The Border Patrol won't waste time responding to a single illegal immigrant.

2. The San Rafael Valley was the location where the classic John Wayne movie *McLintock!* was filmed. (Unfortunately, Kit Monzingo passed away before this book was published. She will be remembered by all who knew her for her sense of humor in the face of adversity and the strength she shared with her husband. She will be missed by all who loved her, and by the borderlands, which needed her.)

Chapter Five

The Unbelievable

"We can't give you any protection—you're on your own."
Unidentified Border Patrol captain

ILLEGAL IMMIGRATION AND SMUGGLING were not always high-profile issues in Arizona. The avalanche of money, drugs, and illegal immigrants was just ramping up in the decade of the '90s. Any difficulties on the border were overshadowed by other events. In the 1990s Arizona experienced a political scandal involving bribes, and by the time the dust settled ten state legislators had resigned.[1]

One result of the scandal was the rise of the Speaker of the House, Jane Hull (R). She championed ethics reform and restored trust in the legislature. Hull's efforts resulted in her election as secretary of state (Arizona's second most powerful office) in 1994.[2] Her career might have ended there if it had not been for a second scandal involving Governor Fife Symington. The sitting governor was convicted of a felony and resigned his office. Secretary of State Hull became governor (Arizona has no lieutenant governor), and a year later (1998) was elected to that post by nearly a two-thirds margin.[3]

It was a time when powerful women were appearing on the Arizona political landscape. In addition to Hull, there was a new United States attorney for the District of Arizona named Janet Napolitano. Napolitano's political star was in the ascendency as she was later elected Arizona attorney general. It is also interesting to note the emergence of another female politician. After serving almost ten years in the State Legislature, Jan Brewer was elected to the Maricopa County Board of Supervisors in 1996.[4] Destiny awaited both Brewer and Napolitano. What awaited Governor Hull was a dose of reality concerning Arizona's international border.

Governor Hull was on a political/social junket to historic Tubac (located off Interstate 19 in Santa Cruz County). At lunch with supporters, she talked with a man who said, "My brother is a rancher in Cochise County, and he is being overrun by illegal immigrants and smugglers." Governor Hull was incredulous.

The man pursued the issue with the skeptical governor. He told her that his brother had backpacks left by the crossers. After an extended conversation, Governor Hull told her supporter that she'd send a highway patrolman to pick up a backpack—seeing is believing.

Hull was one of the first politicians in Arizona to come face-to-face with the changing reality in the Arizona borderlands. There would be a huge wave of illegal immigrants and drugs in Arizona's future.

The Backpack

Rancher Larry Dempster watched the Department of Public Safety patrol car wind its way up the long gravel road leading into his Deep Sky ranch. He gripped the backpack. Behind him were the Whetstone Mountains.

The backpack he held was one of many he found. It contained clothing, personal items, a map, and a pamphlet. The map showed a route from the international border to the north. Dempster's house was indicated as a landmark for illegal immigrants to follow on their trip toward Interstate 10. The pamphlet was from segments of the Catholic Church in Mexico. It explained what to say, how to act, and who to call if the Border Patrol intercepted the crosser. The DPS officer accepted the backpack, and the patrol car drove away.

But the backpack was the least of the Dempster's problems. The triple border fence being built along the border in California would change Dempster's life and the lives of every rancher in the border counties of Arizona. It was business as usual with the state and federal government as a flood of human beings and drugs bore down on Arizona. As the tidal wave surged across the border, many ranchers and citizens of the border counties would find that they were on their own.

BC (Before Coyotes)

Ranchers are like most other Americans. They want to make an honest living and feel their family is safe. As long as no one interferes with their rights, they are generally giving and forgiving, which was how Larry Dempster felt near Christmas years ago when he was working out of doors on his ranch. He noticed a couple come into the open. He saw the woman was holding a tiny infant. He thought, "How desperate they must be to have brought a baby this far." Without thinking, he jumped into his truck and drove over to them.

He offered them food and water, which they readily accepted. They were very polite and very grateful. He asked if there was anybody with them. The man said there were fifteen others. Dempster told the husband to have them come up to the road. In a few minutes the illegal immigrants were clustered around his truck. He gave them all the food and water he had. He didn't feel threatened—in fact the only thing that entered his mind was if he could help. It was a time when not every group was accompanied by coyotes. But that was changing all along the Arizona border.

A Bad Day at the Corral

Several years later, ICE told Dempster that there were seventy to a hundred illegal immigrants or smugglers crossing his ranch every day. Watching columns of illegal immigrants traverse his property, he thought about the number. If it was seventy crossers a day, that meant 490 a week or over 25,000 a year. In five years the total would be almost 130,000.

Despite the burden that the destruction of waterlines, gates left open, and trash scattered everywhere caused, he still didn't feel physically threatened. He continued to offer water when appropriate and help when needed. He saw trees on remote areas of his property with women's underclothes hanging from the limbs, but he hadn't heard of rape trees. The rancher's sense of personal safety was about to change.

The end of a summer day brought Dempster to a corral. Darkness extended out from the familiar land. He stood in a corral brushing a horse. Outside of the corral was his pickup truck. He moved under the neck of the horse and stopped. He was not alone. He saw twenty or thirty backpackers lined up at the east side of his corral—motion-less, staring at him. They were dressed in black with heavy burlap backpacks. They were "mules" carrying dope. It was almost too dark to see the men's faces, but he saw their eyes.

He asked in Spanish what they wanted, but they stood—still and silent—watching. "There's water right here. You can have it if you want it," he said, gesturing toward a faucet. But, they were frozen in place. "It was eerie, like out of a science fiction movie. They didn't make any attempt to communicate." Dempster's heart skipped a beat. He was very vulnerable. The sense of menace was palpable.

His mind raced. What should he do? He was isolated—alone. He moved out of the corral to his truck, reached in, and retrieved a small handgun. He told the smugglers to move on in Spanish and English. They stood their ground. With the gun aimed at the ground he fired a couple of rounds. As if by a silent command, very slowly, without expression or sound, the smugglers turned and moved past the corral.

As the group of smugglers slipped into the darkness another group came over a ridge and walked along a ranch road. There were at least another fifty of them. Dempster got into his truck and raced toward his house to call for help. An hour later, two Border Patrol agents arrived with a dog. The smugglers were long gone.

For the first time he had felt threatened—real fear in a situation he had no control over. A dilemma was beginning to take shape in his mind. He would try to shake it off, but it would remain and grow. And the Border Patrol would add to his concerns.

You Need a Bigger Gun

Dempster's sense of personal vulnerability was soon reinforced. The rancher and a friend were driving on a rural road after picking up trash left by illegal immigrants and saw a Border Patrol vehicle parked on the shoulder. He decided to talk to the agent and pulled up behind him. A Border Patrol captain exited his vehicle, sandwich in hand.

Dempster explained the problems he was having with broken water lines, gates smashed, fences cut, and trash left everywhere. He also expressed his concern about the number of smugglers crossing his land. He asked for the Border Patrol's help.

The captain responded, "We can't give you any protection—

you're on your own." A silent Dempster looked back. The captain asked, "What kind of weapon do you carry?"

Dempster answered, "A twenty-two for snakes."

"You need a larger caliber weapon," observed the captain.

The rancher persisted. "I can tell you where the trails are. I can show you."

In a moment of candor, the captain shared this comment: "We are frankly better off doing nothing. We have been told not to do anything to get in the newspapers or create publicity. I'm better off just sitting here eating lunch and drinking coffee." Among his worries were being accused of mistreating an illegal immigrant or "violating his rights." He explained, "It doesn't matter if the illegal is or isn't mistreated." Just the accusation was considered toxic.

Dempster asked him who was responsible for the "do-nothing policy."

The captain was reluctant to answer. When pushed, he finally said, "The politicians."

This was not good enough for Larry Dempster. "Name them. Name one."

The captain responded by naming a prominent congressman.

A frustrated Dempster came to the realization that he was on his own. He watched the captain return to his vehicle and wondered if he needed a twelve-gauge shotgun or a rifle. Returning to his pickup he concluded, "Maybe both."

Tell Her to Lay on the Floor

Dempster has firsthand experience of how illegal immigrants affect the lives of people living beyond the border counties. Several years ago Larry's wife Carol became ill. She was suffering so much pain she was immobilized, and the family doctor said she needed to go to the Tucson Medical Center Emergency Room immediately because something was seriously wrong.

"The emergency room was full of people," says Dempster. "An hour later they had pretty much rotated everybody through—except Carol." New arrivals kept the waiting room full. There were babies, kids, and old people. It was obvious they were all Hispanic. In fact, the only language to be heard was Spanish.

After the group of people that had come in after Larry and Carol had been seen and the room kept filling up, Larry returned to the admitting desk. "I asked if it was our turn." To Larry's surprise the man spoke very poor English. Larry continued, "So between my Spanish and his English, he communicated 'Just sit down and relax, you'll get there when you get there.'"

Carol had been waiting over three hours, and the pain was increasing significantly. It became obvious that she needed treatment and it wasn't a good idea to wait much longer. But they continued treating people ahead of her—people with obviously minor ailments.

Carol and Larry got up to see if it relieved any of the pain if she moved around. When they returned their seats had been taken, and Carol had nowhere to sit. Larry approached the admitting clerk again. Carol was in excruciating pain. Dempster told the Clerk, "Look my wife is in terrible pain, and there's no place for her to sit and no place to lay down."

"Tell her to lay on the floor," snapped a nurse.

With the nurse trailing, a very angry Dempster stormed down the hall and found a room with an empty bed. "What about this room?"

The nurse answered, "Oh, no. We keep that bed for people that are brought in by ambulance."

Dempster whipped out his cell phone and dialed 911. "I'd like an ambulance sent to Tucson Medical Center Emergency Room." He repeated the request and added, "My wife has to have a place to lie down. Just bring the ambulance and she can lie in the ambulance till she's seen. I'll pay for it."

Moments later a supervisor appeared and presto, after a four-hour wait Carol got a bed and treatment. The ER doctor advised Dempster that Carol could have died because of the delay in receiving treatment.

Which Way to Brooklyn?

It was July 2010. The number of Border Patrol agents numbered approximately twenty thousand nationally. The situation in Arizona had become explosive because of the murder of Cochise County rancher Rob Krentz. Nationally, the illegal immigration lobby had mobilized because Arizona had passed SB 1070 in an effort to provide security to the citizens of Arizona. The Border Patrol had been uncharacteristically busy the last few months.

Early Sunday morning on July 11, 2010, Dempster was speeding along on his main ranch road. He pulled up abruptly. Two dirt bikes, two pickups, and two horse-mounted Border Patrol agents were scouring one of his pastures. Dempster stopped to see what was going on.

The Border Patrol had sighted a group of illegal immigrants crossing onto Larry's property. Since most of the Border Patrol agents didn't know the area around Larry's ranch, he agreed to show them where the gates, layups, trails, drinkers, and pickup areas were.

While they paused at a popular loading area that smugglers frequently cruised, a call came in from the mounted patrol: "We've spotted them."

After having crossed about two miles of rolling land and pastures, they reached the location where the horse-mounted Border Patrol agents had flushed a dozen illegal immigrants out of the bush—including one woman. They were sitting under a mesquite tree. An agent identified them as Ecuadorians and indicated they were still missing a few of them.

Dempster volunteered to unlock some more gates to help with the search. But first he wanted to take a picture of the mounted agents and the trespassers. The supervisor wouldn't allow any pictures, however.

Dempster thought, "After all these years you're still afraid of publicity of any kind. Here they are—the Ecuadorian illegal immigrants are on my property, the Border Patrol is on my property, and I can't take a simple picture on my property." He decided his time was better spent fixing the fences the Border Patrol agents took down during the chase. He wondered, *Whose side are you on?*

Dempster considered, "Why no pictures?" He concluded, "If no publicity is allowed or even a simple snapshot, then it's easy to deny that there are any illegal immigrants."

A couple hours later the Border Patrol had left, but Dempster's day was not over. After repairing the fence, he worked on a drinker the illegal immigrants had broken. A shiver ran up his spine. Someone was standing behind him, less than a foot behind him. He could hear him breathe. Dempster turned.

Rancher Larry Dempster was working in his corral when an
illegal immigrant came up behind him—seperating him from his truck.
Photo by William Daniel.

Face-to-face, the illegal asked Dempster how far it was to Brooklyn and said there were others hiding in the brush that were missed by the Border Patrol. Dempster answered, "It's a long way to Brooklyn." But something else was going on.

The illegal aggressively tapped Dempster's shirt pocket containing a cell phone. There were no "*por favors*" or "*con su permisos*" (please). It was "*Dáme!*" (give me!) He wanted the phone. Dempster told the man no. The illegal demanded money. Dempster said, "No." He wanted food. Dempster told him in Spanish to "Wait here and I'll go for food." Dempster picked up his shovel and walked to his pickup truck. As he climbed into the driver's seat, the illegal got in the passenger side. The illegal ordered Dempster to go.

Dempster ordered him to get out. The man again demanded that Dempster drive. Thoughts tumbled through his mind. There was a revolver in the console between the two men. The rancher considered going for it and forcing the man out of his truck. But was the gun loaded? Was it holstered? He couldn't remember. What if the illegal wrestled the gun from him? What if there were other illegal immigrants in the brush and they were armed? Even if he ended up shooting the illegal while defending himself, he might be sued and lose everything.

Maybe he could use the shovel as a weapon? Dempster reasoned if there was a fight, he'd probably lose to the younger man. The shooting of rancher Rob Krentz and the legal issues Roger Barnett experienced had exposed the vulnerability of ranchers.

Finally, he yelled at the man to get out. The illegal immigrant was weighing his options. In Spanish Dempster yelled even louder, "Get out!" The illegal immigrant decided to get out. Dempster drove off. By the time he returned with the Border Patrol, the man was gone—headed for Brooklyn.

A Rancher's Dilemma

Over the years, the attitudes of many ranchers toward illegal immigrants have changed drastically. The sympathy and empathy toward the illegal immigrants that was once prevalent has disappeared. Ranchers are just trying to make a living and the illegal immigrants do not add to that goal in any way. For most ranchers there are no positives about illegal immigrants and certainly not drug smugglers.

According to Dempster, people on the outside will suggest, just "carry a gun—that's what John Wayne would do." The problem is, John Wayne had a script, and the outcome was always positive. People like Dempster don't have a script, and most outcomes are negative.

It is hard for Dempster to carry a heavy gun all day, stretching fence or working under a machine with a weapon strapped to his side. Hard physical work and guns don't go well together. So guns are left in trucks, barns, and toolboxes where they can do little good in emergencies. And guns have other more important downsides.

When the Border Patrol responds to a call from a rancher, their first question upon arriving is often, "Do you have a gun with you?" Dempster always answers, "Why do you ask?" To which there is no response. There is a suspicion that the Border Patrol is "covering their ass." Ranchers believe they are trying to keep a record that certain people carry guns in case there is an incident for which they can show a history of gun possession.

The suspicion was confirmed by Dempster. He talked to a Border Patrol official who explained how the policy works. If a rancher is present when a group of smugglers or illegal immigrants is apprehended, the Border Patrol is required to ask the rancher if he has a gun with him. If the rancher responds yes, an agent will ask the illegal immigrants or drug smugglers present if they were in anyway harassed, threatened, or "bothered" by the rancher.

If any detainee answers yes, the Border Patrol (unbeknownst to the rancher) will inform the FBI. At that point the FBI will open a file on the rancher. If at a later time there is an incident involving a claim by any illegal immigrant or drug smuggler of harassment against the rancher, the information in the FBI file will be used against the rancher.

And yet, a Border Patrol captain told Dempster he should buy a bigger gun for self-protection. It is a confusing message.

In a conversation between Dempster and Cochise County sheriff Larry Dever, the subject of using a gun in self-defense came up. Dever remarked that there was a strong possibility that criminal charges would not stick, but it wasn't a sure thing. If there were illegal immigrants witnessing the shooting, they could very well lie. And if the criminal charges were dropped, there would certainly be civil suits, he said.

The cards are stacked against a rancher in a civil suit. Because of immigration rights activists, a rancher who shoots an illegal while defending his life could lose his property and livelihood, or spend hundreds of thousands for defense lawyers. As noted in an earlier chapter, a rancher can come close to losing almost everything by allegedly kicking a plastic Jesus.

And all of this begs the more important question, which Larry Dempster has thought long and hard about. Could he shoot another human being? His answer is probably not. "Ranchers aren't killers," observes Dempster. "Don't carry, don't own."

The dilemma for Dempster is that if he is threatened, "I can't shoot them, I'm too old to fight them, and I can't threaten them back.

I can't even keep up with what is politically correct to call them. So I just call them unwelcome."

Protecting the Image of Illegal Immigrants

Dempster believes Border Patrol managers and leadership has little interest in protecting ranchers. In November of 2010, Larry Dempster had a frank conversation with a Border Patrol supervisor. Dempster asked why he wasn't allowed to take pictures of the Ecuadorian illegal immigrants on his own property. He was told, "It is a matter of policy."

"Policy?" responded Dempster.

"The Border Patrol's policy is to protect the image of illegals," replied the supervisor. Dempster couldn't believe what he heard. The supervisor repeated that the Border Patrol has a "policy to protect the image of illegals.

Dempster asked where that policy originated. He was told, "I don't know. It probably goes all the way up to Napolitano. If it were [US Customs and Border Protection Commissioner] Bersin or [Director of ICE] Morton, I'd know it."

Dempster asks, "What is the Border Patrol hiding? Why does the Border Patrol seem more interested in protecting the image of illegal immigrants than the safety and rights of American citizens? And why, in America, is the FBI opening secret files on ranchers?"

He concludes, "It's as if right and wrong has been turned upside down." And Dempster may be right. In April of 2012, the rancher encountered an armed drug scout on his ranch some twenty-five or thirty miles north of the border. If he called the FBI, would they open a file on the smuggler?

Endnotes

1. "Scandal In Phoenix," *Time Magazine*, February 18, 1991.

2. Jane Hull, Wikipedia, http://en.wikipedia.org/wiki/Jane_Dee_Hull.

3. Jane Hull, Wikipedia, http://en.wikipedia.org/wiki/Jane_Dee_Hull.

4. "Governor Janice K. Brewer Biography", http://www.azgovernor.gov/About/Gov_Bio.asp.

Chapter Six

Boots on the Ground

"I've heard the Border Patrol was designed for deterrence, but the Border Patrol was designed to fail."

Frank, Border Patrol agent

LIKE MANY BORDER PATROL agents, Frank is not only willing to talk, but anxious to talk. He also understands that if his identity is made public, his career will be jeopardized—perhaps ended. Frank is not a rookie. His enthusiasm has come face-to-face with reality, but he is still dedicated. He hasn't quit caring or trying—even though his eyes are wide open. In two hours he will be on the border trying to arrest smugglers and catch illegal immigrants. He talks about danger.

"Your danger comes from coming up on mules—people smuggling dope through the mountains. There's a lot of money involved. In a sense I understand what they're doing. It's their work and they got a job to do. There's no work in Mexico and they can get good money to bring seventy-pound bales into the United States with a bunch of other guys.

"Illegals are different. I've come on thirty illegals by myself with no problem. Most will run, but not always. After all, if you stop some Mexicans, most likely they'll be sent back to Mexico and try again in a day or two. The coyote might get angry and throw rocks." Frank notes that rocks are a problem. A five-pound rock can be a deadly weapon—agents have been seriously injured or killed. But experienced coyotes understand that throwing rocks can get them shot if they are in the United States.

The towns of Nogales, Arizona left, and Nogales, Sonora, are divided by a concrete and steel fence, but Border Patrol agents report of having rocks thrown at them and of gunfire. United States Government photo.

Deadly Force

Frank outlines Border Patrol guidelines for using deadly force. The situation has to meet three criteria before an agent can shoot to defend himself. The aggressor must have (1) means, (2) opportunity, and (3) intent. "For example, if I had a five-pound rock (means) in my hand at this distance (opportunity), I could easily kill you if I hit you in the head. Their intent is if they show an aggressive action toward me—either threatening to throw the rock or throwing it."

If a situation occurs like that described above, the Border Patrol agent can take action. But, in reality the agent's hands "are pretty much tied," according to Frank. "That's a lot to think about when things are happening really quick ... one after another."[1]

When to use deadly force is not an academic question. The use or perceived use of deadly force can have unintended consequences, as will be seen with the death of Border Patrol agent Brian Terry.

Cash on Delivery

When Frank stops a group of illegal immigrants coming across the border, he doesn't automatically know who the coyote is. "It's such a big business it could be a juvenile, a woman, or a forty-five-year old man." Human trafficking is big business. The going rate for getting a Mexican to Phoenix could be $1,500 while the fee for an illegal from a Special Interest Country (Border Patrol talk for a possible terrorist from Iraq, Iran, Syria, Somalia, or Cuba) is much more. Chinese are charged minimally $20,000 a head.

Rates for transporting illegal immigrants from South American countries vary. Frank has interviewed a lot of OTMs (Other Than Mexicans). Guatemalans usually pay $3,500 for the trip to a stash house in Phoenix. People from El Salvador are charged typically $5,000. There are organizations (usually connected with the drug trade) all over South America, which facilitate the transportation of illegal immigrants.

It also should be noted that the decline of the United States economy affects the price illegal immigrants pay. For certain groups the price for crossing has been slashed. However, for persons motivated less by the promise of economic gain than political concerns, the price is still high. Among these OTMs are refugees from the "Arab Spring," Iraq, and members of terrorist groups.

The following is not atypical for a person who is economically motivated to cross the border. For example, a person wanting to go to the United States from Guatemala is told the cost and where to go. This usually isn't a cash-up-front business. When the potential illegal reaches the southern border of Mexico, he joins up with perhaps forty other Guatemalans. They pay off the Mexican immigration authorities and cross into Mexico. "They are put on a big truck and shipped up to a railroad," Frank says.

The Guatemalans are often transported on top of boxcars north, until they reach Cananea or somewhere below Texas or Agua Prieta. Frank continues, "This assumes they are not intercepted by other Mexican authorities that rape them, beat them, steal everything, and leave them stranded in the middle of Mexico."

At that point they will meet the coyote who puts them up in a hotel for a night and arranges payment. Frank quickly adds, "They don't have to pay then. They'll call family members that live in the United States or make other arrangements to pay. When the illegal reaches Phoenix, there is usually a time limit on how long before payment is expected."

"That's why," Frank says, "it is not uncommon for forty people to be held in a tiny house while waiting to buy their freedom. It's also why Phoenix is the number two city in the world for kidnappings. It's the cartels against one another. One cartel will kidnap the illegal immigrants from another cartel's stash house." It's big business. With a group of forty illegal Guatemalans (valued at $3,500 a head in the Orwellian world of modern slavery) there is a potential profit of $140,000 to the kidnappers without the overhead or risk. Frank observes that the kidnap victims also might be cut a better deal. "Hey, I'll give you your freedom for half. Pay me and then go on and live the American dream."

Big Business

The Arizona Department of Public Safety reported a person they found running naked on the streets of Phoenix—on Christmas Day, 2009. The DPS took the man back to the drop house he escaped from, and they found another forty-six people. The people were all shackled and blindfolded. There was a room next door where the smugglers tortured and raped the illegal immigrants so they could extort more money out of their relatives. In this instance each person was valued at about $2,000.[2]

The drop houses that the DPS busted in those days (circa 2009–2010) operated 365 days a year and received a new group of forty to fifty illegals every three days. The DPS estimated at that time that there were a thousand drop houses operating in Maricopa County, where Phoenix is located, at any given time.[3] As the alien smuggling organizations became better organized, they brought a new level of professionalism and ruthlessness to the business. Again, because of the current poor economy, fees charged by human traffickers have been reduced for Mexicans in what amounts to half-price sales.

DSO and ASO

According to Frank, "Drug smuggling organizations (DSO) and alien smuggling organizations (ASO) are highly organized along the southern and northern borders of the United States. In the Tucson Sector of the border the DSOs tell the ASOs when they can and can't cross the border. The DSO controls the corridors. Along the Arizona border, it's the Sinaloa cartel."

The United States may be having trouble securing the southern border, but the cartels have tremendous control of much of the borderlands.

Tent City

In the Tucson Sector, most of the dope and OTMs (Other Than Mexicans) are brought through the area between Naco and Douglas, the Tumacacori Mountains, the Tohono O'odham Nation, and the Buenos Aires National Wildlife Refuge because there is less of a chance of being caught. Despite being temporarily more heavily patrolled as the result of rancher Rob Krentz's murder, the volume of dope crossing the border in extreme southeast Arizona has not decreased.

Addressing illegal immigrants Frank notes, "If you haven't taken a walk up in the Tumacacori Mountains or Pajarito Mountains, you ought to. There are lay-ups where they rest ... it's horrible."

Frank pauses, looking for words, and then continues. "To the United States Government, the mountains are a natural deterrent. Oh, no, people aren't going to walk through those mountains. The heck they aren't! I can guarantee at any given time there are at least three hundred illegal immigrants in the [redacted] mountains right now. I've personally busted groups of seventy or eighty illegal immigrants in those mountains. I've watched groups, with a night scope, coming out of the mountains thirty or forty at a time."

Frank considers the Tumacacori area and the Buenos Aires Wildlife Refuge. "Both are really no-man's land." He's seen the Border Patrol pull three busloads of illegal immigrants out of the wildlife sanctuary a night—each containing fifty or sixty illegal immigrants.

"There are huge lay-ups (rest areas) up there. A lay-up is easily identifiable because that's where all the trash is—backpacks, tooth-paste, toothbrushes, clothes, food, clothes, plastic bags, shoes, diapers. There are areas in some mountains where lay-ups literally cover a couple of acres."

Frank describes an enormous lay-up "on top of one mountain that the agents call Tent City." The smugglers and illegal immigrants have stuck sticks from tree to tree and tied so many plastic bags together they can get under it and "it's like a tunnel system." This Tent City lay-up was over an acre in size.

A Border Patrol agent volunteered to take pictures of "Tent City" for inclusion in this book. Unfortunately, someone mentioned the huge lay-up to a Border Patrol supervisor before the Border Patrol agent had a day off. The lay-up disappeared.

"Drug smugglers rarely use lay-ups or the same trails as illegal immigrants," continues Frank. "Smuggling is a very well-thought-out effort. It is extremely well organized. They have two-way radios, cell phones, scanners, and lookouts. There will be ten or fifteen smugglers hauling seventy-pound bundles straight north through the mountains to a highway. It's really tough going, but they do it. They'll dump the load and immediately head south," explains Frank.

Periodically a six-man team will patrol a mountain area. Frank says, "You really need fifty people to do it right." He recalls that the last team he was on caught more than six hundred illegal immigrants in a couple of weeks. The government knows they're there—that they are coming through in huge numbers, but the Border Patrol doesn't even keep a six-man team permanently stationed in most of the mountains because there's not enough manpower.

The Manpower Shell Game

Frank has been told that the Obama administration wants to keep Border Patrol manpower at twenty thousand. "Right now we have 21,400 employees to cover the northern border, southern border, and administrative duties," observes Frank.

There does appear to be a policy to keep the effective strength of the Border Patrol at around twenty thousand. This is despite a recent announcement that the numbers will be increased. It seems the Federal government is playing with the numbers. While Congress declared its intention to increase Border Patrol funding by $600 million, there was an announcement that employee overtime would be cut. In terms of man-hours, this effectively keeps employment at the twenty thousand level.

It also must be remembered that there are three shifts. Therefore, at any one time there are a little more than 6,500 agents actually available to patrol the border and transport and process illegal immigrants. This is a best-case scenario that takes into consideration that President Obama's temporary infusion of 1,200 National Guard troops release some administrative staff to work on the border. But as will be discussed later, the National Guard's contribution to border security is a mixed bag at best.

In reality, the effect of the small number of agents available is serious. According to Frank, during any shift there may be a single Border Patrol agent covering a four-mile stretch on the border with one other agent acting as backup in the northern part of that particular grid.

These numbers help the dope smugglers, who often send a group of illegal immigrants between grids to draw away the meager Border Patrol resources. While the agents are preoccupied chasing the illegal immigrants, the cartel will send through the dope.

Further, illegal immigrants are often recruited as mules, since the drug trains are more likely to successfully evade the Border Patrol and there is no fee going to the coyotes.

What Part of Illegal Don't They Understand?

Many Border Patrol agents have a common complaint about illegal immigrants. They've noticed the change in attitudes observed by others who live in the borderlands. "The thing I'm disgusted about the most with immigration," offers Frank, "is the people coming across have no respect for authority, they have no respect for America. There have been youth groups that have volunteered to clean up a particular canyon. They'll have a trash dumpster full in a couple of hours. We've even had Border Patrol agents picking up trash on the Tohono O'odham reservation.

"What part of illegal don't they understand? Once you're in the country you're breaking the law. Yet they feel entitled. They feel they are owed certain things. As far as I'm concerned they have humanitarian rights, but no legal rights.

"If we try capturing them, they run ... what happens in Guatemala or El Salvador or Brazil if they run? They shoot them, or if they are caught they'd beat the holy crap out of them. Yet they complain about us mistreating them.

"They laugh at us, call us names, run—they've learned not to respect the law north of the border. So, we just have to play the game," says Frank.

Violence

The violence across the border in Mexico has not gone without notice by the Border Patrol. Ever since President Felipe Calderon sent Federales from Mexico City and Mexican military units to dislodge some local Federales with ties and loyalties to particular local cartels, violence has soared. Frank shakes his head. "The Federal Police fighting the Federal Police." The Mexican body count is well over forty thousand for the last three years. (Many intelligence sources place the death toll much higher.)

Frank considers the question of whether the Border Patrol receives any assistance from Mexican authorities regarding illegal immigrants or drugs headed north. He answers, "Never. Not on the border towns, no way. They're all in it. They're all out to make an extra dime."

Violence does spill over into the United States, but it is largely ignored or excused. In Mexico there is a very aggressive press, so citizens are aware of the violence. Its impact is lessened by citizens rationalizing that it's mostly between criminal gangs. In the United States it's mostly not acknowledged because the government and media essentially ignore it.

According to Frank, one of the most violent areas in the United States is what the Border Patrol calls the West Desert, also known as the Devil's Highway. "The West Desert is a seventy-mile stretch of nothing north of the border from Ajo to the west. It's a long grueling march with only two gallons of water. I couldn't do it. The drug smugglers will take the worst possible route to get their dope through."

Bandits will listen to their scanners or hear about a group coming up from a rival cartel and ambush other smugglers. The result is unidentified bodies lying in the desert with gunshot wounds. "Yeah, they get into gunfights with each other, but it doesn't happen as much in my area," says Frank. He looks at his watch. His shift is coming up soon.

Equipment

The drug cartels are well funded. They supply their people with superb equipment such as communication gear, weapons, vehicles, or observational aides. They have night vision equipment and the best binoculars. Frank says, "It's not uncommon for them to have forward observers sitting on hills in the United States with $3,000 Swarovski binoculars. Their radio listening devices are excellent. Plus there are no restrictions on what they can listen to."

The Border Patrol radio communications are really poor in some areas and under certain conditions. "We can call Tucson loud and clear, but can't talk to somebody a mile or five hundred yards away," notes Frank. "As far as we know they [the smugglers] aren't listening to our radios—yet." It is assumed with the resources the cartels have and their appreciation of intelligence that they are working on breaking in to the Border Patrol's radios.

Working a Shift

A typical shift on the border begins by going to muster where agents meet with the supervisors and the field-operating supervisor. They tell the agents what's going on, like "They're working a group in such and such grid or there's a group in the mountains," Frank says. Then the agents get their grid assignments, pick up their vehicles, and head out for their shift.

Every agent does things a little different. Frank likes to start out by "cutting sign" (looking for tracks of people or vehicles crossing an area). He pulls out a big cutting light and attaches it to the patrol vehicle door with a magnet. "I'll just 'slow go' down the line, cutting sign. If I'm near a fence I'll make sure there's nobody dropping over it."

"It gets to be a real game. Observers from the other side will warn groups when a Border Patrol car is close and have them hunker down, then tell them they can go, and this goes on and on.

On the line you want to be as visible as possible, which means lights on and a spotlight shining toward the line. You wait for a sensor to go off—you read a book, whatever. The big no-no is you don't go to sleep." Frank laughs. "Mexico is right there across from you and you can get rocked easy. It can be very boring, or other times every grid is blown up [has crosser or smuggling activity] and there are groups and people everywhere."

The Paperwork We Do Has No Significance

It is at this point in the process that the world turns Orwellian once again. If the Border Patrol catches crossers, they will roll their fingerprints. If they don't come up in the system they get food, orange juice, and a ride back to the Mexican border. "We turn the van around, open the back doors, and say, "See you later." These people are called a voluntary return. There have been illegal immigrants that have been returned to Mexico twenty or thirty times. If at first you don't succeed, try, try again.

"If they're a file, meaning they have a DUI, domestic violence, driving without a license, or previous immigration violation, the crosser is classified as an ER [expedited removal]. They'll become an NTA [notice to appear] illegal, which means on such and such a date they'll have to appear before a judge."

Frank pauses and considers what to say next about the processing procedures. Then, in no uncertain terms, he states, "The paperwork we do has no significance. It is a waste of time and a waste of money.

"If you misspell a name the document is shredded. Then the supervisor reviews your paperwork, and you start over by fixing his mistakes. We shred flats of paper. It's meaningless because the guy is just headed south and will be back tomorrow if they are a voluntary return. Why isn't a GS-5 doing the paperwork? The process takes us away from the border."

"The ER [expedited removal] will be transported by a contractor to Tucson. Someone is paid to do some more paperwork, and the illegal alien is told, you have to appear before a judge on say the twentieth of the month. So be here at such and such a time on the twentieth. Theoretically, on that date the judge will decide whether to give them five days in jail, thirty days in jail, or return them to Mexico."

At that point the ER is an NTA (notice to appear alien). They are released in Tucson without bond—they have already broken a law, and now they promise they won't break another law by failing to appear before a judge. In reality, there is no chance they will appear for the court date. They have been transported to Tucson at taxpayer expense and released into our society. If they are an NTA with a warrant out against them, they will be held depending on the seriousness of the charge.

"The bottom line is the government has participated in and expedited the illegal's criminal activity. Further, the illegal's previous DUI, domestic violence charge, etcetera has contributed in their successful return to the United States," Frank says. And as another bonus, the illegal has bypassed having to pay the coyote any fee.

OTM (Other Than Mexicans) are treated differently. They are typically transported to Tucson, and they are all sent back to their country of origin at taxpayers' expense by plane.

"The Border Patrol Was Designed to Fail"

Frank continues, "I've heard the Border Patrol was designed for deterrence, but the Border Patrol was designed to fail. I don't like failing. Now I like to think I'm doing my job and doing some good, but there's something wrong with the organization.

"The Border Patrol is a good job. I can support a family and have a life, but I could also have that if the Border Patrol was a success. New agents are all gung ho, yeah-yeah boys. Don't get me wrong, I still love the work—I'll be the first to volunteer for tough duty like the Mountains—if there's dope in the River or on the Res, I'll chase it…"

"But the way the Border Patrol is designed, there's always going to be more dope tomorrow and more illegals. I know in the big picture what I do won't make a difference. I know in my mind I kept 250 pounds of dope off the streets, but they're still getting their stuff. I've caught rapists, child molesters, people who have killed somebody while driving under the influence—but there's always more of them coming—all the time."

"There's only two options that will make the immigration problem better. First, these other countries, including Mexico, have to get better. They have to produce jobs. Something has to appeal to the people to keep them there. I don't see that happening.

"The other way, is the United States is going to become like these other countries, which isn't going to make anything better. It'll be everybody is poor and the reason for coming to the United States will disappear."

Bullcrap

According to Frank the numbers of illegal immigrants reported in the country are all wrong—as are a lot of numbers provided by the government regarding the border. The official number used by the government is approximately eleven or twelve million illegal aliens live in the United States. According to Frank, "The real number is much closer to eighteen to twenty million."

In the past illegal immigrants would come to the USA for a job, work, and then return home. Now, the illegal immigrants are here to stay. Frank is quick to add, "The idea these people want citizenship is a bunch of bullcrap. They're Mexican—they don't want to be American. It's only the American politician that wants them to be citizens. They aren't learning English, they don't want to pay taxes, and they are not assimilating."

The bottom line is, "The government wants open borders. Everything else is bull."

Confirmation and Consequences

According to Frank and other agents with boots on the ground, the experiences ranchers report relative to illegal immigrants, drug smugglers, and the Border Patrol are accurate and not isolated. But more to the point for Frank and other Border Patrol agents is, how can they succeed in their mission when they are apparently not allowed to?

Leadership that should be inspiring the effort to secure the border has more than once declared it an impossible mission. "We would need on the order of about four hundred thousand or five hundred thousand border patrol agents to seal the border," declared US Customs and Border Protection Commissioner Alan Bersin in a recent speech. He added that agents would have to be placed "twenty-five" yards apart along the entire length of the border.[4] In a real sense, Bersin is abdicating control over huge stretches of the border.

This "can't do" attitude from the top contributes to a de facto policy of open borders. The unintended consequences of this policy will change the political landscape of the country and ultimately result in the deaths of hundreds of people. All of which leads to the murder that changed America.

Endnotes

1. An international security consultant who has operated throughout the world indicates that this is precisely the problem nonmilitary units have against criminal organizations such as a cartel. Franks description indicates "hesitation." Lack of hesitation provides a strong advantage to highly trained military units, terrorist organizations, or drug cartels. He provided the following example.

   "On July 5, 2002, a gunman opened fire at LAX, killing two Israelis and wounding four others. As National Guard troopers sought out ammunition from their commanding officer or exited the terminal, an El Al ticket counter/security employee without hesitation approached the shooter and shot him in the head. Hesitation is often fatal.

2. Jonathan Paton, interview, July 13, 2010.

3. Jonathan Paton, interview.

4. Alan Bersin, speech, Center for American Progress, August 4, 2011.

Chapter Seven

Black Draw and the Murder That Changed America

"The murder of Rob Krentz took place fifteen miles north of the border. The problem was the Border Patrol was fifteen miles further north of the murder site."

Rod Rothrock, Chief Deputy,
Cochise County Sheriff's Department[1]

GERONIMO TRAIL WINDS EAST from Douglas, Arizona, hugging the border with Mexico before twisting its way northeast toward Portal. It services large ranches that stretch toward and border New Mexico and Old Mexico. The landscape is covered with volcanic rocks, brush, ravines, mountains, valleys, and hardship.

It takes a special kind of person to ranch this land. What was always a tough job became tougher with the invasion of illegal immigrants and drug smugglers. As with other border ranches the federal government to all intents and purposes abandoned the ranches along the Geronimo trail to the cartels and illegal immigrants.

The spoken and unspoken message from the federal government to ranchers was, "We can't protect you, you're on your own." There were of course the bizarre caveats, "And by the way, don't do anything to protect yourself or damage the image of the illegals." As noted before, ranchers struggled to survive in a variety of ways. They often combined a less aggressive version of Roger Barnett's fight to protect his rights and George Monzingo's devotion to attend every meeting he could to get help, even if it meant going to Mexico.

Ranchers Rob and Sue Krentz were vocal. They attended meetings, wrote letters, and campaigned to make their voices heard. They attempted to tell the story that not only was America being invaded; but that if something was not done, there would be violence. In a letter to Congress, they voiced opposition to declaring the Tumacacori Highlands a "wilderness area" (and potentially a drug smuggling corridor).

The Krentzes wrote, "We are in fear for our lives and the safety and health of ourselves and that of our families and friends. Please defend our laws and our rights. We have been refused legal protection of our property and lives when dealing with border issues and the illegals. We are the victims!" They further stated, "It is your duty to protect the lives of the people and their safety ..."[2]

Regardless of Washington's neglect of the border, the ranchers had to persevere. They went on with their routines, enduring the smugglers, illegal immigrants, and danger. Rob and Sue Krentz were no different.

A Timeline to Murder

The Krentz Ranch has been in their family since 1907. The Peterson Ranch and Wendy and Warner Glenn's Malpai Ranch separate it from the border three or four miles to the south. In March of 2010 the area was wide open. The drug smugglers and illegal immigrants were crossing north at will. The estimate that one group out of ten was intercepted was generous. As everyone went about business as usual, events began to unfold that would have unexpected and tragic consequences. A scout for drug smugglers was robbing his way back to Mexico.

> » On Thursday night, March 25, some people staying in Cabins at Cave Creek (above Portal near the Chiricahua Mountains) have their trucks broken into. Among the items taken are two cell phones and a 9mm pistol. Friday morning the Cochise County Sheriff's Office investigates the theft.[3]

> » The Border Patrol on Friday, March 26, discover a large load of dope on Rob and Phil Krentz's property. The Krentz brothers help the Border Patrol haul the dope out of the remote area.[4]

> » Early Saturday morning a man breaks into the home of Everett Ashurst. Ashurst's father, Ed Ashurst, is the ranch

manager for the giant Mallet ranch directly north of the Krentz Ranch. Several items are taken from Everett's home, which will prove to be significant later.[5]

» Saturday morning, March 27, is like any other day for Rob Krentz. He and his brother Phil go to check water lines, pumps, and tanks on their ranches. Rob recently had a hip replacement and isn't very mobile, but there is ranch work that has to be done.

A Trap

Rob Krentz heads out on his ATV with his dog. Around 10 or 10:15 AM neighbor Wendy Glenn hears Rob on the community radio. Wendy hears Rob call Phil and say, "There's an illegal down here. It looks like he might need help. I'm going to check him out. Call the Border Patrol." Wendy notes, "This wasn't unusual—it's very common. Fred Eddington at the Peterson Ranch also heard Rob."[6]

Rob doesn't say he's in trouble. Phil answers his brother's call with, "I'm having trouble hearing you—where are you?" Rob answers, "I am in the Molene pasture. When you get out where you have cell service, call me on the phone." That is the last anything is heard from Rob Krentz.[7]

Rob Krentz has always been kind to illegal immigrants. He gives them food, water, and the benefit of the doubt. If there were another human being in need, he would be there to help. It is no different that Saturday morning at the mouth to Black Draw where he sees a man who looks like he needs help.

What happens next is not known for sure. Someone who sees the crime scene reports that it appeared a large man was lying on his stomach when Rob approached on his ATV. Apparently Rob drives in for a closer look and starts to circle around the man. The man rolls over and sits up with a pistol. Rob roars away on his ATV as the man fires four times.[8] As the murderer departs he drops some items he stole from Everett Ashurst's house.

A report released by deputy medical examiner Avneesh Gupta, indicates that Krentz suffered multiple gunshot wounds. Despite his injuries it appears that he was able to drive up a steep embankment and out of sight of his attacker.[9] The shooting took place before noon.

As time passes there are no more messages from Rob, but his family and friends are not overly concerned. Sometimes Rob works until sundown or later on water lines, and radio reception in the remote parts of the ranch is often poor.

Finding Rob

Ed and Jean Anne Ashurst return from Flagstaff to the Mallet Ranch around 5 PM. About 5:30, Rob Krentz's son, Frank, calls Ashurst. Frank asks, "Have you seen Dad?" He goes on to explain, "He's been missing all day. He was out checking water and called Phil [Krentz] about 10. He saw an illegal down at the south well and wanted Phil to call the Border Patrol. He was going to be home at noon, but he's never shown up."

Ashurst asks, "Have you called the sheriff?"

Frank answers, "No, Dad's probably just broke down."

After hanging up, Ed makes the first of two calls. He calls his son to get his help in looking for Rob Krentz. When Everett answers, he tells his father that he is standing with a sheriff's deputy. The younger Ashurst explains his house was burglarized.[10]

Rancher Ed Ashurst reports that Rob Krentz is missing. Photo by William Daniel.

Ed Ashurst's second call is to Cochise County sheriff Larry Dever.

"It was around six in the evening when I got a call at home from Ed Ashurst," recalls Sheriff Dever. "He said, 'Larry, Rob is missing. He went out and hasn't been seen for some time.'" Ashurst explains to the sheriff that Rob had been missing all afternoon and about his last radio transmission.[11]

The sheriff immediately notifies the Cochise County Search and Rescue Team, which is on a training mission in the Chiricahua Mountains. The team loads its equipment and heads for the scene of Krentz's disappearance.

By 6:30 PM it's getting dark. Ashurst meets Louie Pope, Phil Krentz, and Scott Arena at Rucker Canyon Road, where several Border Patrol units, Frank Krentz, and others have gathered. The area will become a command center.

Ed, Louie, and Phil start looking for Rob along the south part of the Krentz Ranch. Ashurst recalls, "At this point we thought Rob had a mechanical problem with his ATV, a flat tire or run out of gas— something like that. The worst possibility would be he had a health problem. We thought he was just waiting for someone to come out and lend him a hand."[12]

Warner Glenn receives a call at 8 PM from fellow rancher Don Kimball telling him that Rob is missing. Glenn, who is also a lion hunter and renowned tracker, volunteers to check water lines and tanks on the east and south end of Krentz's property. Freddy Eddington from the Peterson Ranch joins Glenn. Bill Snure and a hand that works for him are searching from the southwest.

"Everybody was hoping he had just broken down and because of his health problems needed some help," recalls Warner.[13]

By 8 or 9 PM there are lots of Border Patrol agents, sheriff deputies, and the promise that "helicopters are on the way." The Cochise County Search and Rescue is scouring the area on ATVs.

Despite the number of people searching, there is no sign of Rob. The problem is threefold. First, they are searching a rugged area that covers more than sixty thousand acres. Second, it is a moonless night. And last, a Border Patrol helicopter has not shown up.

According to Sheriff Dever, the Rescue Team coordinator was told that the federal authorities had requested air assets and they were coming. "So, they waited and waited and waited and waited," recalls Dever. "They had a DPS (Arizona Department of Public Safety) Ranger (helicopter) on standby in Tucson. The federal air assets never showed up, so finally we launched the Ranger out of Tucson."[14]

In a short time (around 10 PM), the Ranger is on sight. Almost immediately the helicopter picks up the heat signature of Rob's Polaris—it is still running. The helicopter touches down near the Polaris and Rob Krentz's body is discovered.[15]

At 11 PM, March 27, 2010, there are eight or ten cars parked on the turnoff to Rucker Canyon. A dozen people are present, and more people are gathering.

One of Rob's two sons, Andy, arrives from Las Cruces. Rob's wife, Susan, had been in Phoenix that afternoon visiting her ill parents. She reaches the Rucker Canyon turnoff moments before the tragic news. Rob's other son, Frank, reports that his father has been found—murdered.

Ed Ashurst recalls, "We were all in disbelief. People are crying—what do you say? It's a sad thing." He pauses and adds, "Everyone had dismissed the idea that a smuggler or an illegal had injured Rob. I kept saying that Rob is too smart to let someone get the jump on him—but that's what happened."[16]

Warner Glenn is still searching for Rob when he receives the news. "We were about ten miles away from their location. Everybody was devastated." Warner went home and tried to sleep.[17]

Tracking Bigfoot

At 5:30 AM the phone rings at Ashurst's home. Warner Glenn says, "Matt MaGoffin [an ICE agent], Kelly [Glenn's daughter], and I

Warner Glenn. Photo by William Daniel.

are going to go down there. Will you come and help us?"[18]

ICE agent Matt MaGoffin is allowed to look at the murder scene, which was in the "head drainage of the Black Draw." Soon, MaGoffin notifies Warner, Kelly, and Ed about the killer's track and what to look for. He explains the pattern of the man's boots and stride length. "It was a big size twelve or fourteen waffle footprint—like a work boot," notes Ashurst.[19]

They unload their horses and as Warner rides to the

north to look around, Kelly and Ed ride south along Black Draw. Meanwhile, Matt starts following the trail from the scene of the shooting.

According to Warner, "He was no dummy. He was not just an illegal. He knew what he was doing. He had a long stride, but at no point was he running. Judging by his stride, he was probably at least six feet two." He also knew the territory. At one point he left the Draw, went to a water trough for water, and then reentered the Draw. He was obviously very well acquainted with the area.[20]

Kelly picks up the track south of the Peterson Ranch headquarters with Ed providing protection. "North of this location Black Draw is pretty wide open and not too rough. South of where Kelly found the tracks, the draw really boxes up and is very rocky. There are rim rocks, walls up thirty to fifty feet high," recalls Ed.[21] Shortly thereafter, Warner catches up and confirms they are on the right trail.

Soon MaGoffin joins them. "He's [the killer] had a lot of experience," notes Glenn. As Warner, Ed, and Kelly move down Black Draw, MaGoffin will leapfrog ahead by vehicle and on foot.

The murderer followed Black Draw to the border. Photo by William Daniel.

Between three or four in the afternoon the trio follows the tracks of the killer to Geronimo trail. "When we got to Geronimo Trail there was so much law enforcement activity the tracks disappeared."

Around 4 PM some Border Patrol agents declare they've found the track where the suspect went into Mexico. A skeptical Warner Glenn doesn't think it's time to quit.[22] They will wait until everyone leaves and find the real tracks of the killer, but for Rob Krentz and his family it doesn't matter. The killer probably escaped to Mexico before dark the day of the shooting.

Warmer reflects on the shooting of Rob Krentz. "I'll tell you what it did. It brought the possibility of that happening out into the open. This raised the possibility that the people coming and going through here aren't all good people—and we might have to be more careful."

Warner continues, "The fact that we lost a good friend and a neighbor turns you a little bit bitter against these people. We used to halfway feel sorry for them until it got to be so many of them. Instead of in the hundreds it was in the thousands. And now you realize enough is enough. The fact that Rob was killed brought it to a head. I wouldn't say it made people more fearful, but it made people more watchful—more aware of what can happen."[23]

Locally, the immediate result of the shooting was that the Border Patrol drastically increased the number of agents and equipment patrolling the area. Traffic of illegal immigrants was curtailed, but drugs continued to get across the border. The number of ultralight aircraft crossing the border at night carrying loads of dope increased dramatically.

Impact

Driving to the Krentz ranch in late spring of 2011 to interview Sue Krentz shows how much things have changed, and in ways have become worse. Arizona is burning. The smoke rising from the six-week-old Horseshoe 2 fire billows white into the blue sky. When the fire reaches a building a black pillar explodes upward against the white smoke.

Senator McCain and Sheriff Dever are attacked when they express publically the view that illegal immigrants or smugglers probably started the fires. However, a source within Homeland Security confirms privately that smugglers started the million dollar a day blaze and a large fire near Sierra Vista.[24]

Pulling up to the ranch house, Sue Krentz walks from her porch to greet her visitor. She is a survivor. In March of 2010 a smuggler took away the life of her husband Rob. It was a national news story to most, but to Sue Krentz and her family it inflicted pain that does not diminish with time. In September of 2010 a car struck Sue after she and a friend left a service at Saint Luke's Church in Douglas, Arizona. To many people the coincidence of the accident seemed suspicious.

Sue sits at the kitchen table. She is animated, articulate and outwardly displays little evidence of an accident that almost took her life. She runs through a gamut of emotions and observations.

It is said the murder of Sue's husband pushed SB 1070 (Arizona's controversial anti-illegal immigration bill) through the state legislature. Sue Krentz sees things differently. She doesn't connect the passage of SB 1070 to her husband's murder. It was going to be passed, she believes, and yet her husband's death was linked to the bill. It is a linkage with which she is uncomfortable.[25]

She also notes a recent murder in Hidalgo County, New Mexico. Immediately, the press tried to describe the deceased as a rancher and made an association with her husband's death. The press was trying to say it was an illegal and yet they had no evidence. In Sue Krentz's world it is painful. It is painful when someone calls to interview her and asks how big their ranch is or how many cattle they run.

First, it's bad manners. It's like asking someone how much money they earn or how much money they have in their bank account. But it is much more significant than a display of bad manners. A very strong Sue Krentz leans forward. "It's as if you have a lot of land or cattle or money, it diminishes the impact of your loss."

She reflects on the accident in Douglas, and notes that some people believe it was a warning [directed at other ranchers] to mind their own business when it comes to illegal immigrants or drug smugglers. "I don't know why they would want to kill me, but what are the odds?"[26]

Sue talks about the man that shot her husband. Her view is that the shooter is probably dead; retribution dealt out by the cartels for having so much attention drawn to the border. It changes nothing.

In her mind if the murderer was arrested, convicted, and executed it would do little to alter what has been visited upon her and her family.[27]

Sue Krentz is full of passion and pain and anger. She has been through hell and not of her own choosing. "If the murderer was shot a thousand times it wouldn't change what he did," she says.[28]

Her attention turns to the consequences of the murderer's actions. In a recitation marked with anger, tears, remorse, and steely determination, she attempts to describe how the murder of Rob has affected everything. It's changed the way the family relates to each other and the way others relate to them.

With great eloquence and determination she makes her case that her family members have been made victims by the murder. She looks through booklets—*Victim Information Booklet* and *Your Victim Impact Statement*—from MADD and relates how they apply to their family and all people along the border.

Again leaning across the table she forcefully notes, "If you came on our land uninvited, we could have you arrested for trespassing. We could arrest you for trespassing. But if you're an illegal, there is nothing we can do. We would be violating your rights."

"But what about our rights, our civil rights? What about our right to be safe in our home and on our property? There is so much concern about their rights, that they might be victimized, it is ignored that we are the victims ... my husband and my family and myself."

She indicates that she has been invited to Texas to meet with people who are concerned with the situation along the border and the murder of David Hartley eight months earlier. David and Tiffany Hartley set out to have a day of jet skiing and sightseeing on Falcon Lake, in Texas on the border with Mexico. Members of the Zeta cartel shot David. His wife Tiffany barely escaped with her life. His body has never been found.

But her interest is not to push a political agenda. She is interested in meeting Tiffany Hartley because she considers them both victims. She is angry that so little thought is given to American citizens who are the victims.

When the subject of Brian Terry is discussed, she focuses on the Terry family. She voices a thought that she should or might talk to them. They have much in common. They are victims and yet not treated as such.

In fact, then United States Attorney for Arizona Dennis Burke was actively attempting to exclude the Terry family from making a victim's impact statement at the sentencing of the man who supplied the weapon that killed Brian Terry.[29]

Sue Krentz believes there should be a victims rights law enacted by the state legislature to protect and care for all citizens that have suffered at the hands of criminals who cross the border, whether they are trespassers who trash and steal property or murderers who kill their loved ones. She is determined that victims' rights be protected.

Stepping outside, the smoke from the Horseshoe 2 fire billows in the distance. It has blackened a fourth of the land on which the Krentzes graze cattle and destroyed miles of fences and pipelines. In the drought cattle will have to be moved to lower pastures where grass is scarce. It is another challenge Sue Krentz and her family will meet. Another hardship visited upon them because of the open border.

Nonetheless, Sue Krentz's resolve is clear. "I will not move. I will not sell. I will not apologize."[30]

Making a Difference

Whatever one's political leaning, the murder of Rob Krentz was a tragedy. He was slain on a known route used by drug smugglers. Ten miles north of the murder site a sign (on land ranched by the Krentz family) was erected years ago by the Forest Service. It warns the public of drug smuggling activity. The government knew the area was dangerous, but offered little protection.

There are many who believe that the killer's identity and movements after the killing are not known. Some state that nobody knows or can know if the murderer was an illegal immigrant, or a drug smuggler, or a United States citizen. Some believe he is dead.

However, without equivocation we can say that the murderer of Rob Krentz was a Mexican citizen and a drug smuggler. He did cross into Mexico the same day of the murder and he is still alive. In order to not jeopardize the investigation no additional information is presented here. The only question is whether he will be brought to justice.[31]

Warning sign north of area where Rob Krentz was murdered.

While it does not lessen the tragedy of his death, the murder of Rob Krentz was destined to become a catalyst for a tectonic shift in American politics. And the political earthquake began in Arizona.

Endnotes

1. Rod Rothrock, Cochise County Chief Deputy, interview, August 21, 2010.

2. Sue and Rob Krentz, letter to Subcommittee on National Parks, Forests, and Public Lands, U.S. House of Representatives, November 12, 2007.

3. Sheriff Larry Dever, interview, October 14, 2010.

4. Sue Krentz, interview, June 9, 2011.

5. Ed Ashurst, interview, October 26, 2010.

6. Wendy Glenn, interview, September 1, 2010.

7. Wendy Glenn, interview.

8. Witness, interview, 2010.

9. Ed Ashurst, interview, October 26, 2010.

10. Ed Ashurst, interview.

11. Sheriff Larry Dever, interview, October 14, 2010.

12. Ed Ashurst, interview.

13. Warner Glenn, interview, September 1, 2010.

14. Sheriff Larry Dever, interview, October 14, 2010.

15. Sheriff Larry Dever, interview, October 14, 2010.

16. Ed Ashurst, interview, October 26, 2010.

17. Warner Glenn, interview, September 1, 2010.

18. Ed Ashurst, interview, October 26, 2010.

19. Ed Ashurst, interview, October 26, 2010.

20. Warner Glenn, interview, September 1, 2010.

21. Ed Ashurst, interview, October 26, 2010.

22. Warner Glenn, interview, September 1, 2010.

23. Warner Glenn, interview, September 1, 2010.

24. Homeland Security employee, 2011.

25. Sue Krentz, interview.

26. Sue Krentz, interview.

27. Sue Krentz, interview.

28. Sue Krentz, interview.

29. William La Jeunesse, "U.S. Attorney's Office Rejects Family of Murdered Border Patrol Agent as Crime Victims," August 11,2011, Fox News, http://www.foxnews.com/politics/2011 /08/11/us-attorneys- office-rejects-family-slain-border-patrol-agent-as-crime-victims.

30. Sue Krentz, interview.

31. Law Enforcement, Homeland Security, interviews, 2011.

Chapter Eight

Politics and Damned Politics

"The President is holding the border hostage."
United States Senator Jon Kyl[1]

THE MURDER OF RANCHER Rob Krentz by a drug smuggler brought together two powerful tides of history that had previously been running parallel to each other. In the five years that preceded the murder, events were occurring on the border, but there was a whole different series of battles that were going on in Phoenix.[2]

One of the politicians who was instrumental in getting many of the major bills regarding immigration out of the state legislature in the last five years was former state senator [District 30] Jonathan Paton. Better than most, he understands the local and national politics that brought SB 1070, Arizona's anti-illegal immigration bill, into being. He is also an astute political analyst.

Johnathan Paton

From a strictly political point of view—local, state, and national—the Democratic Party understands that it is the Republican female voter and independent female voter who decide close elections. Paton observes that in the last two elections these two blocks decided the winners—they put Obama over the top, for example. These two groups are the most prized voters for two reasons. They are the swing voters who are most likely to vote.[3]

Republican women vote in larger numbers than any other demographic group. The reason is that women live longer than men and the longer someone lives, the more likely they are to cast ballots. Democrats have consistently wooed Republican women over social issues. For example, in Arizona the Democrats have emphasized social issues to Republican and independent woman in large cities. Social issues resonate with these two groups of people—women's right to choose, education, and health care. By peeling off enough of these swing voters, the Democrats have been able to win in close districts.

The New Normal

Before the 2010 midterm elections, Paton was visiting a group of women in the Tucson Foothills. They were fairly wealthy, educated Republican and independent women. They all identified themselves as socially liberal and fiscally conservative. Paton asked, "What do you think of SB 1070?" They responded, "We love it." He continued with, "What do you think of the border situation?" They answered, "It's a travesty."[4]

This meeting illustrates a sea change that most Democrats were and are missing. The two groups Democrats depend upon to win elections in swing districts no longer view the illegal immigration and the border situation as a social issue—the murder of Rob Krentz was the last straw in a long process. These voters view it clearly as a security issue. Previously, immigration had always been seen in the same light as abortion or education. The border is now viewed as a separate matter with its own constituency.

The change in attitude was a major miscalculation of people in Washington, D.C., and also those in Arizona who were against SB 1070. They didn't realize there was such a large constituency of moderate women who were 100 percent for SB 1070 and 100 percent against the lawsuits that attacked SB 1070.

In 1996, perennial GOP candidate Joe Sweeney was running against Jim Kolbe in the primary for an Arizona's eighth Congressional seat. Sweeney called for the deployment of National Guard troops to the border. Most people could not believe what they heard—it seemed to be "unbelievable." Fast-forward to 2010 and US Representative Gabrielle Giffords, a Democrat who succeeded Kolbe, was supporting the deployment of National Guard troops to the border.

There has been a complete culture shift from what was normal then and now—the "new normal."[5]

Political Point of No Return

In 2004 enough signatures were gathered to place Proposition 200 on the state ballot. Proposition 200 required that individuals provide proof of citizenship before they could vote or apply for public benefits in Arizona. The conventional wisdom was, "There's no way this thing is going to pass. People are too reasonable to let this thing pass."

Opposition to Proposition 200 was bipartisan. The established political parties opposed it. Republican senators John McCain and Jon Kyl, Democratic governor Janet Napolitano, and other government officials campaigned against it.

The establishment was shocked. Not only did Proposition 200 pass, it passed overwhelmingly. It received over 64 percent of the vote total. It passed in liberal Pima County. In addition, despite being called racist, Proposition 200 received a majority of Hispanic votes.

Proposition 200 was a first step. A bill enacting the intent of Proposition 200 was passed by the legislature and signed by Governor Napolitano. Arizona had reached a political point of no return. What followed was a series of bills, most of which were sponsored by Republican state senator Russell K. Pearce.

In 2005, State Senator Tim Bee and then State Representative Jonathan Paton sketched out the next bill on a napkin in a restaurant. The result was a bill they cosponsored called the Human Smuggling Act. The act essentially stated that if a person brings someone into the country illegally they could be charged with a class four felony (punishable by one and a half to three years in prison.) Democratic governor Napolitano vetoed most bills coming out of the State Legislature relating to the border and illegal immigrants, but she signed the Human Smuggling Act.

Bee and Paton reasoned that it wasn't just people on this side of the border who were at risk from the effects of human smuggling. People from Mexico were dying in the desert, and sometimes being raped, robbed, or murdered by human smugglers. They also included in the bill that if a person is smuggled into the country for purposes of prostitution or forced labor, it is a class two felony. At that point, Governor Napolitano didn't have much choice politically but to sign the bill.[6] It is difficult to veto a bill that essentially outlaws slavery.

A series of bills followed. One dealt with bail for illegal immigrants. SB 1265 stated that if a person is in the country illegally and charged with a capital offense, they will not be able to be bailed out while waiting trial, nor be sent back to their country of origin. The Democratic governor also signed the bill, which conformed closely to federal law.

During this period of time the legislature split along political lines every time an anti-illegal immigration bill was considered. However, sometimes bills would split the Republican Party as well. One such bill (HB 2779) was the Employers Sanction Bill. The bill required employers within Arizona to verify that employees were in the country legally. Knowingly violating the law for the first time would result in a suspension of the employer's business license. A second offense would result in a "business death penalty." The employer's license would be permanently revoked.

Governor Napolitano signed the Employer's Sanction Bill. Napolitano wrote, "Immigration is a federal responsibility, but I signed HB 2779 because it is now abundantly clear that Congress finds itself incapable of coping with the comprehensive immigration reforms our country needs. I signed it, too, out of the realization that the flow of illegal immigration into our state is due to the constant demand of some employers for cheap, undocumented labor."[7] The bill is one of the strongest of its kind in the United States.

It is interesting to note that in 2010 President Obama directed the Justice Department to challenge Arizona's Employers Sanctions laws in court.[8]

The political fights in the legislature continued and were brutal. Governor Napolitano did not sign any additional significant bills regarding illegal immigrants that emerged from the legislature. According to Paton, many of the bills passed were termed "veto bait." "We knew the bills would go to Governor Napolitano, and we knew she would veto them," notes Paton. It was a constant battle and neither side was ever satisfied.[9]

A Huge Miscalculation

It was during this time that the illegal immigration lobby and their supporters took to the streets. They held huge demonstrations across the country. The largest protests were held in Phoenix and Los Angeles. Thousands of protestors, including a vast number of illegal immigrants, gathered in Phoenix carrying American flags upside down and waving Mexican flags. The intent was to demonstrate their strength—"Look how many people we have. These people matter. See, we are showing them our power."[10] The Arizona State Capitol was at the epicenter of the Phoenix rally.

What the demonstrators didn't realize was that every time they demonstrated, they were stoking the anger of Middle America. Paton recalls talking with Kyrsten Sinema, who was one of the supporters of the demonstrators and one of the most liberal members of the state legislature. She confided that in the end the demonstrations were a mistake because they horrified the rest of the state—the people watching it.[11]

While not all people demonstrating were illegal immigrants, many were. People were saying, "You're here illegally and you're protesting in the country where you broke the law?" The protestors didn't get it and that disconnect was destined to carry over to SB 1070. Not only didn't the groups that organized the demonstrations get it, but neither did the establishment.

Congress was more interested in pursuing "immigration reform" than listening to what was happening at the grass roots of America. Many leading Republicans in Washington were caught in this disconnect regarding popular sentiment. On the state level, this disconnect caused a huge rift in the Republican Party that is still being felt today.

At this point there were all kinds of political battles going on in Phoenix—and they were still disconnected from the border issues.[12] In Phoenix, people were concerned with drop houses and labor centers. In many ways it was a cultural issue. Mesa was turning into a community that looked more like a Hispanic community than the Mormon community it had been.

On the border people were concerned about hundreds and thousands of illegal immigrants crossing their property and sometimes breaking into their homes, destroying water tanks, and making ranching, already a precarious and difficult way of life, unimaginably harder.

Again, few legislative votes actually concerned stopping illegal immigrants at the border. There was a vote regarding sending Arizona National Guard troops to the border—a vote that then State Legislature member Gabrielle Giffords voted against. Mostly, the legislature was concerned with what to do after the illegal immigrants were already here. In Phoenix, no one was really focusing on what was going on in Portal, Douglas, Arivaca, or along the Geronimo Trail. The border was like the canary in the coal mine and people didn't notice that it was dying.

Many people had reached a point where they didn't trust the federal government. They felt when the government said they wanted to do everything comprehensively in a single bill regarding "immigration," it was code for amnesty. Paton notes, "People aren't going to go for it. People don't believe that the government would live up to their end of the bargain of sealing up the border."[13]

President Obama Clears the Way for SB 1070

The only thing separating major illegal immigration legislation from becoming law in Arizona during the preceding four years was Democratic governor Janet Napolitano. President Obama's appointment of her as secretary of Homeland Security changed the political balance of power of state government in Phoenix.

The Republican leadership in the Legislature realized the day that Napolitano resigned as Arizona governor there would be nothing to stop illegal immigration legislation. The first year belied this assumption because of the financial crisis Arizona was struggling to cope with.

As Governor Brewer and the legislature started to address the state's financial condition, a bill emerged from the legislature to address the status of illegal immigrants within the state. It was political dynamite.

Many in the state legislature decided if the United State would not enforce immigration laws, the state must fill the vacumn. Senator Russell Pearce, Representative Jonathon Paton, and Senator Al Melvin carefully crafted SB 1070 to mirror the federal illegal immigration law. In fact SB 1070 contains more protections against profiling than federal law. Nevertheless, activists charged it could lead to profiling and discrimination.

It is interesting to note that activists did not protest the federal illegal immigration law, which offered much more opportunity for profiling and discrimination. This caused some observers to wonder if they were in reality less interested in racism than their fear SB 1070 might be enforced and discourage illegal immigration into the United States.

One of the most significant aspects of the law according to State Senator Al Melvin was to shut down sanctuary cities. Melvin stated during an interview, "If SB 1070 doesn't shut down sanctuary cities in the state, then the legislature will have to start withholding funds from these municipalities."[14]

Governor Brewer signed SB 1070 on April 23, 2010. A week later, she signed a second version of SB 1070 that had even stronger safeguards against racial profiling.

The previous five years had been full of political turmoil, but Governor Jan Brewer emerged with widespread national notoriety and a growing popularity. However, there would be consequences for the taking on the federal government.

The Rise of SB 1070

Jonathan Paton received a phone call from a friend shortly after voting for SB 1070. She asked, "Did you vote for SB 1070?" He answered yes. There was a long pause. She then said, "Wow, I don't know if you should tell people that. Things are just exploding. There are demonstrations, all these things on the news ... It looks like there's going to be a big backlash and anybody that voted for SB 1070 is going to be in serious trouble."[15]

Paton recalled the huge demonstrations that had been held a year or two earlier across the country by the illegal immigration lobby. There were all the groups and commentators on television predicting dire consequences. But Paton also remembered the tremendous resentment that those demonstrations had created in many Americans.

Paton knew the anti-SB 1070 demonstrations would cause the same resentment across the electorate. "But even I didn't grasp how deep the resentment to the demonstrators was going to be and not just by the typical white male conservatives, but among middle-of-the-road, upper-income women."[16]

The political landscape had fundamentally changed with the murder of rancher Rob Krentz and the passage of SB 1070. An incident along the border in a tiny corner of Arizona changed national politics. The political interests of an important segment of Middle America and the people on the border had been joined.

The problem was and is, while much of grassroots Americans were getting it (that illegal immigrants and drug smuggling were security issues) the federal government appeared oblivious. The ruling elite started to label a huge number of mainstream Americans as terrorists, radicals, and ignorant. However, in reality the American political ship had sailed and the administration was blinded by its self-deception, clinging to what has been described by some as a pro illegal immigrant agenda.

Arizona Senator Jon Kyl met one-on-one with President Obama in June of 2010 regarding Arizona's border issues. According to Kyl, the president said, "If we secure the border, then you all won't have any reason to support comprehensive immigration reform."[17] Kyl continued, "In other words they are holding it hostage." The White House denied the senator's assertion, but Kyl stood by his story.

A Challenge to Federalism

The denial of the border crisis by politicians within Arizona was ended with the passage of SB 1070. The state bill united the interests of the state of Arizona with the interests of the citizens on the border. The effect went far beyond the borders of Arizona.

SB 1070 exposed the power vacuum that the federal government's abdication of power regarding the border and illegal immigration had created. Some states and municipalities followed Arizona's lead and passed even stronger illegal immigration laws.

As predicted, the supporters of the illegal immigration lobby came out of the woodwork at home and abroad. However, in many people's minds, they inadvertently made the case that Americans had to choose between compassion for illegal immigrants or for their own security and economic interests. As in Arizona, many Americans decided illegal immigration was no longer a social issue, but a security and economic issue.

The story was no longer about the survival of ranchers on the border, but about the survival and future of the country. With SB 1070 the battle was joined. In response, opponents of SB 1070 turned to anyone with any gravitas that might speak out against the Arizona bill, from Mexican president Felipe Calderon to Arizona's first Hispanic governor, Raul Castro.

Endnotes

1. "Kyl: Obama Won't Secure Border Until Lawmakers Move on Immigration Package," *FOX News*, June 21, 2010, http://www. foxnews.com/politics/2010/06/21/kyl-obama-wont-secure-border-lawmakers-immigration-package/.

2. Jonathan Paton, interview, July 13, 2010.

3. Jonathan Paton, interview.

4. Jonathan Paton, interview.

5. Jonathan Paton, interview.

6. Jonathan Paton, interview.

7. Jeannie Shawl, "Arizona governor signs tough sanctions for employers hiring illegal workers," *Jurist Legal News & Research*, July 3, 2007.http://jurist.org/paperchase/2007/07/arizona-governor-signs-tough-sanctions.php.

8. JJ Hensley, "Supreme Court asked to review Arizona employer sanctions law" *The Arizona Republic*, May 29. 2010.

9. Jonathan Paton, interview.

10. Jonathan Paton, interview.

11. Jonathan Paton, interview.

12. Jonathan Paton, interview.

13. Jonathan Paton, interview.

14. Al Melvin, interview 2010.

15. Jonathan Paton, interview.

16. Jonathan Paton, interview.

17. "Kyl: Obama Won't Secure Border Until Lawmakers Move on Immigration Package," *FOX News*, June 21, 2010, http://www.foxnews.com/politics/2010/06/21/kyl-obama-wont-secure-border-lawmakers-immigration-package/.

Chapter Nine

An Honest Man

"I know how the system works."
Former Arizona governor Raul Castro

WHEN ARIZONA GOVERNOR JAN Brewer signed SB 1070, she was in reality approving a modest bill that did nothing but mirror much of federal immigration law. The biggest difference was that the state law was much more stringent in establishing that racial profiling could not be used in carrying out the provisions of the bill. No such limitation is present in the federal law.

Oddly, the federal government could have sidestepped the controversy by embracing the bill and welcoming the cooperation of the state with immigration as they do with illegal drugs coming across the border. Instead, the administration pushed back with all the subtlety of a blunt instrument.

In addition, it illustrated that LaRaza, MEChA, the ACLU, President Felipe Calderon, a large number of American politicians, and alien smuggling organizations (ASO) might not have shared values, but they sometimes had shared interests. Many of them also had a shared response—outrage.

With a seemingly knee-jerk reaction, President Obama, who taught law at University of Chicago, immediately called SB 1070 misguided while the secretary of Homeland Security Janet Napolitano and Attorney General Eric Holder condemned the bill without having read it entirely.[1] It was a classic case of leading by impulse. SB 1070 had hit a nerve.

Real Discrimination

Seeking support against SB 1070, opponents turned to Raul Castro, Arizona's first Hispanic Governor. Castro was born in

Cananea, Sonora. Francisco Domingo Castro and his wife Rosario
Acosta Castro legally immigrated to the United States in 1918,
bringing with them Raul (age two) and ten other children. They
settled in Pirtleville, near Douglas, Arizona, and became citizens. His
father, who had been a union organizer in the mines of northern
Mexico, worked in the mine near Douglas.[2]

Raul Castro attended elementary school in Pirtleville. A sixth
grade teacher told Raul that he was very bright, but wouldn't amount
to anything because he didn't work hard enough. Raul thought, "She
must like me or she wouldn't have taken the time to tell me that." He
resolved he would never disappoint her.

After the sixth grade he went to school in Douglas. He had to
walk the five miles from Pirtleville to school because the school bus
didn't carry Hispanics. He said to himself, "This is not right. This is
not fair." He recalls that Hispanic children could only swim at the
Douglas public pool on Saturday mornings because the pool would
be cleaned that afternoon.[3]

Castro's father died, leaving behind a widow and ten children. A
twelve-year-old Castro saw his brothers dropping out of school and
going to work in the smelter. He went to his mother and asked, "I
see my brothers getting up at five in the morning, going to work, and
coming back at five in the afternoon. Is this going to be my life? What
am I going to be when I grow up, Mother?"

She answered, "You're going to be whatever you want to be."[4]

Despite hardships and discrimination Castro persevered. He
graduated high school, went to college in Flagstaff on an athletic
scholarship, and received a teaching degree. Unable to find a teaching
position because of discrimination, he became a hobo, a professional
boxer, and a field worker.

Upon returning to Arizona, Castro got a job with the State
Department. He worked at the American Consulate in Agua Prieta,
where he issued border crossing cards and visas. He would tell his
fellow citizens, "I'm not your lawyer, but I am here to protect your
human rights."[5]

The American consular general from Juarez came to inspect the
consulate in Agua Prieta and after three days talked with Castro.
"Raul, I've seen your work for the last five years. I think you have a

lot of ability, but I would recommend you quit the job." He indicated that Hispanics didn't have a future in the State Department.

"In those days diplomatic service was strictly Ivy League or anybody east of the Mississippi," notes Castro. "Anybody west of the Mississippi was considered just a bunch of drunken cowboys." Castro resigned and decided to go to the University of Arizona Law School. He was denied entrance because he was "Mexican."[6]

"They told me I couldn't have an outside job (his outside job was teaching Spanish at the university), and it was their experience that Mexicans didn't do well in law school." A determined and persuasive Castro called the president of the university. He was granted entrance.

Arizona Today

Raul H. Castro's life is the all-American success story. He became a Pima County superior judge and then was appointed by Lyndon Johnson as ambassador to El Salvador. After four years he became ambassador to Bolivia. Upon returning to Arizona, he was elected governor and served from 1975–77. His term was cut short when President Carter appointed him ambassador to Argentina.

At the age of ninety-five, Raul Castro lives in Nogales with his wife of over fifty years, Patricia Steiner Castro. Their home, built in 1906, sits near the border with Mexico. Arizona is not the same place as it was during his youth. Discrimination has been reduced and opportunities increased for people from all walks of life. Castro sits in his living room, surrounded by mementos of his and Patricia's service abroad.

Castro recalls how the ebb and flow of the American economy has always affected the

Raul Castro, Arizona's first hispanic governor. Photo by William Daniel.

number of Mexicans coming across the border. With chronic high unemployment and low wages in Mexico there is always a pool of labor willing to come north. "When the American economy is good, labor from the south is welcomed. When it is bad, nobody wants them. That's just the way it is—that's just the way the cookie crumbles."

According to Castro, "This bill (SB 1070) that has been passed is pretty well ill-conceived in the sense that what we need is more diplomacy—more communication between both governments, which we haven't had. President Calderon met with the president just three days ago instead of a year ago to try to work something out."[7]

At the same time, the former Arizona governor argues that "It's not right for anyone to jump the fence or build tunnels to come in. It's an illegal act. If it's an illegal act it's a no-no." He picks up a copy of SB 1070 and notes that "under no circumstance will a policeman stop a person because of race, color, or national origin."[8] Castro admits that it sounds good but is afraid it will be ignored. He recalls how he has been stopped in the past because of his appearance.

This is the conflict that the former governor struggles with. He weighs his fundamental allegiance to law and order and his past experience with discrimination. A conflict born from the time in his life when there were no persons of Hispanic origin teaching, and none in law enforcement or government, to now, where Hispanics are common. But the truth is, profiling still exists. SB 1070 didn't create it, nor would the bill's demise change that fact.

The eminently fair Castro also recognizes that the federal law, which SB 1070 mirrors, is not immune to the abuse of profiling. An area rancher indicated his support for SB 1070. Castro listened carefully as the man remarked how difficult it is to get any help on a remote ranch from law enforcement. The delay in response time or no response from the Border Patrol can have fatal consequences.

The federal government's emphasis that illegal immigration is a matter for the federal government has had an enormous chilling effect on local law enforcement's response. Often if a rancher calls local law enforcement about illegal immigrants and even drug runners he is referred to ICE or the Border Patrol. The rancher tells Castro, from his point of view, at least SB 1070 gives local law enforcement more latitude in dealing with the issue. Castro nods and agrees. "I hadn't considered that. It is certainly a valid point."

The former ambassador addresses his view on what is happening in Mexico regarding drugs. There have been fundamental changes occurring south of the border. "Number one is the consumption of drugs in the United States has increased over threefold. The demand for the drugs is not in Mexico or Latin America. It is in the United States. If Americans were not using drugs, there wouldn't be a problem." Castro says Latin America's willingness to supply the drugs is the other side of the equation. It has changed the fabric of Latin American society.[9]

"That's where diplomacy comes in. the United States and Mexico have to get together. We can't just blame the other side." He adds that the American drug user has to take responsibility for the violence in Mexico. "It's become a monetary situation."

"The drug cartels are buying off the police, the mayors, and the military. They're all scrambling to bring drugs into the United States. If anyone bucks it, they're killed. Yesterday they found ten bodies in Nogales, Sonora. If there wasn't any money in it, the violence would end," he says. At the same time, he insists that Mexico has a duty to prevent its citizens from traveling illegally across the border.

A Cautious Man

Castro observes that the threat to the Mexican government from the cartels "is a really serious problem." He believes diplomacy has failed. He looks back to earlier times when the two countries were good neighbors who would work things out. "The government of Mexico is unstable and that will affect us," Castro warns.

Castro considers the possibility that the Mexican government is doomed. "Yeah. There is a definite dilemma. Look at my case. I'm fifty yards from Mexico. I look into Mexico from my back porch. I'm practically in Mexico. When I go upstairs to bed at night, I don't turn on the lights in the room. Because at two or three o'clock in the morning is when the shooting starts.

The machine guns—I can hear them. I haven't been to Mexico in the last eight months."[10]

Having lived for years in Latin America and Argentina, Castro believes he is more aware of what is going on—how the system works—than many other Nogales residents. For example, when he answers the phone he never gives out any real information.

The former governor notes that 50 percent of the phones in Nogales are tapped. This figure is stunning. Questions quickly arise. Who is tapping them? Are they cell phone calls or landlines? How could anyone keep track of the phone traffic? The former governor stands firm. "I know how the system works." He illustrates his point by referring to a building that he asserts is operated by the DEA for this purpose.[11]

In truth, it appears many of the phone systems in the borderlands are at risk. This goes beyond the issue of our government's legal phone taps and the more controversial but real forms of "electronic rendition" being carried out in northern Mexican states.[12]

The ability of cartels and Mexican authorities to listen in is substantial. Cartel intelligence in the borderlands is extensive and runs the gamut from technical to human capabilities. Speaking anonymously, an expert in international security matters confirmed and explained how the cartels, with the assistance of certain Mexican Army resources, have the capability to tap into cell phone or hardwired conversations without any difficulties.

Bought Off

While there has been illegal immigration and drug trafficking for years across the border there are differences today, says Castro. The sheer number of crossers is enormous and the amount of money involved is huge. "Even some of the United States government employees are being bought off—the immigration and Border Patrol people." This is happening at every level of government.[13]

"In my day, forty or fifty years ago, it was unusual to find any American employee being bought off by a cartel. Of course, the drug trade was not nearly as highly organized in those days. The cartel system itself didn't exist. It was families that pursued drug smuggling." Castro observes that many of these same families are involved in the cartel organizations of today, but that they "pretty much protect each other. Almost like unions—they are well organized, we're not."[14]

President Obama and President Calderon: Core Values

In a speech before a joint session of Congress on May 20, 2010, Mexican president Felipe Calderon criticized Arizona's passage of SB 1070. Before a cheering crowd of Democratic senators and congressmen, he lectured the United States. He stated, "It is a law that not only ignores a reality that cannot be erased by decree but also introduces a terrible idea using racial profiling as a basis for law enforcement."

In English, Calderon spoke about the risk when "core values we all care about are breached." The issue of core values might well be questioned. As will be noted in chapter 14, the Mexican government's involvement in the drug trade is pervasive.

Former diplomat Raul Castro was critical of the speech by the President Calderon before Congress. "You do not criticize a country when you are the guest of that country. You do not criticize a person's home when you are in their home." Castro believes that President Obama enabled the Mexican President to make the speech. "I have the idea that he [Calderon] probably asked Obama, and Obama agreed that he could say those things," says Castro.[15]

Solutions

Raul Castro is a strong supporter of law and order. He is not a strong supporter of SB 1070 because of his concerns about human rights violations that he thinks might occur. He is not easily categorized as relates to immigration. He believes our number one priority should be securing the border. As noted, he believes the Mexican government has a responsibility to help with this endeavor, not enable illegal immigration.[16]

Castro is a compelling advocate of an effective guest worker program that doesn't grant permanent residency or citizenship. It would offer an avenue for a worker to come to the United States legally and return home. It would also offer protection and rights to the guest worker as well as ensure no American is displaced from a job.

The former governor doesn't think the average illegal immigrant has any desire to become an American citizen. "We talk endlessly about making citizens of the Mexicans that come to the United States.

Citizenship is not the issue. Really, it is not. Those people living in the United States are not concerned about becoming American citizens. Their big concerns are to be able to work, wages, and being able to support their family."[17]

"We turn around and always talk about citizenship. That's not the issue. You can't use that as an attraction to let them stay in the country. The family is primary to them, not citizenship. The idea they want citizenship is a false assumption which hurts the immigrants' cause."[18]

A View to the South

Former Governor Raul H. Castro steps onto his balcony. Behind him is a panoramic view that looks across the border into Nogales, Sonora.

Raul Castro and his view across the border. Photo by William Daniel.

The border fence snakes its way between the two border cities. Below him, is a small brick house. He says that the night before last it was filled with thirty illegal immigrants waiting for transportation up to Tucson.

"Probably $2,000 each," he observes matter-of-factly. In what is sometimes touted as the best-guarded city on the American border, the illegal immigrants come through an unguarded fence. It's the way things work. It's the system.

In his ninety-five years Raul Castro has traveled a long way. He has overcome much. He is the product of two cultures, but has the heart of an American. He is all that is good about legal immigration. He is all that is good about America.

Beyond Diplomacy

Raul Castro has no illusions about the border. While he is uneasy about SB 1070, he is no advocate for open borders or extending citizenship to illegal immigrants. He is critical of Mexico for allowing the uncontrolled flow of its citizens into the United States. He also condemns the dependence of many Americans on drugs. His experience as a diplomat and serving in Latin America makes him keenly aware of dangers that others do not even consider. When speaking about illegal immigration, drug smuggling, and violence, he is firmly attached to reality.

Raul Castro is experienced in the ways of the world and diplomacy. But to fully understand what is happening along the border and to our country, one must look at another world and the business of drug smuggling.

And it's a world a man named Eduardo understands perfectly.

Endnotes

1. "Holder Admits to Not Reading Arizona's Immigration Law Despite Criticizing It," *FOX News*, May 14, 2010, http://www.foxnews.com/politics/2010/05/13/holder-admits-reading-arizonas-immigration-law-despite-slamming/.

2. *Raul H. Castro: Two Cultures, Many Challenges*, directed by Sy Rotter and LuisCarlos Romero-Davis, UA Center for Latin America Studies, State of Arizona, 2008.

3. Raul Castro, interview, May 28, 2010.

4. Raul Castro, interview.

5. Raul Castro, interview.

6. Raul Castro, interview.

7. Raul Castro, interview.

8. Raul Castro, interview.

9. Raul Castro, interview.

10. Raul Castro, interview.

11. Raul Castro, interview.

12. Intelligence analyst, interview, 2010.

13. Raul Castro, interview.

14. Raul Castro, interview.

15. Raul Castro, interview.

16. Raul Castro, interview.

17. Raul Castro, interview.

18. Raul Castro, interview.

Chapter Ten

The Straightest Business

"The border is never the way it seems. The weirder it is, the closer to the truth it is."
Zack Taylor, supervisory Border Patrol agent (retired)[1]

SOMEWHERE IN SOUTHERN ARIZONA, Eduardo sits in a small office bringing up a Mexican newspaper on the computer. Eduardo is charming, intelligent, and extremely likeable. As a onetime connected man he knows everything and everybody. The following is an inside look at the cartels and drug smuggling in Mexico and the United States from the viewpoint of Eduardo and cartel members.

Deep in the Heart of Mexico

Eduardo begins, "What is the best way to explain how Mexico and the drug cartels work? When it comes to drug crossing, everything is in segments. Mexico drug cartels pay off the political people over there. Let's say they are going to fly drugs from Chihuahua to the center of Durango—Durango, Durango—that's where most of the drugs like marijuana come from that are going to the border. They fly from there to Caborca, Sonora; Magdalena, Hermosillo; or a smaller state." Eduardo goes into great detail. He describes how a plane will "carry approximately 350 kilos of marijuana [almost eight hundred pounds] in blocks of ten or thirty kilos each [twenty-two to sixty-six pounds].

"One of the main things is they must be fifty kilometers [thirty-one miles] from the border. That is as close as they can get by airplane, because of the American radar. It picks them up. What they do when they are going to fly is that they usually leave about four or five o'clock in the morning from Sierra or Durango. They fly for maybe two hours in a Cessna 210 or Cessna 206.

"Let's say they are going to Caborca—most of the people these days land in Caborca. Before they leave Durango, they will call the federal officials and Army officials there [in Caborca]. They will pay them about ten to fifteen thousand dollars. Once that is paid the same feds will help unload and put the load in the trucks.

The Army guards the loads and transports them to a safe place. It may be a stash house in town or a little ranch outside a city. The goal is to move the load as close to the border as soon as possible. Once the Army gets the load within a kilometer [a little over a half mile] of the border the mules pick up their loads."

Teamwork

Often there will be two teams of mules that carry one half of the load each. Each team has two points. One man goes a mile ahead and the other man two miles ahead. They are both heavily armed in case something happens, which isn't unusual. A third man usually trails from behind. The armed men are in contact with each other and spotters on hills warn them of trouble ahead or following them.

According to Eduardo, a major problem, in addition to the Border Patrol, who may intercept 5 or 10 percent of the drugs coming across are the border, are the "banditos." They wait on the American side of the border. The mules are tired after carrying forty or forty-five kilos (eighty-eight pounds to one hundred pounds) and are vulnerable. The banditos may kill everybody and take the load—these men are usually connected with a rival cartel.

Eduardo estimates without hesitation that two out of ten loads are stolen. It is a major problem. The bodies with gunshot wounds found in the desert are victims of these ambushes. This is common in the Santa Rita Mountains and around the Buenos Aires National Wildlife Refuge.

In another interview, an informant indicates that some of the groups of mules are much larger because of the frequency of loads being stolen. Accompanying these loads it is not unusual to have five or ten heavily armed men. Also, a lot of the banditos work out of Arizona because they would be killed in Mexico.

The informant considers the death of BORTAC agent Brian Terry in passing. Manuel Osorio-Arellanes was with a group of five to eight armed men who were confronted by four BORTAC agents on the night of December 14, 2010. It was during this confrontation that agent Brian Terry was killed and a wounded Osorio-Arellanes was taken into custody.

Official versions floated initially indicated that Osorio-Arellanes was a bandito or part of a "rip crew." The informant smiles and shakes his head. He doesn't think it is true. He indicates that the shooter was back in Mexico before dawn, but doesn't offer any further details; our agreement is to talk about drugs.

The Nation

Once a load crosses the border there are a lot of places the smugglers can go. "Sometimes, about one out of fifty times, the drug cartels have a deal with the Border Patrol. Not all Border Patrol do it, but they do it. They get paid and they bring the load all the way to Tucson. They get paid twenty grand—thirty grand a load. That's to pick it up and drive it for an hour in their Border Patrol cars."

The informant notes, "Most of the times the drugs go to ranches with the owners already tied to the cartels and they get paid well so the burros land [lay up] there." A lot of the ranchers are Native Americans. This is because a huge amount of drugs [estimated as high as 75 percent] come across the Tohono O'odham Indian Reservation, also called the Nation.

Law enforcement is more limited on the Nation, even though Native Americans are subject to federal law and tribal law. The tribal police on the reservations are underpaid, stretched thin, and often not well motivated, according to several informants. Another issue is the Border Patrol presence on the reservations is more limited both in numbers and authority than in other areas. An exception to these problems is an elite unit made up of Native Americans called the Shadow Wolves, who are very effective.

Zach Taylor (former supervisory Border Patrol agent) says that there are very few Border Patrol agents on the reservation within a ten-mile strip north of the border.[2]

If caught, a Native American may never be reported to the federal authorities. If he is tried in a tribal court under a lesser charge, there is a tendency toward leniency. Life on the reservation is hard, and drug money is easy. As a Border Patrol agent related, "It's easy to pick out who is working with the cartels—they will have an expensive truck and a dilapidated home. You can't blame them."

Drugs also come through the Nation because the border between Mexico and the Nation (albeit part of the international border) is less defined. In fact, the border splits the Nation in half. There has been a lot of intermarriage and there are blood ties between families in Sonora and on the Tohono O'odham reservation.

But the routes across the reservation aren't the only way north. Every route that goes from south to north along the border is a potential corridor, and as soon as one is patrolled more heavily other corridors are used. An informant says it's a good business and the odds of getting caught are slim. "Maybe one or two out of ten get caught, but you got to remember if they (the Border Patrol) get three thousand pounds it means at least twenty or twenty-four thousand pounds gets through—and some of the loads they think they got are give-ups so the others make it." He leans forward, "There are so many routes, and the nights are so dark, and the land is so big that you can bring as much as you want."

After the drugs are dropped at a ranch, the owner of the ranch or some other people will take them the rest of the way to Tucson as soon as he thinks it is clear. Normally the drugs are pushed north in less than a day. The rancher will usually get about $10 a pound for letting the mules lay up. If the rancher moves the load to town, he'll get $35 a pound.

Sometimes mules bypass ranches and walk all the way up to Interstate 10. As they get close to the interstate, they alert a confederate by cell phone that they will be at a certain mile marker in so many minutes. As they emerge from the brush, a large truck with a camper will pull over and the mules dump their loads. In less than a minute the truck is headed west and the mules are headed south. An informant observes, "They are very fast but you got to remember everything is really checked out. If you don't count the give-ups only one in twenty loads is busted."

The mules know enough to dump their loads if they are about to be caught. Then, most often the worse that can happen is they'll be given a sandwich and maybe held overnight. If they have no record, ICE or the Border Patrol will drive them back to the border.

Tucson: A Middle Point

Eduardo explains "Once the drugs get to Tucson, then somebody picks them up—usually the buyer or the middle person. The middle guy picks up the load, weighs it, and reports to the owner how much it is. Then the owner will want it sold. It will be sold in about twenty-four hours. Keep in mind that Tucson is just a middle point—nothing stays there. Tucson is just a resting point. Let's talk numbers."

"The middle guy—he's the guy that makes a $100 a pound. Say he gets a thousand-pound load, just to round it up. He will make $100,000 …"

There is a long pause. "That's a $100,000 to weigh it and sell it to somebody up north. So the middle guy sells it. Usually to a white boy—people from Atlanta, people from Cincinnati, Columbus, people from Florida; you're talking Boston or New York. These people bring money—lots of money … most likely a million or $2 million in cash. They buy it in Tucson.

"The owner sells the weed to the middle guy for maybe $400,000. The middleman sells the weed to the buyer for $500,000. That's how the middleman makes a $100,000 in twenty-four hours." The buyer will normally just buy from the same middleman.

At that point, the buyer from Columbus or Boston will take the dope he just bought, "Dress it up and load it the same day. They move fast because of the heat."

After the purchase is made in Tucson, the buyer will bundle everything in fifty-pound blocks. He'll take it out of Tucson and drop, for example, eight hundred pounds to Atlanta and a thousand pounds to New York City.

"The Atlanta guy will then drop a fifty-pound bundle to a person who covers a block. So in Atlanta those sixteen people sell it to street people. Three pounds to one person, five pounds to another, and so on. "And they do it daily. This thing repeats every day."

"The demand for the drug business is there. You don't have to order—you don't have to do anything, it's there."

All the cartels and farmers have to do is produce the product. "The Mexicans produce and produce and produce. There are more

Real Heat: Real Power

"American officials ... it is funny ..." An informant stops and considers what to say. He explains that there was a lawyer he did business with. After they established a relationship, the lawyer volunteered that he knew other drug dealers that wanted to do business. The informant was an owner and middleman who didn't just work with anyone. There wasn't a lot of reason to risk working with a new person.

He tells his lawyer that he doesn't want to work with anybody new. "I told him I was my own boss, and this lawyer says, 'come on.' I say, 'Who is this guy?' The lawyer said he is a white guy with a lot of money—a lot of power. I say, 'Why does he want to meet me?' The lawyer said, 'cause you got good stuff.'"

"What does he carry?" The lawyer answers, "A million—two million." The informant continues, "Then when I met him, he was a big-time politician." The man started buying weed and continued for over a year. In that period he made millions.

"It was very exciting because when I got to meet this guy, I went a couple steps up in my business and started making millions consistently—I was a young guy."

After a year the politician retired. He quit the drug business and built a big house in Mexico, on the coast. He made crime pay, but how? "Because he had eyes above him—looking out for him. He is one of the few people I see get away with it. The one who succeeds is one out of fifty and I think it was him. You usually end up dead or in prison."

buyers than drugs. This is why there is so much killing, because people are stealing."

In short, there is not enough supply. "There are more buyers than supply. It's really weird. I've seen fifteen to twenty tons of weed in one chop."

Mexican Justice

Turning his attention to a computer monitor, Eduardo talks about a particular shooting of a police official in Sonora. It caused public outrage for a day or two and then, like all the killings south of the border, was forgotten. "There's so much killing. That police guy. That police guy I guarantee you was in the business ..."

"Matter of fact ... it's just getting crazy ..." He points to a picture of a man in a Mexican newspaper displayed on the screen. "See this guy? I first met him in 1999. He was in charge of Nogales. Every cartel has a man in charge of their cities. He was like a sheriff for the cartel. He was a lieutenant for El Chapo Guzman." (Guzman is the head of the most powerful cartel in Mexico—the Sinaloa Cartel).

"He was a big shot. Other drug people from different regions want to get in, but he doesn't let them. That's why he's allowed to be in charge."

Eduardo explains how he knew the man and adds, "He probably killed twenty-five or thirty people in the last month." He also says that the man killed the police official. "That's why he was arrested.

"This guy when you meet him—you don't think of him as a killer. You think of him just like you. This guy is really mellow. He don't drink, he don't do drugs. He don't do anything. He's just a straight-up killer. And he controls Nogales for the drug cartel. How much money is he worth? Probably fifty or sixty million dollars."

He made his mistake killing the federal official. If he hadn't killed him he would still be free. It is not good business for a guy to kill a public official above a certain level or if he is too connected. "That's a big no-no." There was too much publicity in United States newspapers.

Eduardo says, "The murderer should get a fifty-year sentence, minimum, but he'll pay off the Mexican government with $5 or $10 million and be out in sixty months. While he is still in prison, he will run his business, as long as El Chapo backs him."

The Crooked Business Is the Straightest Business

There is a discussion about how money moves in the drug world. In the United States, money from deals is flown across the country in private jets to private airports. There is no customs—there are no problems, except for the volume of the money that is to be sent to Mexico. It comes in duffle bags. Although the exchange of money between the owner (the cartel) and the middleman is handled in different ways by different cartels, the method described below is not atypical according to Eduardo.

"At this level with drug cartels everything is done by your word. I owe you a million dollars; I'll pay you on Friday. OK. We don't go 'I'll kill you.' We don't say anything like that. The crooked business is the straightest business." It's straight because people in the drug business ultimately can't get away with anything vis-à-vis their compadres or organization.

"They'll find you. They'll find your family. And they don't have to tell you that. You know it. So the drug business is the straightest business. Your word is all you got. You break it you're done. Done." The penalty for double-crossing the cartel is much more certain than the probability of being caught by Americans.

Another informant laughs at American enforcement efforts. "You Americans go to all the trouble to hunt down and fill tunnels, but you let hundreds of ultralights fly dope over the border and don't do nothing. You don't shoot them down or nothing. It is a joke."

The overall low rate of drug seizures results in a large number of drug owners and middlemen having huge amounts of cash ... truckloads of cash. They have to clean their dirty money.

Doing the Laundry

The traditional way of simply moving the cash across the border is losing favor though it is still done. Some people will try to fly it south, but it is not the recommended way. Eduardo says, "There's lots of ways. In the old days you'd hire skinny women who would put on thousand dollar 'pregnant suits' and they'd walk $300,000 across the border at a time. You'd send four or five across a day. Other ways were to conceal it in packages like diapers or dog food—$100,000 a package." The money was rarely discovered.

The amount of money confiscated by ICE or the Border Patrol is miniscule, according to another informant. "If they get half a million they think it's a big deal, but we're sending five million in behind it. It's the old give-up thing. Let them think they got something big, but they don't got shit."

Today, money goes south to be laundered, stays in the United States, or a combination of both. But whether it stays above or below the border, laundering drug money depends on whom you know. "Everything is through connections," Eduardo states. "Everything is through big connections. First of all, Mexican bankers. Money exchange houses. Real estate. Private owners. Let's look at the banks. You go talk to the director of the bank. You say, "I got $5 million and I need to clean it."

"The director of the bank says, 'We need to pay four or five people on top of us.' The director will charge one and a half percent. For seventy-five thousand he will get three of four people to sign the right documents and your money is in."

"You take the money to a money exchange house and have them transfer the money in parts to the bank. The banker will tell you when and how, because there are days you can and days you can't. Only him and the owner know about it. It goes into your account. The account will show that the money has been there five or ten years. After six months you can do pretty much anything you want with the money. Some people will leave the money in the Mexican banks. Other will move it to, say, Spain."

The amount of drug money being laundered is staggering. It is in the realm of hundreds of billions of dollars. And some very big American financial institutions have been and are involved in cleaning some of these billions. One of these was Wachovia Bank, which was later bought by Wells Fargo.

Wachovia's involvement in money laundering started to unravel in April of 2006. A DC-9 jet belonging to the Sinaloa Cartel landed in Ciudad del Carmen and was busted by Mexican soldiers. Not only was it carrying 5.7 tons of cocaine (valued at over $100 million), but also a paper trail that showed how the cartel bought the plane.[3] The DEA (Drug Enforcement Agency) and the IRS followed the trail for almost two years and discovered the DC-9 was bought with money laundered through Wachovia Bank.[4]

The bank was closely watched and it was found that billions of dollars of cash from Mexican exchange houses, wire transfers, and travelers checks were flowing into Wachovia. But as noted earlier, a lot of weird things go on when talking about the border, and the Wachovia affair was to be no different. Criminal proceedings for not maintaining an effective anti-money laundering program were brought against Wachovia (not against a single individual), but the cases never reached the courts.[5]

In 2010, the case was settled. Wachovia was essentially put on a year's probation and had to forfeit $110 million. They also were fined $50 million for not monitoring funds that were used to transport twenty-two tons of cocaine.[6]

To make matters worse, it appears that Wachovia had laundered $378 billion (the equivalent of half of Mexico's GDP) from Mexican currency exchange houses without "providing proper anti-laundering strictures."[7]

It is hard to overstate the influence of money laundering by the cartels. Antonio Maria Costa, head of the UN Office on Drugs and Crime, asserted that internationally many banks were saved during the 2008 monetary crisis by drug money. "The system was basically paralyzed because of the unwillingness of banks to lend money to one another." Costa claimed to have seen evidence that drug money and organized crime money was the "only liquid investment capital available to some banks on the verge of collapse last year."[8]

While most high rollers in the world of drug smuggling like to bury their money in hundreds of accounts around the world, others prefer simple property investments. They give the seller cash for the property and the seller says it's a gift to avoid taxes. In Mexico, buying ranches is a common way to clean drug money. The informant sitting across the table smiles. "I got some ranches."

He ends his interview with swagger, confidence, and a parting comment, "Despite what the white boys think, we run the show."

Payoffs or Policy?

The testimony of cartel informants reinforces what many people along the border have known for years. The Mexican Army is actively involved with the drug trade as well as human trafficking. It also illustrates that at the higher levels, drug traffickers have little fear that their product will be stopped and confiscated by ICE or the Border Patrol.

In fact, it demonstrates a growing problem with American law enforcement discussed by former Arizona governor Raul Castrol—corruption. The amount of money involved in the drug trade is staggering. So large that in some cases even the largest banks have succumbed to its power.

The question is, how much of the failure to stem the flow of drugs across the border is a result of incompetence, corruption, policy, or just plain denial? To gain insight into this issue it's important to return to the border, because the dope never quits.

Endnotes

1. Zack Taylor, interview April 28, 2011.

2. Zack Taylor, interview.

3. Ed Vulliamy, "How a big US bank laundered billions from Mexico's murderous drug gangs," *The Observer*, April 3, 2011.

4. Vulliamy, "How a big US bank laundered billions from Mexico's murderous drug gangs."

5. Vulliamy, "How a big US bank laundered billions from Mexico's murderous drug gangs."

6. Vulliamy, "How a big US bank laundered billions from Mexico's murderous drug gangs."

7. Vulliamy, "How a big US bank laundered billions from Mexico's murderous drug gangs."

8. Anny Shaw, "Drugs money 'saved the banks from collapse' during global crisis, claims UN drugs and crime chief," *Mail Online*, December 13, 2009, http://www.dailymail.co.uk/news/article-1235512/Drugs-money-saved-banks-collapse-global-crisis-claims-UN-drugs-crime-chief.html.

Chapter Eleven

The Dope Never Quits

"You just get pissed at the incompetence of the government..."
Ed Ashurst, manager of Mallet Ranch[1]

ED ASHURST IS ONE of the men who tracked the murderer of Rob Krentz to the Mexican border. He manages the Mallet Ranch, which sits north and east of the Krentz Ranch. It is bordered on the north and northwest by the Chiricahua Mountains, and to the east is the rugged country where the Apache chief Cochise waged guerilla warfare against the United States in the late nineteenth century.

Jack Tunks is a member of the Cowboy Hall of Fame and foreman of the Red Tail Ranch thirty miles to the north. He is a man of few compliments, except when it comes to Ed Ashurst. When asked about Ashurst, Tunks takes a break from branding. "He's one helluva cowboy. Ed can ride any horse in the state. If he tells you that a tree is going to fall over in five minutes, you don't need to start checking the tree; you better start getting out of the way."[2]

Coming from the west on the highway you pass a high rounded hill before arriving at the lane to the Mallet Ranch headquarters. The reality of ranch life near the border appears. Sitting on top of the hill is an MSS (mobile surveillance system) truck-mounted radar unit. It has a range of ten miles. The hill is twenty-two miles north of the border. Waiting outside the ranch headquarters is Ed Ashurst—a twenty-first-century cowboy.

A Revelation

Having worked on the huge Babbitt Ranch in northern Arizona, Ashurst was more than able to manage any ranch in the country. But the Mallet Ranch was to offer challenges he had never encountered.

Some of the busiest human trafficking and smuggling corridors in the country cross the ranch.

Ed's first encounter with illegal immigrants was on Thanksgiving Day 1997. Ed and his wife Jean Anne awoke to discover seventeen crossers in their yard. They were covered with black plastic to stay warm. "At that time it was all worker types. There were no drugs. I'd hear about drugs ten or fifteen miles away or out in the mountains, but I never saw any drugs or had any evidence of drugs coming through the ranch yet," says Ashurst. "There were no guns. Just illegals—hundreds of them."

Ashurst is not a man to stand back and watch. He had a ranch to run and the illegal immigrants were making his job more difficult. He picked up mountains of trash from crossers and helped capture groups of illegal immigrants numbering 200, 120, 114, 50, 60, and 40. He didn't count groups under forty. The activity did not let up as the next year passed into the next. "The number was constant and astounding," noted Ashurst.

He recalls about how he "helped" catch bunches of illegal immigrants. "I say I've helped, because the Border Patrol would not have caught any of them if I had not found them, called the Border Patrol, led the Border Patrol by the hand, and said, 'There they are.'"

The numbers of illegal immigrants increased through the early 2000s. The attitude and backgrounds of the illegal immigrants changed during these years. But there were also signs that not all of the traffic was from illegal immigrants. The area was experiencing a growing crime wave— the result of drug smugglers. "Typically, drug smugglers will drop their loads and rob or steal as they return to Mexico. The routine is drop the dope going north, burglarize a home going south," observes Ashurst.

For example, a guesthouse on the Mallet Ranch was broken into multiple times, but according to Ed, "It was no big deal. We stopped keeping anything in there and half the time we wouldn't call the law. What was the use?" In the thirteen years the Ashursts have lived on the Mallet Ranch the guesthouse has been broken into fifty times.

Don't Phone Again

By 2008 crime was becoming more and more brazen. On March 6, 2008, Ashurst and his wife saddled a couple of horses, loaded them in a trailer, and left the Mallet Ranch headquarters at 7 AM. They met their son at the old IV Bar Ranch headquarters, which was a little over a mile away. They gathered and sorted a couple hundred yearlings.

Ed and Jean Anne returned before one o'clock. Jean Anne noticed the door to their house was ajar. They discovered thieves had stolen nine firearms, their wallets, checkbooks, credit cards, and social security cards, but didn't ransack the house. They also stole all the Ashursts' clean socks and left behind their filthy socks.

Ashurst notified the Border Patrol and the sheriff's office at 12:40 PM about the break-in. His next move was to phone his neighbors. Among them were Rob and Sue Krentz, Dean Nelson, Hal Mortenson, Rick Snure, Don Kimble, and the Rodeo Grocery Store, asking for any and all help available to help catch the burglars.

What is of particular interest is that from 1 PM to 3:30 PM Sue Krentz made repeated calls for assistance on Ed's behalf to the Border Patrol, both in Douglas and Lordsburg. The Douglas Border Patrol station is only thirty miles from the Mallet Ranch.

The irony is, not only were they the last to respond for the call to help, but they also ended up in the wrong place. They barged into the ranch house of Sue and Rob Krentz, telling Sue that there was a robbery going on. Sue explained that the robbery occurred at the Mallet Ranch. They insisted, "We heard it was here. Get out of the way." Afterwards, they showed up briefly at the Mallet Ranch and left.

In the process of looking for tracks before the arrival of the authorities Phil Krentz, Louis Pope, and Ashurst caught a group of twenty-four illegal immigrants hiding in a culvert under the highway and another group at the Price Canyon turnoff. At 6:30 PM Ed Ashurst called off the search.

Sitting in his burglarized home, Ed made his last call to the Border Patrol at 8 PM. He talked to the shift supervisor and asked why no help was given. He is told, "Don't phone again. We have no plans to help you in this kind of situation."

After 2008 the drug traffic across the ranches above the Geronimo Trail exploded and continues to grow.

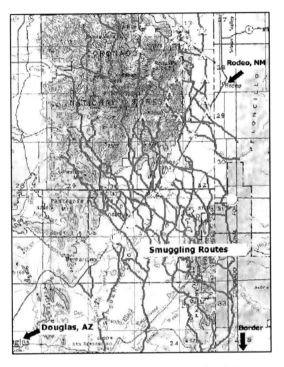

Major routes used by smugglers crossing north of Geronimo Trail as of 2011 and 2012.

Deliberate Incompetence?

In the wake of the public uproar that occurred after the murder of Rob Krentz, Arizona governor Jan Brewer, Senator Jon Kyl, Senator John McCain, and others pressured the administration to send National Guard troops to the border. Senator McCain and Senator Kyl recommended deploying five to six thousand National Guard troops to the Arizona-Mexico border.[3]

The Obama administration reacted strongly. National Security Advisor James Jones and the White House Terrorism Czar John Brennan called McCain and Kyl's efforts "unwarranted interference."[4]

Nonetheless, on May 25, 2010, President Obama announced

1,200 National Guard troops would be sent to the two thousand-mile-long border with Mexico. Of this number almost half were assigned to Arizona.

Ed Ashurst is outspoken in his views, but he cooperates with the Border Patrol when they ask his help. Ashurst met with Supervisory Border Patrol agent Mark Monin in August of 2010. Monin was looking for a place to establish a camp for the soon-to-arrive National Guard troops as well as a location for an observation post.

The observation post would be equipped with the latest gear in order to assist the Border Patrol in intercepting smugglers and illegal immigrants. Since the locations Monin was looking at were on the Mallet Ranch, he needed Ashurst's approval. Ashurst recommended a hill that was accessible to a nearby highway. Monin agreed—that's where they would put the observation post.

Something bothered Ashurst. He asked why they were putting an observation post twenty-two miles north of the border.

Monin replied that no suitable place had been found on the border. However, Ashurst recalls him saying they had found a spot on a ranch very close to the border with a view ten miles to the east and ten miles to the west, but it had been rejected.

According to Ashurst, the Border Patrol and National Guard responded, the hill (which was exactly twenty-one miles south of Ashurst's hill) would be too time-consuming to get up and down and it was too far away from town.

It was mystifying to Ashurst. Why would they select a hill twenty-two miles north of the border for an observation post that was in actuality farther from a town than the hill rejected right on the border? Why would they claim the access was too poor to use the border hill, when it was really more accessible than the hill Monin had selected on the Mallet Ranch?

The rancher located on the border had pleaded with the Border Patrol to put the observation post on his hill. He had personally witnessed countless loads of dope and groups of illegal immigrants pass within sight of his hill a mile north of the border.

Shortly after Ashurst's meeting with Monin, a F150 pickup was found on the Fairchild Ranch, eleven miles north of the rejected border hill and eleven miles south of the accepted Mallet Ranch hill. The truck was so overloaded with dope (in excess of a thousand pounds), both rear tires had blown out.

The truck would have been seen coming across the border from an observation post on the border hill, but would not have been seen by the proposed observation post on the Mallet Ranch. That same week in August three additional pickups passed through the same area, all of which would have been easily detected from the border hill. This does not take into account the countless loads coming through on the backs of mules.

As part of his attempt to inform people about what is going on along the border, Ashurst writes Border Manifestos, which are widely circulated. Concerning the observation post, Ed Ashurst writes, "To me the significance of this is profound. Why would the Border Patrol and our National Guard pass up an opportunity to establish a lookout in an excellent spot right on the border, only to choose a spot of lesser quality twenty-two miles north of the border? Is this mere coincidence? In my opinion, no. It is planned and deliberate incompetence."[5]

A veteran ICE agent remarked on the importance of the selection of the hill on the Mallet Ranch and not the border hill. "An observation post on the hill a mile north of the border would have effectively shut down the border ten miles each way."

In one of the last stakeholder meetings Ashurst attended, "I told Congresswoman Gabrielle Giffords (Dem., AZ) and then Border Patrol sector chief, Robert Gilbert, that 'I have had no less than a dozen Border Patrol agents tell me their superiors purposefully do things to make them unsuccessful.' I thought they were going to have me arrested. After the meeting, an out-of-uniform Border Patrol agent hugged me and thanked me profusely for telling the truth."

New Strategies: Old Responses

2011 brought new techniques of drug smuggling to the border. Plasma cutters were being used on the high fences along the border. These saws can cut quickly and neatly through the metal fences, drugs can be transferred across the border, and the cut fence set back in place to disguise the existence of the opening.

More importantly, the use of ultralights piloted by smugglers and laden with 200 or 300 pounds of drugs each are becoming much more frequent along the border, and the area north of the Geronimo Trail was no exception. It is the policy of the Border Patrol and ICE not to shoot the ultralights down.

A pilot assigned to the Davis-Monthan Air Force Base in Tucson relates how at night, radar screens will light up with scores of blips as ultralights cross the border from Mexico. He got in trouble one night because an ultralight got caught in his jet wash (the turbulent created behind a jet engine exhaust). He was told in no uncertain terms to be more careful—it's expensive to treat injured ultralight pilots.[6]

As the invasion by the cartel ultralight air force increased, the presence of the National Guard on the hill near the Mallet Ranch headquarters became less frequent. Finally, in January 2011, Supervisory Border Patrol agent Monin negotiated another agreement with Ashurst.

A Joint Task Force North out of Fort Bliss, Texas, would be allowed to get "real-life training" for an Army Air Missile Defense brigade that was going to be transferred to the Middle East in a month or two. They would set up their million dollar radar rigs on the hill every night.

Soldier sets up barbed wire for protection. Photo courtesy of Ed Ashurst.

Ashurst visited the unit one night. He noticed they had strung coils of barbed wire around the perimeter of the observation post. The commander of the six-man unit explained that the wire was needed " to protect us in case we are attacked." (This particular incident took place shortly after the murder of BORTAC agent Brian Terry.)

The rancher countered, "You've got firearms, don't you?" The men looked around at each other. Finally, a soldier said they had one gun. Ashurst couldn't believe what he was hearing. He almost asked, "Do you have bullets?" A roll of barbed wire and a single gun was protecting six soldiers and millions of dollars of high-tech gear. Ashurst snapped some pictures and left.

Dusk and no weapons in sight. Photo courtesy of Ed Ashurst.

As he walked back to the ranch headquarters, he wondered, "Why would the American government allow unarmed soldiers to sit on a hill, essentially without protection, after Brian Terry was murdered in a firefight by a group of men armed with AK-47s less than a month earlier? These people are out of touch with reality."

Reality Check

During this period the head of Homeland Security, Janet Napolitano, cited statistics about the relatively low crime rate on the border as compared to other areas in the country. In response Ranchers

Louis Pope (Rob Krentz's brother-in-law), Phil Krentz (Rob Krentz's brother), Roger Barnett, Fred Eddington, Scott Arena, and Don Kimball met with Ed Ashurst.

"We made a map of the area which covered from the southeastern corner of Arizona going west about twenty miles to the Silver Creek area, and going north about thirty miles to the area around the towns of Portal, Arizona, and Rodeo, New Mexico. On this map we made marks recording violations to United States law committed by illegal aliens for the last two years. We did not use government statistics, but recorded incidents that we knew had happened firsthand, many of which we had witnessed." It excluded the city of Douglas.

Don't Look!

Ashurst relates a final story. It is about a friend who has a green card, works in the United States, and visited relatives in Mexico recently. "He [the friend] was with his wife and two young daughters in a Ford SuperCab pickup. The girls were in the backseat. My friend was at a busy intersection stopped at a red light in Juárez."

"He said, 'Two cars were behind me and an SUV pulled up beside one of the cars, rolled down the windows, and stuck machine guns out the windows. They blew the car off the face of the earth—I don't know how many dead there were. There were stopped cars all four directions. And nobody looks. My little girls started crying and turning around. I told them to be quiet and don't look—don't look! Everybody just looked straight ahead. The light turned green and it was business as usual."

In Mexico, the people on the street claim the level of violence is so extreme that Ciudad Juarez in two years will become "La Ciudad Fatal" (the City of the Dead).

Ashurst is afraid that kind of violence is headed north and our government is saying, "Don't look!"

By summer of 2011 Geronimo Trail is again lightly patrolled. You can drive on the Trail from Douglas past the famous Slaughter ranch and not encounter a single Border Patrol vehicle. But scouts for drug smugglers crouch along the border fence waiting for dark. And the dope never quits.

Scouts waiting to cross the border are the only sign of life.
Photo by William Daniel.

To many ranchers, Homeland Security appears to have a policy of benign and intentional neglect regarding the border—a policy they feel directly threatens the safety, security, and lives of every American. And a dog named Bandit may prove them right.

Legend

arrest or capture of 40 illegals or more ☒ ⟨38⟩

dope loads found ● ⟨213⟩

stolen vehicles ⟍⟋

dangerous encounters; assaults, burglaries, forced entries etc. ! ⟨132⟩

dead illegals found ✝ 16

high speed vehicle chase between drug haulers and law enforcement ↥ ⟨14⟩

murder ✶ ⟨1⟩

fires started by illegal aliens ⟶ 100000 ACRES PLUS BURNED $40000000 cost to taxpayers ⟨9⟩

illegals spotted with firearms ⟶ ⟨12⟩
or ammunition caches

outlandish residents ? ⟨4⟩

$100,000,000ºº Loss to Private sector — loss in real estate value personal property etc.

Loss in wildlife habitat — immeasurable ?

This map does not represent total incidents, only things that have
for sure been documented, and are very conservative in estimate.
The vast majority of these events here recorded happened in the last
two years (2008 thru 2010)

No attempt was made to record anything except the incidents
from Silver Creek east to New Mexico and the Mexican border
north to the Portal area.

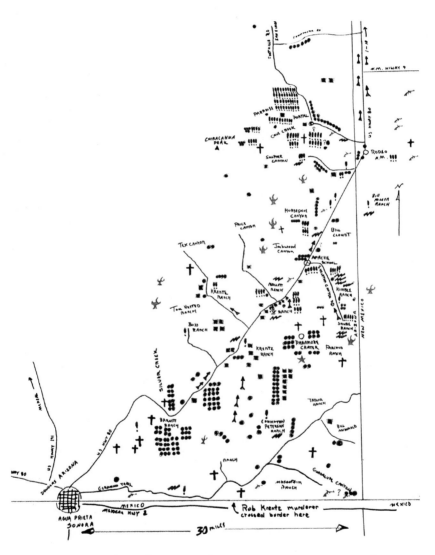

Ranchers chronicle crime in their area over a two-year period.

Endnotes

1. Ed Ashurst, interview, October 26, 2010.

2. Jack Tunks, interview, May 12, 2011.

3. "National Guard Troops On Mexico Border: Stalemate Frustrates Lawmakers," *Huffington Post*, May 26, 2010, www.huffingtonpost.com/2010/05/20/national-guard-troops-on_n_582929.html.

4. Michael D. Shear and Spencer S. Hsu, "President Obama to send more National Guard troops to U.S.-Mexico border." *Washington Post*, May 26, 2010.

5. Ed Ashurst, "Border Manifesto Two," *The Federal Observer*, August 10, 2010, http://www.federalobserver.com/2010/08/10/ashurst-border-manifesto-2/.

6. Pilot, Davis-Monthan Air Base, interview, 2011.

Chapter Twelve

Security on the San Pedro

"Who are you and what are you doing here?"

Hamdy Singury1

WALT AND MAY KOLBE own and operate a picturesque inn on the San Pedro River a few miles north of the border Arizona shares with Mexico. It is known as a premier birding area. Behind their home are four cottages and the San Pedro River. The inn offers facilities for horse owners who like to ride the fifty-seven thousand acres of the San Pedro Riparian National Conservation Area. The idyllic setting has been marred in recent years by the influx of illegal immigrants and smugglers that stream up from the south. They follow the San Pedro River north—past the Kolbes' Inn. The Kolbes' experiences had been similar with those shared by many landowners and citizens along the borderlands. But that was about to change.

Walt and May came to understand the most important problems coming from the south were not illegal immigrants looking for work or even drug traffickers. It had rained Monday night and the ground was still wet when Walt performed his Wednesday ritual of collecting trash that illegal immigrants dump on their property. He found a muddy backpack near a fence line and dumped it in the trash. The couple left for several days, returning on a Sunday.

It was about suppertime, and Walt was in the kitchen. May came into the kitchen from the outside with a backpack in hand. "Did you throw away this backpack that was in the garbage?" she asked.[2]

"Yeah, I threw it away," Walt, answered.

"Where did you find it?" asked May.

"Down by the fence, about a hundred yards from our house," he responded.

"Did you look in it?" she asked.

Somewhat irritated, Walt answered, "No, I didn't look in it. I don't know what vermin is crawling around in there."

"Well, I did," said May.

May produced a book about six by eight inches. Inside were notes made in Arabic, Spanish, and English. There was a phone number for Iran and a phone number for Canada inside. It was wet and pages had bled through, but they were still very legible. There was the notation Champotón, Campeche.

Walt and May Kolbe hold photos of diary pages.
Photo courtesy of Walt and May Kolbe.

Walt advocated calling Cochise County sheriff Larry Dever in the morning. "He's the only law enforcement agent I trust in Cochise County," he said. May suggested writing an email to Walt's brother, Jim Kolbe. At that time Jim was a member of the United States House of Representatives. Shortly before midnight May sent an email to Jim in Washington, D.C. Within five minutes there was a reply. Jim wrote, "Call the FBI in the morning. The FBI will be out there before you can even hang up the phone."[3]

Walt spent a sleepless night thinking about the book. Early in the morning he told May that he was going to call the FBI, "but once the FBI gets hold of this diary, it's going to disappear into a black hole. It'll be gone forever. We'll never see it or hear anything about it again."

He decided first to call Bill Hess, a senior reporter with the *Sierra Vista Herald*. He phoned Hess around 6:30 AM expecting to leave a voice mail. But the reporter was already at work and answered. Walt told him about the discovery. Shortly afterward Hess and a photographer were looking at the book. "You can photograph anything but the two phone numbers," said Walt. Hess spent the next hour interviewing Walt and May.[4]

The FBI Responds

By 8 AM the reporter and photographer had left. Walt assumed the FBI office in Sierra Vista was open by then and called. After being put on hold for twenty minutes, an agent picked up. Walt explained he and his wife had found a diary-like book written in what looked like Arabic, Spanish and English. He also indicated it contained a phone number for Canada and Iran.

A not very interested FBI agent replied, "Oh, well...could you bring it into the office sometime?"

A surprised Walt answered, "We weren't planning to be back in Sierra Vista for a week."

"That's OK, just bring it in at your convenience."

A stunned Walt answered, "OK." He hung up and looked at May. "You won't believe this. He said 'Bring it in at your convenience.'" May fired off an email to Walt's brother, Jim. Three minutes later an angry Jim Kolbe called.

Congressman Kolbe said, "What? I can't believe this. This can't be true!"

Walt responded, "He said bring it in at my convenience."

After a short talk, Congressman Kolbe hung up the phone. About fifteen minutes later Walt received a call from the Sierra Vista FBI agent. "We thought maybe we should come out and look at that thing. Would this afternoon be OK?" offered the agent nonchalantly.[5]

Walt agreed and hung up. Within minutes the phone rang again. The same agent that had phoned before announced, "We are leaving town right now and will be to your house just as fast as we can get there." Jim Kolbe had notified the FBI liaison office in the Capitol Building of the problem. The liaison office called FBI headquarters and Walt and May were getting action.

A few minutes later two FBI agents stood inside the Kolbe's home, diary in hand, ready to exit. Walt asked for a receipt and got it. As the agents exited Walt asked, "Do you have any interest in the backpack? There might be something important in it."

The agent replied, "Oh, good idea. We ought to take the backpack." Holding a second receipt Walt and May watched the agents prepare to go.

Walt asked, "Would you like to see where we found the backpack?" Walt showed them the bottom wire on a barbed wire fence at the edge of his property. The wire had caught the backpack. Walt and May give the credit for this event to their dog Bandit, who was very protective and hated intruders.

"At that time we were getting more than three hundred crossers every night," noted Walt. "Bandit would bark at them and chase them off. We think he (the man with the diary) probably turned around and went back south through the fence in a hell of a hurry and got the backpack snagged on the fence. He probably came back to try to find it, but Bandit doesn't give up."[6]

A determined Bandit. Photo courtesy of Walt and May Kolbe.

At first, the diary disappeared down an FBI black hole like the Kolbes expected. Then, the FBI finally acknowledged it and suggested it was just a bunch of love letters.

The Reappearing Diary

The seriousness of the matter and what really concerned the Kolbes was that the government had just raised the terrorism level "to the top notch" and were telling people if they saw anything suspicious to notify the FBI. The Head of the Department of Energy had notified Congress that the largest nuclear plant in the United States (the Palo Verde Nuclear Power Plant near Phoenix) might be a target of terrorists.[7]

Also, a month after the diary was found, a fifteen-member terrorist cell was shut down in Montreal. According to an August 2002 report of the Canadian Security Intelligence Service (CSIS), "… with the possible exception of the United States, there are more international terrorist organizations active in Canada than anywhere in the world."[8]

A later event added further credence to the value of the diary, even though the FBI publically minimized the document's importance. In 2006, Walt and May attended a dinner where the keynote speaker was a United States congressman from Colorado's Sixth District—Tom Tancredo. Walt met the Congressman after the speech and said, "The border problem is very important to us because we found a diary…"

Tancredo responded instantly. "Yeah, I saw that diary in the Foreign Affairs Subcommittee on Terrorism." Somehow, the unimportant diary Walt and May found was important enough to be discussed in the committee.[9]

The Mystery Man

The Middle Eastern man crossing Walt and May Kolbe's land demonstrates the ease with which potential terrorists can cross the border. What illustrates the tragedy from a national security perspective is that a watchdog named Bandit was more effective than our entire national security apparatus.

So, in this instance, who was the mystery man crossing Walt and

May Kolbe's property? Was he a potential terrorist? Was he a threat to national security? Or was he "harmless" and just another "illegal immigrant"?

It is clear the government did not address this—publicly. The government has a policy of keeping the public uninformed about events occurring along the border. The question arises: Does the policy of secrecy work in the public interest or just in an agency's self-interest? What are the secrets in the diary that the FBI has kept to itself?

Hamdy Singury, a Middle Eastern intelligence expert who is also a professor at the University of Arizona, reviewed photos of the diary. He determined the name of the man that crossed the Kolbe property was Wail, an Iraqi citizen who lived south of Bagdad. Wail was also a member of the Shia minority. The diary indicated that his motivation for leaving was because Saddam Hussein and his Bath party were then still in power and persecuted the Shias.[10]

It was also clear from the diary that Wail flew out of Iraq. Wail wrote, "This is the best day of my life. I will not forget it. I never thought I would leave."

Singury explained how people travel out of the Middle East without papers. "You go to the most corrupt countries in the area and get papers." Since Wail had made drawings of the Great Pyramids in his diary it is most likely he flew to Egypt."[11]

Wail's next move, Singury said, was to find an equally corrupt government to which he wanted to travel. Wail selected the Mexican Consulate and was given a visa to enter that country. Wail and the wayward diary journeyed from Egypt to Champotón on the Yucatan Peninsula.

Singury observed, "He was a young man and judging by his grammar had the equivalent of a middle school education."[12]

According to the diary, accompanying Wail were at least three other Iraqis. They were Anwar, Hodge Hassan, and Babu Kanol Fahad. Hassan was a much older man and a mentor to Wail.[13]

The tone of the diary changed. Somewhere in Mexico, Hodge Hassan died. Hassan's last words were, "Take care of your brothers." Wail continued toward the Arizona-Mexican border without papers, guided by a coyote. On a rainy night, the journey of Wail, Babu, and others took them near the inn of Walter and May Kolbe. It was there he lost his diary.

Was Wail a terrorist? Hamdy Singury addresses the issue with a laugh. "No, there is nothing in his writing to indicate he was a terrorist." Singury leans forward. "Americans do not understand that terrorists are very intelligent, highly motivated, and usually well educated. Wail's diary shows a simple young man who was having a bad trip."[14]

Wail's diary. Photo courtesy of Walt and May Kolbe.

Fallout

But other Iraqis or persons traveling with Wail did not leave a diary behind. As Singury points out, you need to be able to ask everyone entering the United States without exception two questions: "*Who are you and what are you doing here?* And they must be able to prove it."

He describes a conversation he had with a law professor at the University of Arizona. The professor was complaining about the passage of SB 1070. Singury remained quiet. The professor asked, "What do you think about SB 1070?" Singury replied, "It is your country and your law."

The professor pushed for an answer. "No, what do you think?"

Singury responded, "You Americans are funny. You ask the police to protect you and yet you make it impossible for them to do it. Then, when you are attacked you blame the police when it is you who have caused it."[15]

The question of whether the public interest would have been better served by releasing the contents of the diary is a difficult question. In order to make intelligent decisions the public needs to be informed. To deny the public information to make these decisions can legitimately be based upon national security or privacy concerns.

However, as noted within this book, information is often withheld by the government or manipulated for self-serving promotion or agenda-driven purposes. Whether the information in the dairy was worthy of concealment is up to the reader.

A Numbers Game

In the end national security and the open border is a numbers game. Among the millions of illegal immigrants who are entering or have entered the United States, it is estimated that 10 to 17 percent are criminals. Since the effect of intentionally permitting a million or more criminals to enter into the country doesn't bother some politicians, it is doubtful that permitting a few thousand terrorists to enter matters to them either. But it should.

Among the OTMs (Other Than Mexicans) illegally entering the country there are members of Hezbollah, Hamas, and al Qaeda—and more are coming. The going price for smuggling a member of Hezbollah into the United States is about $25,000 to $35,000.

At some point there will be terrorist events. The true significance of Wail's diary is that we are unprotected. Seven years later, the reluctance of our government to ask the two simple questions "Who are you and what are you doing here?" of *everyone* entering the country demonstrates a national death wish.

A Ticking Bomb

A well-placed security expert (speaking on terms of anonymity) believes the most important border issue the country faces is the possibility of a group crossing the border with a weapon of mass destruction (WMD.) He states, "The current threat of a nuclear event in the United States is the most serious it has been since the Cuban Missile Crisis."

The assembly of a nuclear device is not an overwhelming task. The theoretical design of a nuclear weapon and the triggering device is pretty straightforward. From a design point of view there are more than enough detailed bomb plans floating around (thanks particularly to the father of the Pakistani atomic bomb, Abdul Qadeer Khan, and the Chinese People's Republic). And then there is the relatively simple solution of using a dirty bomb.

The international security expert observes, "There is a plentiful supply of weapons-grade uranium available in the world." It does not take a large amount of weapons-grade uranium to create a devastating weapon. For example, a quantity of weapons-grade uranium no larger than a tennis ball can create a weapon with a potential yield of ten megatons. The bountiful supply is mainly a result of the breakup of the Soviet Union.

This weapons-grade uranium is often poorly guarded, improperly stored, and inadequately accounted for. No one really knows where all of it is located. The biggest problem is that it is incredibly, stunningly cheap.

The same source reported that the United States has been scurrying around the globe buying these wayward inventories of weapons grade-uranium. This is an area where the United States government has been very successful and lucky. However, it is an area where you have to be successful 100 percent of the time. In this endeavor, Israel has been exceedingly helpful.

It must be emphasized that the public tends to dismiss this threat because of the government's lack of emphasis of the danger. In truth, the government is combating the threat of a WMD being brought into the United States vigorously. However, the effort is severely handicapped because of the open borders.

It is a serious enough issue that a source within the management of the Border Patrol who had been unwilling to talk earlier came forward to express his concerns about an upsurge of OTMs entering the county (circa 2011) from Arab countries not friendly to the United States. Agents with boots on the ground are noticing the spike.[16] The Border Patrol had no knowledge of their identities or their intent. And worse yet, Walter and May Kolbe's dog Bandit has passed away. So we may not be as well protected as we were.

The experience of Walt and May Kolbe raises many questions. For example, why is the government so apparently uncommitted to border security as compared to airport security? It is one of many disconnects that surround the federal government's policy regarding the border—an anomaly.

And one of the most important ways to understand the border situation is to look at actions and anomalies. Anomalies expose intent, methods, and motives. And no one is more experienced with the peculiarity of government actions than Cochise County sheriff Larry Dever.

Endnotes

1. Hamdy Singury, interview, November 10, 2010.

2. Walt and May Kolbe, interview, September 10, 2010.

3. Walt and May Kolbe, interview.

4. Walt and May Kolbe, interview.

5. Walt and May Kolbe, interview.

6. Walt and May Kolbe, interview.

7. Jeanne Meserve "U.S. official: Arizona nuclear plant may be target," *CNN U.S.*, March 20, 2003, http;//articles.cnn.com/2003-03-20/us/nuclear.plant.threat_1_arizona-nuclear-plant-power-plant-palo-verde?_s=PM:US

8. Walt and May Kolbe, interview.

9. Walt and May Kolbe, interview.

10. Hamdy Singury, interview, November 10, 2010.

11. Hamdy Singury, interview.

12. Hamdy Singury, interview.

13. Hamdy Singury, interview.

14. Hamdy Singury, interview.

15. Hamdy Singury, interview.

16. Border Patrol supervisor, interview, 2011.

Chapter Thirteen

Border Law

"I am here to investigate Cochise, Santa Cruz, and Graham County..."

Senior FBI Agent

FOUR-TERM COCHISE COUNTY SHERIFF Larry Dever is on the front lines of the crime wave shoving its way north from Mexico. When he was campaigning in 1997, he was asked what was the greatest issue that Cochise County would face in the future. "I had this sense that the border was going to throw something at us. Something we didn't understand and hadn't seen before. I would tell people that when I was campaigning. It was like a premonition."[1]

In 1998, the avalanche of smugglers and illegal immigrants began invading Arizona and the border states. In 1999, Dever warned that the Sinaloa Cartel had moved into Agua Prieta and Nogales, Sonora. By 1999–2000, 640,000 illegal immigrants were caught crossing the Arizona border. Over half of the illegal immigrants streaming north into the United States crossed through the Tucson Sector.

Sheriff Dever works seven days a week. If he is not running the Sheriff's Department, he is taking the message about the border crisis to the American people. Not only is Cochise County and Arizona under a relentless assault from across the border, but also from the federal government.

It is early morning. It will be a long day. Between work and his next trip to Washington, D.C., Sheriff Dever puts his phone away, takes off his hat, and begins to talk. The politics of the border never stop. It is just before the 2010 midterm elections, and Dever tells about a meeting he learned of a day earlier.

"John Morton, the assistant secretary over ICE [Immigration and Customs Enforcement], Dennis Burke (US attorney for Arizona), and Congresswoman Giffords want to have a meeting with the Krentz family next Tuesday to discuss the 'case' [the murder of Rob Krentz]."[2] A usually reserved Sheriff Dever is not happy. The sheriff thinks he should have been the first one asked.

According to Sheriff Dever, "Some family members were suspicious that it was a political ploy or they were going to be using the Krentz family for some other nefarious purpose. They're capable of both." Dever shakes his head. In the end the Krentz family talked it over and called the meeting off. [3]

A Good Listener

US Representative Gabrielle Giffords had represented Arizona's Eighth Congressional District since 2007. The southeastern Arizona district is diverse and sprawling. It includes a long stretch of borderlands extending from New Mexico toward Nogales and northward to Tucson. Giffords, a Democrat, was narrowly reelected in November 2010 despite a historic surge of Republican election victories that swept the GOP into a majority position in the US House of Representatives. As a gun-owning, Second Amendment champion, the blue dog Democrat had strong support among some ranchers.

Washington politicians who do "fact-finding" missions to the border are few and far between. When they do visit the border, it is often used as a photo opportunity. They helicopter in, spend a few hours, and then they head back for the Potomac. They depart with the illusion they have learned something, but do little.

Giffords was different. Even though ranchers make up a small part of her constituency, she visited the border often and was very candid with the ranchers. During a visit to a border ranch, the rancher complained that the Senate had never confirmed President Obama's "border czar," Alan Bersin. Giffords responded, "That's why he's a czar. He would never get confirmed by the Senate because he had a housekeeper and cook working in his San Diego home who weren't here legally."[4]

Giffords, a native of Tucson, would also accompany ranchers to remote areas on horseback or by mule to witness what the ranchers faced every day. She supported tighter border security and increased use of National Guard troops. Many ranchers appreciated her because they felt she was one of the few politicians that genuinely cared about their plight.

> Among those ranchers was John Ladd of Cochise County. His ranch lies west of Naco and is directly north of the border. "Gabby Giffords helped. Her big deal was making the Border Patrol accountable. She didn't solve it, but we had lots of meetings with her and she did something. She was the first politician that seriously questioned what the Border Patrol was doing. She really got involved after Rob (Krentz) got killed."[5]
>
> Ranchers lost an ally after a madman shot Gabrielle Giffords on January 8, 2011, in Tucson. Ladd notes, "When she got shot it was completely different with the Border Patrol. It was like a 'Well, your girl isn't here anymore' attitude. I didn't agree with all her votes, but she was a good friend to us."[6]
>
> Giffords resigned from the House of Representatives on January 25, 2012. The people of Arizona and the country wish nothing but the best for Gabrielle Giffords.

Dever discusses federal government involvement in the Krentz murder case. "They're participating to the extent they can, but this is not a federal case. It's a murder. We are very certain that it involves a smuggler who is a 'frequent flyer' back and forth across the border.[7] "I'm guessing their big concern is this guy is not new to them. That they are aware that this guy ought to be in jail and should have been in jail long before he ever killed Rob Krentz."[8]

The Murder Investigation

The murderer of Rob Krentz was very familiar with the area and had probably taken the same smuggling route many times. Dever believes that "It was a circumstantial meeting that went bad. The guy had a gun and he killed Rob. Rob had two guns and never got to use them." Rob also had his dog with him.

It's the sheriff's opinion that the dog was on Rob's Polaris four-wheeler and may have even bitten the shooter before it was shot. "The dog was still alive many hours later when we found Rob," notes Dever. "The dog was still trying to be as protective as it could. After the animal was put down, the bullet was extracted and impressions were made of the mouth in case it had bitten the murderer. Saliva samples and tissue were sent to a lab in Phoenix."[9]

Rob Krentz suffered from multiple gunshots, and his dog was shot once. Dever theorizes that after the killer shot the dog, Rob probably yelled, went for his gun and then was shot. After being shot, Rob accelerated away from the killer.

Dever thinks Rob Krentz's killer might have been associated with smugglers arrested the day before, but he wasn't with them. In this case the killer would have been acting as a scout farther north on the smuggling route.

Good Leads: Bad Luck

Sheriff Dever hasn't given up hope of bringing the murderer to justice. "Three days after this thing happened, I wouldn't have bet you a dime we would have been near ever solving it. But then things just kind of started coming together." He credits his detectives, who were turning over every rock and following up things that under ordinary circumstances they probably wouldn't have thought much of, but some of them pointed toward a suspect. "Sometimes you get lucky, but you have to be trying to be lucky," says Dever.

Unfortunately for the murder investigation, the results coming back from the lab were not helpful.[10] Despite the setback, the investigation has gained new momentum from unexpected sources. The new leads may well explain why Burke and Morton wanted to meet with the Krentz family. Regardless what many think, the effort to bring the murderer of Rob Krentz to justice is proceeding. There are leads that are genuine.

Burned Too Many Times

In the summer of 2010 there was new activity by the federal authorities in Santa Cruz, Graham, and Cochise County. A new special agent in charge joined the FBI operation out of Sierra Vista. One rancher received a phone call from a prominent official in the Justice Department announcing his arrival and telling the rancher the agent was a good guy and could be trusted.[11] Another rancher confirmed that the new agent was not necessarily replacing anyone, but was on special assignment.[12]

Rancher George Monzingo said the new FBI man showed up at a periodic "stakeholders" meeting. These meetings are gatherings of ranchers, Border Patrol agents, politicians, ICE agents and others to discuss concerns of all parties on the border. The rancher's interest was piqued because of the questions the agent was asking. "I didn't know what he was after or what he was doing there. It made me suspicious."[13]

Another rancher met the FBI agent when he visited his remote ranch. The straight-talking rancher asked directly what the agent was doing. He reportedly answered, "I am here to investigate Cochise, Santa Cruz, and Graham County..."[14]

The agent reportedly said in a visit to one ranch in Cochise County that he was talking to everybody—ranchers, lawmen, citizens, veterans, and politicians. The agent told the rancher that if they could just work together it would help everybody. He went out of his way to explain that of all the people he talked to or tried to talk to, only one would not return his call. He said that man was Sheriff Larry Dever.

According to Dever, "The guy's never contacted me." That was to change when Sheriff Dever ran into the complaining FBI agent in 2011 on the Malpai Ranch. Dever accompanied Arizona senator Jon Kyl and a couple of other senators to the ranch and had lunch. The FBI agent was there, as well as his boss.

Dever chatted with the agent. "I talked to him quite a while. It was a friendly, casual conversation. It wasn't long after that, I was attending the Brian Terry memorial service and sat by his boss, and we got along fine." Dever smiles and shakes his head. "It was subsequent to that, the agent got hold of one of my commanders and tells him I won't talk to him."[15]

The sheriff described how he used to travel south of the border and work with Mexican public officials (like his predecessors Sheriff Jimmy Judd and Sheriff Jimmy Willson did). "They [the Mexican officials] knew that I knew that they were involved in illegal activity—in the drug business. Not all of them were, but some of them. It'd drive the feds nuts every time I would go south and break bread with those guys," says Dever, laughing.

"The way I dealt with those guys [Mexican law enforcement], I'd tell them up front that I'd catch them if I can. We'd take the drug trade business and take it off the table so we could talk about other law enforcement issues—our common thieves, our common murderers, or whatever. And it worked just fine."[16]

"I'd get back from one of the meetings across the border and I'd get phone calls from the federal agents. They'd ask, 'Do you know who you were meeting with?' I'd answer, 'Yes I do.' The thing is I was doing my job the best way I knew how to do it. They can investigate that as much as they want."

Sheriff Dever describes how the cordiality of the intermittent meetings in Mexico changed. "One day, we were sitting down having lunch and they all flat just looked at me. One guy, a chief of police, said, 'Mr. Dever, you need to understand that you are not dealing with the same people down here that you are used to dealing with—and neither are we.'" The sheriff has not been back to Mexico since that warning. Occasionally, one of the men will come to Cochise County. In fact, one of his old contacts has helped him with the Krentz investigation.[17]

Previous Encounters

Sheriff Dever has had previous encounters with the FBI and others involved in the unfolding border crisis. In 1979, a radical, separatist pastor from the south side of Chicago heard God speak to her. God told Pastor Frances Thomas that she was to take her followers and settle in Miracle Valley, a small community in southern Cochise County (three miles north of the border). She believed in the power of faith healing, the principle of separatism, and the primacy of God's law over man's law.

When Pastor Thomas and over three hundred of her followers migrated to the small and diverse community of Miracle Valley she practiced what she preached. This resulted in crisis after crisis, the death of four children, a failed jailbreak, a van blown up with dynamite, and ultimately a shootout.

After years of extraordinary provocations by Pastor Thomas and restraint by Cochise County authorities, the situation came to a head. On October 22, 1982, Pastor Thomas was allegedly told by then Phoenix police captain Harold Hurtt (serving as Governor Bruce Babbitt's mediator with the Church) that Cochise County deputies were going to serve warrants in Miracle Valley. By this time the pastor had achieved de facto sovereignty in Miracle Valley, and her reaction was essentially, "The hell they are."

On the morning of October 23, 1982, then-Sergeant Larry Dever and approximately forty other deputies encountered several hundred armed church members in Miracle Valley. After a ten-minute pitched battle two church members lay dead. A deputy would eventually die from a beating he received and the majority of deputies were injured. Included in the injured was Sergeant Larry Dever, who was shot in the face and side with two shotgun blasts.

The outcome of the shootout was three legal proceedings, a storm of outraged protest around the world, and the spectacle of Jesse Jackson defending Pastor Thomas, an outspoken fan of cult leader Jim Jones. (Thomas once asked Cochise County sheriff Jimmy Judd if he had heard of Jim Jones. Judd answered, "Yes, ma'am." Pastor Frances Thomas then declared, "Well, the punch is already made.")

The FBI investigated Cochise County and the Sheriff's Department for thirteen months and submitted the results to a federal grand jury. Among those investigated was Sergeant Larry Dever. The US attorney general dismissed the grand jury.

Captain Harold Hurtt later became chief of police for Phoenix and Houston. In a bizarre twist of fate, he is now director for the US Immigration and Customs Enforcement's Office of State and Local Coordination.

The full story of the shootout is available in two volumes by this author: *Shootout at Miracle Valley* and *Shootout at Miracle Valley: The Search for Justice*. They illustrate how political ambition distorts law and order. The consequences of this distortion are deadly. The mistakes made in dealing with the challenge of this cult are eerily similar to what is happening on the border today—except today's events are being played out on a worldwide stage and the outcome could be cataclysmic.

September 11, 2001

According to the sheriff, "As recently as the late 1990s human smuggling was mostly nonexistent here [in Arizona]. People came across the border on their own."[18] But after 9/11, crossing became more difficult because of more resources being sent to the border. Prior to that it was almost like a "gentlemen's game." There were rules of engagement. "OK, you got me today, but I'm going to get you tomorrow. I'd spend the night watching the fence, and when I left the smugglers across the fence would wave. It's a very high-stakes game now and deadly serious—absolutely, deadly serious," states Dever.

There is an impression that illegal crossing has decreased recently, but Dever notes, "In general, human trafficking through Cochise County is more discrete now—much more in remote areas. Although recently down by the river on the western edge of the Ladd ranch, fifty to sixty illegal immigrants came up over the border. It was after 10 PM and the Border Patrol never saw them. There was a man operating a couple remote cameras via the Internet from San Antonio, Texas, that saw them. The crossers marched straight through the fence single file. The guy operating the cameras alerted the Border Patrol, who descended on them.

"Less than a half mile down the fence, bundles [of dope] were going over the border. The other guys were decoys," continues the sheriff. A truck drove up and was loaded right in front of another camera. The load continued north without a problem. The drug traffic continues through the area unabated.

John Ladd, whose family homesteaded his ranch in 1896, is outspoken. "In general, the Border Patrol manages the border for politicians. They don't try to manage it to stop the flow. The bottom line is it's all about politics. It's not about securing the border."[19]

The managers at Homeland Security and the Border Patrol may be focused on politics, but the cartels are concerned about profit. The smugglers are much more sophisticated and organized. "They watch us. They have scouts on both sides. They have observation points that you can see on the other side and we ferret them out every so often on this side," explains Dever.

The Pinal County Sheriff's Office reports there are parts of Pinal County that law enforcement doesn't control (such as in the Vekol Valley.) This demonstrates that the power of the cartels extends beyond the border counties. According to Sheriff Dever, "control" in Cochise County tends to be very situational. "It's much more mobile here. It's more like Wackamole. You hit them in one place and they pop up in another."

The Public Is Our Enemy

US Immigration and Customs Enforcement Assistant Secretary John Morton, as well as Director of Homeland Security Janet Napolitano, claim that a record number of people were sent back to Mexico in 2010.[20] Shortly after announcing the record deportations, a report surfaced that indicated five weeks were added to the period reported, and nineteen thousand persons reported deported had actually been deported in the previous year.[21] This would seem to indicate that Homeland Security worked the numbers to make them what they wanted.

Dever responds, "So what? There are a record number of those people that come back." By "those people," Dever means criminals.

He recalls being in a briefing with former Tucson Sector Chief David Aguilar of the Border Patrol. Aguilar was explaining all the "wonderful" things the Border Patrol was doing. Dever says, "After a while an assistant station chief from Douglas gets up and spews out all these numbers—the feds love numbers. Then he says something that I never heard before—a number you could never get out of them. He says, '10 percent of the people we capture entering our country have serious criminal records in the United States.'"

As the briefing concluded Sheriff Dever asked, "Did I hear the figure correctly that 10 percent of the people crossing have serious criminal records in the United States already? I need to have that number because the public needs to know. It's critically important to the public commentary." The assistant Douglas Station chief said the number was correct.

Tucson Sector Chief Aguilar interrupted, "Sheriff, I trust you absolutely and implicitly. But if our enemies ever got ahold of that information, it could be very damaging."[22]

Dever wondered what enemies Aguilar was talking about. "Then it became very clear to me that David was talking about the general public!" Aguilar was afraid the statistic would lead to criticism and ridicule of the Border Patrol's efforts.

Dever feels the public needs to understand that all the people coming across aren't just hapless people looking for work. There are some bad people mixed in with them. "The last number I heard out of the Border Patrol in Tucson was about a year and a half ago [summer of 2009]. The figure had risen from 9 or 10 percent to 17 percent."[23]

In all reality, the percent of persons crossing illegally who are bona fide criminals (beyond the criminal acts of illegal entry, remaining in the country illegally, stealing Social Security numbers, and driving without insurance or a driver's license) could be higher than 17 percent.

"It's not hard to figure out that the percentage of criminal aliens returning who have been charged and convicted is increasing. The bad guys are continuing to come back again and again and again to continue their criminal ways. So, you can deport all of them you want, but as long as you allow them to return you have accomplished nothing," concludes Sheriff Dever.

"I was having lunch with a senior Border Patrol agent who was nearing the end of his career," recounts Dever. The man was talking about what they do. Dever stopped him. "I'm getting this vision in my head. Tell me if I'm right. You guys are like wildlife biologists who study fish. You go out on the lake and shock the lake. Fish float to the surface and you go out and pick some of them up and take samples. You examine some of them and may hang onto a few. You throw all the rest back into the lake and make a report to your bosses what you found."

The senior Border Patrol person leaned forward. "That's exactly right, Larry. We take samples and we report."[24]

No Permission to Succeed

It seems like everyone has a reason for failure. "ICE will say, 'We have scant resources,'" Dever continues. "There is nobody that understands scarce resources better than a sheriff." Sheriff Dever takes a long pause. "After all these years and all this time, my question is why? Why don't you have the resources you need to solve this problem?

"The answer lies in Congress. Or it lies in statements like Janet Napolitano makes that 'You don't need to worry about the border.' She said that—that, 'You don't need to be concerned about that border. It's as secure as it's ever been.' That statement is an indictment."

A common theme when talking to many Border Patrol agents is, it appears to them that a basic policy exists at the highest levels that they are not permitted to succeed in any meaningful way. Dever is asked if he agrees with the statement and if so, what is that about?

Sheriff Dever considers the statement. "Yeah, I agree with that. What I think about the reason for it is very clear and we'll get to that. But I do agree with the statement. In fact, a couple of weeks ago I was talking with a couple of my deputies who said the Border Patrol agents in their area are complaining they are being purposefully deployed to areas of low traffic."

Dever reports a conversation he had with a Border Patrol supervisor during an encounter with illegal immigrants near St. David. The sheriff asked, "I hear you guys have been instructed not to catch guys anymore?"

The supervisor responded, "Pretty much. I was in the briefing where I was instructed to go to my guys and tell them our mission was to scare people back. We're not to catch anybody." The reason for it was because Washington (Homeland Security) needed to demonstrate that they were causing the numbers of crossers to decrease. Dever adds, "Other Border Patrol agents have been told that they are to report only half the number they catch."[25]

Another source indicates that the Border Patrol has a "Catch and Release" program nicknamed by some agents as a "Charlie-Romeo."[26] In many cases, if illegal immigrants are intercepted, they are not held. They are not processed. They are simply released, which is thought of as being "deterred." There has been conjecture that the policy of catch and release could have very well freed the man who would later murder rancher Rob Krentz.

The Border Patrol Is Designed to Fail: Part Two

"It's evident that they are designed to fail," says Dever. "Take the Ladd Ranch. It borders Naco on the west and goes down to the river on the south. You have the Naco Border Patrol Station that you can see from the ranch house—a fully staffed station. You have the border fence, which is solid fence until you get to the far west end, and then you have 'Normandy fence.' There are fourteen cameras on that ranch, lighting all along the roadway. And yet every week there are at least three or four groups that cross there successfully—smugglers and illegal immigrants.

"My question is this. If you have the fence and you have the lights and you have the cameras and you have the people—all the stuff you say you need to stop this, why aren't you doing it?

"It's not that it can't be done. I've seen it done. To me it's a matter of tactics and planning and strategy—and maybe to the point that it's not a lack of that. It's exactly what you've been told. The tactics and strategies employed are designed to fail. Now why?"[27]

What is Homeland Security's motivation? "When it comes to everything else border-related—drug smuggling, gunrunning, kidnapping, money laundering—the DHS, DOJ, and all of those people use the words 'partner and empower local and state law enforcement to participate and cooperate.' When it comes to illegal immigration they not only don't want our help, they sue us. They have totally politicized it. It's not being dealt with as the serious threat to homeland security that it is.

"All of those things are intertwined—illegal immigration, drug smuggling, gunrunning, kidnapping, murder—but they take illegal immigration off the table. They say, 'That's our turf and you aren't to invade it.' It's said that they want the votes and both parties have made a run for them." According to Dever, "It's all politics."[28]

Would You Care About Me If I Couldn't Vote?

"We don't need comprehensive immigration reform," Dever says. "We need comprehensive immigration enforcement. Not just on the border, but in the interior. We need to fix the legal immigration system to make it much more fluid—like a guest worker program. I say this to the very hard-line anti-immigration people and pro-immigration people. If you believe the issue is who is going to get the vote, let's just take that off the table. If you came into this country illegally there may be a way for you to make amends—to pay a penalty, pay a fine. You can come out of the shadows and take up legal residence. You are not going to be a citizen. You will never be a citizen and never have the right to vote."

Dever doesn't close the door to citizenship for illegal immigrants now in the United States. They simply are not going to achieve that goal by having broken the law and paying a fine. "If you want to be a citizen and have the right to vote, and you snuck in here, you're going to have to sneak back out and stand in line behind all the people who are trying to do it right."

To Sheriff Dever, "The test of your sincerity of wanting to allow these poor people to step out of the shadows is to take the right to vote and citizenship out of the equation." In effect, it is a litmus test for whether a person is really concerned about illegal immigrants' well-being and not that person's greed for votes. It answers the question of how many politicians would be interested in the issue of illegal immigrants if they were not seen as a potential voting block.

"Taking the vote out of the equation will never happen. Because the real intent of politicians is gaining votes, not the welfare of the illegal immigrants or the country," concludes Dever.[29]

Corruption

It has been asserted that the level of drug smuggling, human trafficking, gunrunning, and money laundering could not exist without the cooperation on some level of government officials, bureaucrats, and agencies. Drug smuggling is a growth industry due to the increasing demand for drugs in the United States, and as the amount of money involved increases so does the threat of corruption.

Dever calls the idea that the current level of crime could not exist without the cooperation of officials "interesting." He elaborates, "You take sanctuary city policies. They're against the law. People who have open sanctuary policies are violating federal law, yet there is no prosecution. While the federal government may not be openly advocating breaking the law, they actually become a de facto corrupt organization in failing to deal with the problem.

"You have de facto sanctuary cities," according to Dever. "They don't have open sanctuary policies, but they establish policies that limit or forbid the police involvement or ability to investigate criminal activity. They therefore become de facto partners in a corrupt business.

"I think it's the ultimate irony. Here you have a guy [Harold Hurtt, director for the US Immigration and Customs Enforcement's Office of State and Local Coordination] who was chief of police in Phoenix that has sanctuary policies and chief of police in Houston

Information Sharing—with the Cartels

While some illegal immigrants may be reluctant to share information with law enforcement, it appears that the government is not so shy about sharing information with cartels. A case in point is EPIC (El Paso Intelligence Center.) Located near the Border Patrol Headquarters in El Paso, EPIC analysts sift through information to determine relevant and irrelevant data regarding smuggling, cartel activity, and border security. Most of the alphabet agencies, like ATF, DEA, FBI, ICE, and others are said to share information with EPIC.

EPIC is very thorough. They even listen to and analyze a particular type of Mexican folk ballad called narcocorridos (drug ballads), played not only on the radio in Mexican border states, but in the streets, as well as in the United States. The songs are a form of journalism, reporting on arrests, drug bosses, operations, and shootouts. Such songs have indicated potential cartel hits and plans, as well as chronicled past crimes. However, even EPIC can be screwed up by politics.

A source within EPIC reported that the administration was pushing the agenda that personnel from certain Mexican law enforcement agencies be included in some EPIC conferences to facilitate cooperation between the two governments. The source recalled that it was especially upsetting to him and other employees. As the EPIC employees looked across the room at the Mexican representatives, they "knew" an unspecified number of the Mexican representatives were on the payroll of one or more of the cartels.[30]

that has sanctuary policies. He has argued openly about the chilling effect of law enforcement on illegal immigrants. It tells you what direction Homeland Security wants to go."[31]

Homeland Security has created a situation that encourages not prosecuting illegal immigrants, asserts Dever. "They say they only have thirty-three thousand jail beds to house prisoners. But they are deliberately reducing the number of beds they have by revisiting contracts with sheriffs who house federal prisoners and federal housing facilities. They've tweaked the housing requirements and rules so a lot of the jails aren't going to be able to comply. So, this will reduce the number of available beds in the country for illegals."

The rationales for these policies are political, according to the sheriff. "I think it all comes back to the political support system. The people who argue the chilling effect of state and local law enforcement engaging in preventing illegal immigration are incorrect. People in 'sanctuary cities' aren't reporting criminal activity now. How can you suggest that is going to change just because local law enforcement becomes empowered to help enforce immigration law?"[32]

Dever has been challenged about illegal immigrants not reporting crime, but has many examples. "People [illegal immigrants] become victims of crimes every day and they aren't reported. Every day on the border women are raped, people are robbed, and until people get caught we don't know about it."

Profiling

Civil rights groups and liberals have criticized SB 1070 because of their fear that it might lead to profiling. To Sheriff Dever the only real problem would result from his department being stretched so thin. The Cochise County Sheriff's Office has eighty-six commissioned deputies. The eighty-six deputies patrol an area of over 6,300 square miles, twenty-four hours a day, 365 a year. One half of all illegal immigrants cross the border through the Tucson Sector. One half of all marijuana entering the United States comes through the Tucson Sector.

Dever points out the obvious. "From the geographic proximity of Mexico to the Tucson Sector, most of the people involved in drug smuggling will be Mexican. That's not profiling, that's a fact."

Dever tells the story of the first black police chief in Savannah, Georgia. "Not long after he became chief, there was a bank robbery and a cop was nearby. The cop shot the bank robber, and the robber was killed. The news media showed up and the chief was there.

"A reporter asks, 'Chief, the suspect in the bank robbery—what color was he?' The chief answers, 'He was a black man.' The reporter asks, 'What color was the officer that killed him?' The chief responds, "He was a white man.' The reporter follows up with, "Do you perceive any racial implication?' The chief says, 'Bring me some white bank robbers and I'll kill them too.' Then he looks at the reporter and adds, 'What kind of a world do you live in that would cause you to ask me a question like that?' The chief turned and walked away."

Dever concludes, "Bring me Anglo drug smugglers, and we'll arrest them. Bring me Mexican drug smugglers, and we'll arrest them. We don't care."

No Intention to Secure the Border

"When we first started getting run over from across the border I thought, this isn't our problem. It's the federal government's problem. We didn't have the time or manpower or resources to deal with it," Dever recalls. It was a sentiment echoed by local law enforcement all along the border. And it was true, nobody had the resources and it was a federal responsibility.

According to Sheriff Dever, "Their failure to accept their responsibility dumps the problem in our lap—law enforcement, citizens, everybody."

"I made a conscious decision to go to talk to anyone and everybody who had an idea or interest, suggestion, solution, or whatever—on either side of the equation and anywhere in between. That's what I've been doing and it's taken me to all the places I've been."

Once the decision was made to engage the border issue, he hasn't wavered. "It's been pretty grueling, but this is something you either do or you don't. There is no halfway.

"That's what I've been telling the Feds, because they have always set a low target. They have to set their sights higher, because there's never been an intention to secure the border; there isn't one today—by anyone's definition."[33]

"They try to say the border's secure and then they say they don't know what it means. The language they use now is 'operational control.' When I first heard that I thought, that's interesting. What does that mean? Nobody could tell me. I couldn't find a single Border Patrol agent top to bottom who could define what operational control meant."

Operational Control

The government has come up with a definition for operational control. In an urban area the concept is "seconds to minutes." It means that you have seconds to minutes to apprehend someone crossing the border before they disappear into an urban area and assimilate. So they deploy their resources accordingly—using lighting, cameras, and heavy fencing.

In less densely populated areas they employ the concept of minutes to hours to respond to an incursion from the border. It doesn't require as dense an enforcement population because you have more time, but the reaction must still be in minutes to hours.

Finally, in an area like the Tohono O'odham reservation they use the concept of hours to days.

"The deficiency with their strategy is their inability to detect incursions," observes Dever. "To me securing the border depends on knowing when anybody or anything crosses that border. Through technology, aerial surveillance, and personal observation—whatever it is. Then and only then will your operational control strategy serve its purpose."

"*But*," Dever emphasizes, "they have all of that on the Ladd Ranch. And that is my fundamental point! There is the matter of intent—and Homeland Security is content to act like fish biologists."

Paying the Price

Sherriff Dever's life has been consumed by his career. "It has taken a lot of my attention away from family things I would have been involved in because I'm traveling. I've missed a lot of stuff with my kids growing up because of running our search and rescue team, the SWAT team, building our narcotic task force. Anytime anything of any significance happened I was there.

"The truth is, right after Rob Krentz was killed it took a lot of wind out of my sail. I felt empty. How could this happen? How could we allow this to happen? And I know things happen for a reason, but this was so needless and unnecessary. That was the sense a couple of my detectives had—they broke down and cried. This made no sense whatsoever.

"I'd get up in the morning and look in the mirror and wonder if I was running out of gas? And I never would answer the question. I kept asking it, until the ACLU sued [regarding the possible involvement of the sheriff, if SB 1070 should be ruled constitutional] and it made me really angry. Then the Department of Justice came along and I got angrier. And my tank overflowed. I'm back on fire. The lawsuits were a golden opportunity. They've elevated the conversation to a place where I've been trying to get it for years."

The sheriff pauses. "It's been my whole life, my whole career. It's going to end one of these days and I'm damn thankful of it."

Across the Border

As Sheriff Dever points out, even when the Border Patrol has all the tools, money, and personnel available they don't secure the border. And if you are not willing to secure the border, how do you cope with the rise of a Narco Nation to the south?

Endnotes

1. Sheriff Larry Dever, interview, October 14, 2010.

2. Sheriff Larry Dever, interview, October 14, 2010.

3. Sheriff Larry Dever, interview, October 14, 2010.

4. Rancher, interview, 2010.

5. John Ladd, interview, March 7, 2012.

6. John Ladd, interview.

7. Sheriff Larry Dever, interview, October 14, 2010.

8. Sheriff Larry Dever, interview, October 14, 2010.

9. Sheriff Larry Dever, interview, October 14, 2010.

10. Sheriff Larry Dever, interview, February 14, 2011.

11. Rancher, interview, 2010.

12. Rancher, interview.

13. George Monzingo, interview, 2010.

14. Rancher, interview, 2010.

15. Sheriff Larry Dever, interview, March 28, 2011.

16. Sheriff Larry Dever, interview, October 14, 2010.

17. Sheriff Larry Dever, interview, October 14, 2010.

18. Sheriff Larry Dever, interview, October 14, 2010.

19. John Ladd, *Gaming the Border: a Report from Cochise County, Arizona*, Center for Immigration Studies, August 10, 2010.

20. "U.S. deports record number of migrants in 2010," *FOX News Latino*, December 29, 2010.

21. *Unusual Methods Helped ICE Break Deportation Record*, Andrew Becker, Center for Investigative Reporting, December 6, 2010, http://latino.foxnews.com/latino/ news/. 2010/12/29/deports-record-number-migrants/.

22. Sheriff Larry Dever, interview, October 14, 2010.

23. Sheriff Larry Dever, interview, October 14, 2010.

24. Sheriff Larry Dever, interview, October 14, 2010.

25. Sheriff Larry Dever, interview, October 14, 2010.

26. Intelliegence analyst, interview, 2011.

27. Sheriff Larry Dever, interview, October 14, 2010.

28. Sheriff Larry Dever, interview, October 14, 2010.

29. Sheriff Larry Dever, interview, October 14, 2010.

30. Employee, EPIC, interview, 2010.

31. Sheriff Larry Dever, interview, October 14, 2010.

32. Sheriff Larry Dever, interview, October 14, 2010.

33. Sheriff Larry Dever, interview, October 14, 2010.

Chapter Fourteen

A Narco Nation

"Mexico is looking more and more like Colombia looked twenty years ago, where the Narco traffickers control certain parts of the country."

Hillary Rodham Clinton, Secretary of State[1]

VETERINARIAN GARY THRASHER HAS seen life change on both sides of the border. He has traveled to most of the cities and many of the small towns of Northern Mexico in a career that started in 1982. With over three decades of experience working in Mexico and Arizona as a large animal vet, he has become familiar with the politics, people, and changes that have taken place south of the border. "The border was just a barbed wire fence that was about eighty-five years old when I started my practice. Most of the people crossing were vaqueros or rural people looking for work," notes Thrasher.[2]

Almost all of the work Thrasher did when he started practice was inspecting cattle in Mexico for the United States. In those days there were big differences in the health of the Arizona herds and Mexican herds, which had brucellosis, tuberculosis, and many other things Mexican ranchers hadn't cleaned up. The USDA (United States Department of Agriculture) had fence riders checking the deteriorating barbed wire fence to keep Mexican cattle out of the USA for fear of hoof and mouth disease.[3]

In those days the fence along the border was the responsibility of the Boundary Commission made up of representatives from the US and Mexico. "Every two years they are actually supposed to go and physically spot from one monument to the next—line of sight." Thrasher laughs, "That's why the new fences we are building go around the monuments so they can maintain the line of sight."[4]

Money Laundering, Cowboy Style

Thrasher remarks, "Cattle is big business and the importance of cattle imports into the United States from Mexico is more than of a passing interest." The amount of revenue going south to Mexico amounts to over $500 million annually.[5] Unfortunately, the cartels have found that cattle are a great way to launder drug money. Cartels own hundreds of ranches in Mexico. They buy cattle from other ranchers using drug profits and export the beef to the United States. The result is clean money.

This method of money laundering has been mostly untouched by the Mexican and American governments. However, the extreme violence of the Gulf and Zetas cartels in Tamaulipas has resulted in thousands of ranches being abandoned. The State of Sonora has been relatively less violent, and the Sinaloa Cartel continues to operate efficiently. In Sonora there is a mixture of ranches owned by the cartel and by non-cartel ranchers.

The "independent" ranchers have to walk a tightrope between the Mexican authorities and cartel hierarchy. Many of the more prominent ranchers cultivate relationships with the state governors. Such relationships help balance their positions vis-à-vis the drug lords.[6] This strategy works in areas where the Mexican government still exercise some control over the countryside.

As Secretary of State Clinton pointed out, however, the cartels control some parts of the country. In most cases, the cartels essentially run the Mexican border towns.

Gary Thrasher estimates that approximately one-fourth of the beef entering the United States from Mexico belongs to the cartels.[7] It is a number that is growing.

More significant, of course, is the number of illegal immigrants and the flood of illegal drugs that enter the United States. Which is why it is important to understand what is occurring south of the border and the role the United States has played and still plays in those events.

Poison Pills

Economic conditions and policies in the United States have had a powerful influence on Mexico and immigration. World War II created a labor shortage, and the first of several Bracero (manual labor) programs were negotiated between the United States and Mexico to allow Mexicans to legally work in the States. In theory, the Bracero Program established minimum standards for the guest workers.[8] In reality, these standards were often abused and the program was eventually ended.

With the demise of the Bracero Program and increasing unemployment in Mexico, the Mexican government created the Maquiladora Program within designated areas along the international border.[9] The program allowed the construction of plants in Mexico by foreign manufacturers, which did such things as parts assembly and shipped the products duty-free back to the companies where the parts originated.[10]

A Maquiladora factory in Mexico.

Employment and the number of plants increased dramatically, especially after NAFTA (North American Free Trade Agreement) took effect in 1994. The plants boomed. But in the end, free trade turned out to be a poison pill for Mexico, which dramatically impacted the United States' problem with illegal immigration.

While NAFTA helped the Maquiladora Program, it devastated Mexican agriculture. Because the United States subsidized as much as

40 percent of American farmers' net income, grain and corn poured into Mexico below cost. Mexican farmers were forced off their farms by the millions. The Maquiladora program employed some of these economic refugees from the countryside, but could not begin to absorb them all. And a second poison pill was being forced down Mexico's throat.

Adding dramatically to the misery in Mexico was the 1994 devaluation of the peso. The value of the peso had been set against a certain number of dollars. This did not reflect necessarily the actual value of the currency, but provided economic stability. Under extreme pressure from outside interests, including the American government and Wall Street, newly elected Mexican president Zedillo let the value of the peso float. The Mexican government was told there might be a modest adjustment to their currency if they let the peso float and settle at its actual value.

Interestingly enough, four to five billion dollars in foreign investment left Mexico days before the secret decision was made public. Champagne flowed on Wall Street and tears flowed in Mexico. The value of the peso would fall some 300 to 400 percent. Savings disappeared and the price of food soared. Millions faced a desperate situation. The United States offered a bailout for a condition it had to a large degree instigated.

Finally, by the year 2000, the globalization of the world economies stemmed the boom in Mexico's Maquiladora Program. Outsourcing multinational companies found cheaper labor in the factories of Taiwan, Korea, India, and China.[11] The effect was devastating for Mexico. The Maquiladoras had fueled a population boom as well as an economic respite for many from a subsistence existence. A middle-class had grown up, but also a huge population of young people who were now looking for nonexistent jobs.

In short, NAFTA, globalization, American farm subsidies, and Wall Street contributed enormously to the mass migration of illegal immigrants crossing into the United States starting in the mid-and late 1990s.

The economic decline in Mexico caused by the factors described above contributed significantly to the dependency of Mexican society and institutions on the drug economy. And even worse, the United

States helped ensure that it was a growth industry by failing to interdict drug smuggling in a meaningful way. Further, efforts of drug
prevention through education and treatment provided to addicts
by the American government has been feeble at best. America, by
benign neglect, has essentially provided an open and rapidly expand-
ing market for Mexico's drug lords.

The result: the Mexican citizens who did not go north were left
with an entrenched political system that was struggling to keep up
with new realities—and refusing to change.

The Mafiosa

Gary Thrasher notes, "The people of Mexico seventy-five years
after the Revolution (1910–1920) were divided into a caste system
and a socialist system." The caste system satisfied the peons—the
lower class. "They [the government] gave them all kinds of benefits
because that was the response from the Revolution. The peons supported the Revolution. They are the base for the PRI [Partido Revo-
lucionario Instituciona, or Institutional Revolutionary Party)."[12]

"The PRI was controlled by old-line, wealthy families. They kept
the majority of the wealth for themselves. They also kept the Mafiosa
[what the cartels are called inside Mexico] in line." This relationship between the PRI and the Mafiosa continued until the year 2000
when the PRI lost power.[13]

Prior to the shift in the political landscape, the Mafiosa were able
to focus their efforts on their drug trade, and the PRI could maintain
political power. It was a marriage of convenience. It also disguised
how weak and vulnerable the government had become. At that time,
the Mexican Army was still revered as the powerful force that ultimately held the country together—the government's ace in the hole.
But times were changing.

Colombia: A Dress Rehearsal

Secretary of State Clinton noted, "These drug [Mexican] cartels
are now showing more and more indices of insurgency; all of a
sudden, car bombs show up which weren't there before. It's looking
more and more like Colombia looked twenty years ago, where the
narco-traffickers control certain parts of the country."[14]

But truth is frequently the first casualty when the American government speaks about the situation in Mexico or along the border. A day after Clinton's remarks President Obama stated, "Mexico is a vast and progressive democracy, with a growing economy, and as a result you cannot compare what is happening in Mexico with what happened in Colombia twenty years ago."[15]

Despite the political spin, the Colombian experience is important. Two decades ago, as cocaine trafficking into the United States grew, the American government initiated more aggressive and concentrated efforts on disrupting the drug supply from producing countries—in particular Columbia.

Colombia was lurching toward the status of a failed state under the growing power of the drug lord Pablo Escobar, the head of the Medellin Cartel. On December 2, 1993, the United States helped Escobar fulfill his wish: "I prefer to be in a grave in Columbia than a jail cell in the United States."[16]

The destruction of the Medellin Cartel was the result of an effort that has had a direct influence upon the Mexican situation of today. A group called Los Pepes (Los Perseguidos por Pablo Escobar, or People Persecuted by Pablo Escobar) had formed to fight Pablo Escobar's Medellin Cartel. Los Pepes has been popularly described as a "vigilante" group organized around the many enemies Escobar had made over the years. Los Pepes death squads eventually drove Pablo Escobar into the ground.

Los Pepes was a conglomerate of people with special interests. Among them were members of the rival Cali Cartel. The American government along with the Cali Cartel helped finance Los Pepes, and American contractors and Special Forces participated in missions. An inside source notes, "It was a warm relationship of mutual convenience ... information was shared."[17]

In reality, the death of the Escobar did not curtail Colombian cocaine production. The Medellin Cartel was replaced with the less audacious Cali Cartel and the cultivation of coca leaf in Colombia increased by 50 percent between 1994 and 1996.[18]

Colombia continued on course to become a "Narco Nation" until the United States carried out the threat to decertify it as a cooperating nation in the fight against drugs. "Decertification had powerful trade, aide, financial, and diplomatic ramifications. It applied a huge penalty for the government and business to continue its culture of corruption. It turned the culture of corruption back toward action," says former DEA official Anthony Coulson. It brought the Cali Cartel down and "allowed Colombia to become a democracy again.[19]

A major consequence of the US effort in Columbia was that Mexican drug lords were no longer simple middlemen for the Colombians; they took over the drug routes into the United States and the distribution of drugs in the United States. The last Colombian drug kingpin with a presence in Arizona was forced out about ten years ago. The stage was set for the drug economy in Mexico to boom!

A Secret Meeting and a Secret Report

In the early '90s, as the drug habit in America exploded and the Mexican drug lords grew in power and influence, the United States took notice. The most powerful member of the US Cabinet had a secret meeting with Carlos Salinas, president of Mexico from 1988 to 1994, regarding the Mafiosa.

The meeting would prove prophetic. The American cabinet member offered aid to help combat the growing influence of the Mafiosa in Mexico and drug trafficking into the United States. The number of $400 million was tossed around, but the reception was cool. The cabinet member pressed President Salinas, who reluctantly agreed to accept the money. Salinas repeatedly said in effect, "I'll take your money, but it won't do any good." The cabinet member recalls, "I finally got it—he was involved in the business somehow."[20]

It would later be revealed in a Swiss banking secret report that Salinas' brother Raúl played a central role in Mexico's drug trade, raking in huge bribes to protect the flow of drugs into the United States. In addition, Raúl used his considerable wealth to funnel drug money into his brother's presidential campaign. In fact, when Carlos Salinas became president, his brother Raúl assumed virtual control of all drug shipments through Mexico.

According to the secret report, "Through his [Raúl's] influence and bribes paid with drug money, officials of the Army and the police supported and protected the flourishing drug business … Raúl Salinas commandeered government trucks and railroad cars to haul cocaine north, skimming payoffs upwards of $500 million. On what some of his reputed former associates referred to as 'green light days,' he arranged for drug loads to transit Mexico without concern that they might be checked by the Army, the coast guard or the federal police."[21]

The secret report implied that some family members of Raúl's were implicated in criminal activities (noting credible witnesses) and questioned how President Salinas could be ignorant of the schemes of his brother.[22]

The report adds credibility to the conversation George H. W. Bush's cabinet secretary reported having with Salinas. Why would the Mexican government have taken $400 million dollars to fight the drug trade when they were profiting so much from it? For the Mexican government it was found money. When President Salinas said, "You are wasting your money," he was being truthful.

The Ghost of Fast and Furious Past

Between 1995 and 1998, the US Customs Service conducted a sting called Operation Casablanca. The sting was conducted inside and outside of Mexico and exposed the enormous money-laundering operations of Mexican economic institutions.

Though touted at a huge success by Customs and the American press, Operation Casablanca was a major screwup. It was eerily similar to today's botched ATF gun running scheme called Fast and Furious in its structure, methodology, and lack of meaningful supervision. The big difference is a government agency used Fast and Furious to send guns to the cartels, while Operation Casablance laundered money.

"The problem with Casablanca was that Customs was actually laundering more money for cartels than they were seizing money," observes retired DEA official Anthony Coulson. Further, the cartels fully realized that Customs was laundering the money and considered the seized money as an acceptable fee for cleaning their drug proceeds.[23]

Like the ATF with Fast and Furious, Customs was operating in Mexico without notifying the Mexican government. In addition they were laundering huge amounts of cash and getting very little return in terms of achieving a law enforcement objective—like bringing down drug kingpins. "Customs wasn't getting anything but a commission for laundering money," says Coulson. Customs had lost perspective on what the initial purpose of the operation was.[24]

"In the end much, much more money was laundered than ever seized and no drug trafficker (minor or major) was ever prosecuted. Although *some* bankers and financial people were arrested and prosecuted it was an afterthought scramble, like when Fast and Furious blew up," observes Coulson.

When the money laundering operation became public the Mexican government was outraged. They accused the United States of trying to embarrass Mexico. At the June 8, 1998, UN Drug Summit, President Zedillo said Operation Casablanca violated Mexican sovereignty and that no one "is entitled to violate another country's laws."[25]

President Clinton apologized, and the outcome was an agreement that was to cripple America's anti-drug efforts for years to come and cost the lives of many informants. Attorney General Janet Reno and her Mexican counterpart signed the Brownsville Agreement in July of 1998, which in a practical sense was directed not at protecting Mexican sovereignty but at preserving an environment in which the Mafiosa and Mexican government could continue their relationship unimpeded.

The agreement forbade the US government or its agencies any involvement in areas that might interfere with Mexico's sovereignty. If it was thought any action might affect Mexican sovereignty, the United States was required to get prior permission from Mexico. As will be noted later, the Obama administration would symbolically shoot the Brownsville agreement in the head with the ATF's Fast and Furious operation.

Unlike the ferocious response to the violation of Mexico's sovereignty led by President Zedillo, President Calderon's comments regarding Fast and Furious have been mild. A member of the Mexican intelligence community claims this is because the latest Mexican president "has been bought and paid for by the United States."

The Brownsville Agreement took place at a time when Mexican presidents still exercised some independence of Washington, D.C., and did not really consider drugs a major problem.

A long-standing belief in Mexico that drugs are an American problem and a Mexican opportunity permeates all levels of law enforcement in Mexico. Salim Dominguez, a former Border Patrol agent, recalls being on the shooting range with a new graduate from the Mexican Customs Academy. Dominguez asked what the Academy thought about narcotics. The young graduate replied, "They taught if you get involved in the interdiction of narcotics and you get hurt or killed, your family is on their own, because you put yourself in that position because of your own stupidity. Narcotics is a cash crop for Mexico and only a problem for the United States government."[26]

A Culture of Corruption and Violence

There are major cultural characteristics that allow the Mafiosa to prosper and grow. They make the threat from the south, in terms of both illegal immigration and drug trafficking, especially dangerous to the United States.

First the obvious: the cartels are extremely violent. They routinely burn, decapitate, and torture their adversaries. Former Sonoran governor and presidential candidate Eduardo Bours noted in a Foreign Affairs forum in Phoenix that much of the extreme ferocity and brutality exhibited in Mexico is a result of behavior learned from their French and Spanish colonial masters.[27]

This tendency is illustrated with the tradition in the Mexican drug culture of *plata o plomo*, which translates as "silver or lead." The Mafiosa use this as one of its prime methods of gaining cooperation, whether with a Nuevo Laredo cop or a United States Border Patrol agent—either cooperate with the cartel and get paid (silver) or take a bullet (lead). And they really mean it. That is why Mexico is littered with dead policemen, journalists, mayors, priests, and civilians. It tends to make honest people mind their own business, leading to the illusion that there are few honest people south of the border.

Former Sonora Governor Eduardo Bours.

Bours, in his Phoenix speech, also indicated that Mexico had inherited a culture of favor.[28] It is the culture of favor that justifies the practice of *la mordida* (the bite). Mordida is present in nearly every aspect of public life in Mexico. Whether it's obtaining a building permit, bringing equipment into the country, buying a hunting license, or being stopped by a policeman, the specter of "the bite" is omnipresent. Mordida has a centuries-long tradition, and it promotes corruption by anyone in a position of power. It is a cost of doing business. There is the price for the service, plus the bite.

Part of the power of mordida comes from the poverty of so many Mexican citizens. Local law enforcement personnel often make dishwasher wages. In Mexico, becoming a policeman is sometimes viewed as a job of last resort, and this often draws a type of person who is uneducated and vulnerable to bribes.

Cochise County chief deputy Rod Rothrock trained a group of police in Agua Prieta. They were poorly paid and had no previous police training. They literally didn't know how to properly cuff a suspect. Almost all of them lived outside of Agua Prieta and went to and from work in uniform by bus—usually a half hour each way.

In addition, every day when the uniformed police left the station to go home, they had to leave their weapons locked up in the police station. They were always in danger but they hardly made a living wage. To provide for their families, there was almost no choice but to take mordida. Rothrock reports he hasn't done any training south of the border since the cartels took complete control.[29]

Another tradition that allows the Mafiosa to operate is the deeply held belief that "everybody has a price." This belief is a direct outgrowth of mordida and reinforces the lack of respect the Mafiosa have for anyone in authority. The Mafiosa assumes that almost anyone can be bought, because they have been successful in bribing most people they approach.

Finally, there is often an attitude in Mexico of "going along." Former Sonoran governor Bours was asked, "Are you frightened for your safety because of the cartels?" Bours responded, "No, because I treat everybody equally."[30]

All of which sets the scene for the political revolution at the ballot box that brought carnage to the people of Mexico, unimaginable wealth to the powerful few, and a challenge to American law enforcement that has not yet been met.

Goodbye to the Good Old Days

Before the onslaught of Mexico's bloody war on drugs it was business as usual. The oligarchy and the Mafiosa ruled Mexico. The government was in essence a tool of both of these powerful groups. This is best demonstrated by how power was exercised before the Mexican elections turned everything upside down in the year 2000.

Two of the leading power brokers in those days were Magdalena Ruiz-Pelayo and *Comandante* Guillermo Gonzalez Calderoni. Ruiz-Pelayo was the secretary to the leader of the PRI party. Gonzalez Calderoni was in charge of the Mexican Federal Police and a leading anti-crime figure.[31]

When a Mafiosa leader wanted the government to do something, it is said they often went to Ruiz-Pelayo, who informed leaders of the PRI of the request. Party members fed the requests to the proper individuals within the government.[32]

Sometimes these requests from the PRI ended up in the lap of Comandante Gonzalez Calderoni. Many in American law enforcement held the comandante in high esteem. He is best remembered for hunting down the drug lord Pablo Acosta, who operated along the Texas border. Acosta was killed in a shootout, and Gonzalez Calderoni hailed as a hero.

In reality, the comandante is reported to have received a million dollars for getting rid of Pablo Acosta, who was replaced by Amado Carrillo Fuentes. The comandante eventually fled to the United States and a gunman shot him outside his lawyer's office in McAllen, Texas, in 2003.

The Rise of PAN and the Fall of Mexico

In the year 2000 Mexico elected a non-PRI president for the first time. As noted, the PRI was the party that emerged out of the Mexican Revolution. It was socialist in nature, though run by a group of wealthy landowners. It had not addressed the issue of mordida, and economic challenges were not being met.[33]

The PAN (Partido Acción Naciona, or National Action Party) had been a relatively conservative party that had become center right. What added new life to the party was the rise of a middle class and business class that wanted change, based on facing issues pragmatically and not by a strict ideology.[34] Again, as will be illustrated, it is important to remember that both parties are in the final analysis creatures of the cartels and an oligarchy made up of two hundred wealthy Mexican families.[35]

Vicente Fox led PAN to the presidency of Mexico in 2000. Despite Fox's charismatic style, many Mexicans were disappointed with the results of his administration. The consequence was a very contentious 2006 presidential election won by PAN candidate Felipe Calderon (with a less than 1 percent margin of victory.)

President Calderon took on the problem of mordida, which normally would have been a good thing. Some say he had even made some progress in that area. The problem was at that point in the history of Mexico, it was irrelevant—it was like rearranging the deck chairs on the Titanic.

The relationship that the PRI had pursued with the Mafiosa was what kept the peace in Mexico. The Mafiosa and the PRI had unwritten agreements, which both sides kept for the most part. For example, the Mafiosa generally agreed not to sell drugs to the citizens of Mexico. This agreement kept drug use low in Mexico while it was in effect.[36]

Another agreement between the Mafiosa and PRI was the restriction of guns to civilians. The Army had always considered it one of their prime missions to prevent gun possession by the masses.[37] The agreement meant the Army could provide guns to the Mafiosa group(s) it favored and still fulfill their primary goal.

The Government also gave the Mafiosa de facto parallel authority. It allowed the Mafiosa to grow as an almost shadow government. As long as the Mafiosa's single goal was monetary, and because the criminal organizations provided so much income to the country's gross domestic product, the government permitted organized crime enormous latitude in their operations. They were in effect given a "license to kill" as long as it just involved their "business."

In return, the government helped keep the peace between the

Mafiosa groups by selling rights to smuggling corridors to individual organizations based on the highest bid.

The going price (when the government still influenced who got what route) was for example five million dollars a month for the Nogales corridor. The payment was due at the beginning of each month and would periodically rise as competing cartels bid for the same route.[38] This did not mean there were not bloody conflicts and struggles for dominance by Mafiosa groups, but there were not as many.

As noted, the Mexican Army has played a key role in the protection and transportation of drugs throughout Mexico, up to and often across the border into the United States. It supplied, and still does, much of the infrastructure for the entire drug industry. Services provided by the Army would go so far as to actually guard the huge amounts of cash being amassed by some Mafiosa drug lords.[39]

The PRI would go to almost any length to maintain this balance, but losing an election has consequences—even in Mexico. The people wanted a change, but it was more than they bargained for.

The Collapse of the Agreements

The disintegration of the unwritten agreements between the government and the Mafiosa started under Vicente Fox. A major reality was becoming apparent. The demand for drugs in the United States had grown beyond what anyone had imagined. The United States drug interdiction efforts had failed, as well as American drug treatment and prevention efforts. The supply of drugs flowing into the United States soared and the price dropped.

Retired Colonel John Gold, an intelligence expert with the Army, saw it coming. He was assigned to the southern California HIDTA (High Intensity Drug Trafficking Area) unit with Congressional approval. The issue the 150 separate law enforcement agencies that dealt with drug trafficking across the Southern California border were encountering was the same phenomena that would threaten the existence of the Mexico state. Colonel Gold worked with HIDTA "because the drug organizations that we were facing had more money at their disposal than many countries."[40]

Because of the massive wealth of the cartels, the relationship the Mafiosa had with the Mexican Army and government was no longer in balance. The separate Mafiosa organizations had so much money at their disposal absolutely anybody could be bought or killed for any reason. In reality, the Mexican government (state and federal) no longer controlled the smuggling corridors into the United States.

Calderon and Mexico were at a crossroads—just like Colombia had been when the cartels became rivals for state power. The balance between the Mafiosa and the government had been destroyed. It was also becoming obvious that large groups within the Mexican Army and Mexican government had favorites among the cartels. Something had to be done to preserve the state.

What resulted was a new agreement. It involved one of the most powerful men in the world, Chapo Guzman, and one of the weakest, President Felipe Calderon.

Now You See Him, Now You Don't

When President Calderon came to power there were four or five major cartels. These included the Sinaloa, Gulf, Tijuana, Juarez, and La Familia cartels. The leader of the Sinaloa Cartel, Chapo Guzman, is not only one of the world's richest and most powerful men, but also one of the most intelligent drug lords. Guzman is like a master chess player, and he saw the value of a pawn pretending to be a king.

President Calderon was missing for six days. White House Photo.

In 2006 Chapo Guzman set up a meeting with the new president of Mexico. It is reported that the new president met with Guzman in the foothills of the Sierra Madre Mountains in the state of Sonora. Reports differ; some say it was a meeting with the aides to the president, while others insist it was a face-to-face meeting between Calderon and Guzman.

Hiding in Plain Sight

A decade ago Mexico's most famous drug lord, Chapo Guzman, was in a Mexican prison and serving a twenty-year sentence. In prison he was debriefed by the DEA, but other American government agencies wanted interviews. Guzman asked that those interested make an "application." They provided their names and the areas they wanted to focus on during their interviews. Guzman considered their applications, did the math, and figured he was looking at extradition to the United States.[41] There is a saying: "In Mexico it is your God-given right to escape prison." Guzman exercised this right on January 19, 2001, and became the most seen criminal in hiding in the Western Hemisphere.

Years ago the United States Embassy in Mexico City was constantly hosting parties, formal and informal. The staff would meet with counterparts from different embassies, government officials, businessmen, and others. During these parties, gossip and occasionally significant information would be picked up.

These social get-togethers also extended to "off-campus" drinking parties. Customs agent Richard Cramer, who was stationed at the embassy, attended several of these functions with a person new to the embassy staff. The new staffer related the following story.

At one of the off-campus parties that Cramer and the new staffer attended, there were a remarkable number of attractive women present. The new staffer circulated and nodded to a man who was accompanied by several other men. As he moved on, he noticed women occasionally pointing at the man.

After he left the party he learned the man was Joaquin "El Chapo" Guzman, the leader of the Sinaloa Cartel. It should be noted that Richard Cramer was arrested in 2009 on accusations of drug smuggling.[42] El Chapo has raised the ability to hide in plain sight to an art form.

Former DEA agent Anthony Coulson notes that when Guzman travels in Mexico he is accompanied by hundreds of guards and vehicles. "It's like a battleship moving around the Mexican countryside, and yet everybody claims they can't find Chapo."[43] While the Mexican government insists it cannot find him, in February 2011 he was seen strolling along a sidewalk in Nogales, Sonora.[44] But then, he has friends in high places.

Among those supporting this allegation is retired DEA official Anthony Coulson. The twenty-eight-year veteran of the DEA, who ran the agency's drug enforcement efforts out of Tucson, was skeptical at first. Then evidence surfaced that added credence to the report. Initially, one of the most compelling pieces of evidence was that the Mexican president disappeared for a period of six days when the meeting was said to have occurred.[45] His location was unknown to almost everyone, except Chapo Guzman.

More importantly, despite the public relations blitz north and south of the border about President Calderon's war on the cartels there has been remarkably little progress made. Coulson says, "He wasn't performing. There were little victories, but that was because the DEA went out and co-opted some general or admiral for help—outside the mix, unknown to Mexican authorities beyond the DEA's trusted circle."[46]

Coulson further observes, "You could see steamrolling—the strengthening of cartel control." The situation has become so serious that today the Mexican government controls little of Mexico outside of Mexico City. Control rests with the oligarchy and the cartels.[47]

The Coming Blood Bath

In 2006 the two most prominent cartels were the Gulf Cartel and the Sinaloan Cartel under Chapo Guzman. Despite his powerful position, Chapo Guzman's control was confined mostly to an area some three hundred miles from the border and to the south—in central and southern Mexico. Guzman decided it was time to move north both in Sonora and the Baja. He had his eyes set on the highly profitable Sonora-Arizona drug routes and the Tijuana corridor that would give him access to the California market.

The Gulf cartel controlled Mexico's Gulf Coast and some areas along the Texas border. Its attempt to maintain and extend control of Texas drug corridors was being strongly challenged. To combat their competition they recruited highly trained Mexican special forces troops to join them—the Zetas.

Crime Pays

The Zetas originally consisted of about thirty soldiers lured away from the Mexican Army's elite Grupo Aeromóvil de Fuerzas Especiales (GAFE) with a promise of higher pay. They had received military and anti-drug training in the United States and when they became the military wing of the Gulf cartel they were a potent and efficient force.

Many of the original group that formed the core of the Zetas have been killed or captured. However, the Zetas have replaced the finely honed military expertise of the original group with huge numbers that achieve their goals through the unparalleled use of brutality and force.

The Gulf Cartel may have had the Zetas, but Chapo Guzman had the 2006 agreement with President Calderon. It revolved around a live-and-let-live arrangement. Guzman indicated that where possible he would assist Calderon and in return he wanted to be left alone—sort of. In fact, he used the Mexican government to pursue his ambitions. In what was described as a "peace token" Guzman gave the Calderon Government the "exact location" of drug kingpin Alfredo Beltrán Leyva.[47]

The Beltrán Leyva Cartel was once allied with Guzman and was essentially, "The corruption arm of the Sinaloa Cartel. Not only were they connected to the Colombian cartels, but the cops, judges, and prosecutors of Mexico."[48] Another "peace token" occurred when Guzman "gave up" Beltrán Leyva cartel member Edgar Valdez Villarreal, better known as El Barbie in August of 2010. Again, it gave the appearance that the central government was effective, when in reality it was only effective in helping Chapo Guzman.

It was during the period between 2006 and 2010 that the Gulf Cartel splintered—devoured essentially from within by the virulent Zetas who had been hired to protect it. The Zetas emerged as one of the most dangerous crime organizations in the world, and the government of Felipe Calderon had its hands full. The rise of the Zetas placed it in direct conflict with the Sinaloa Cartel.

Finally, an event that occurred in 2007 was to affect the lives of thousands of Mexican citizens. In 2007 a residence allegedly belonging to a Chinese businessman was raided. Over $200 million in cash was confiscated (see photo). The money was to pay for the importation into Mexico from China of pseudoephedrine, for the express purpose of manufacturing methamphetamine.[49] The problem was, the $200 million belonged to Sinaloa drug lord Chapo Guzman. Chapo was not happy. It was this event that lead to the "Insurrection."

The Insurrection

By 2008 all hell was breaking out in Mexico. With the Sinaloan-government connection still intact, Guzman decided on a move to keep both the Zetas and the remnants of the Juarez Cartel busy. More importantly, his next move would also conveniently require a large number of Mexican Army troops to be deployed in the north and east. He poured thugs into Juarez and created the most violent and dangerous city in the world. The Zetas, Zeta wannabes, and Juarez cartel loyalists fought back.

In response to the unbridled killing and public outrage, Calderon reacted as Guzman wanted. The president had no choice but to

Chapo Guzman sends thugs into Juarez.

deploy large numbers of troops north. The ongoing insurrection conveniently drew attention, both military and public, away from Guzman's growing areas and methamphetamine production facilities. At the same time it weakened the Juarez cartel and drew substantial number of Zeta forces from their primary corridors into Texas.

The popular media and politicians insist that this move by Guzman was and is an effort to gain control over the drug corridor north from Juarez. This is not true. According to Anthony Coulson, "The killing fields in Juarez were not for drug territory or trafficking corridors. Its only value to Guzman was as a distraction that kept attention away from his business."[50] And business was good.

As Juarez and Mexico bled Guzman's power grew. He expanded his control south and into Central America. In Honduras thousands of local gang members allied themselves with his cartel.[51] The flow of tons of pseudoephedrine to his meth production facilities was reestablished. The result is that today there is more and cheaper meth available to the American addict than ever before.[52]

At the same time, Guzman solidified his grip on the Tijuana drug corridor and rebuilt the California drug business to levels not seen in years.

A Dilemma

President Calderon faces a dilemma. The PRI will regain power in the 2012 elections. The story will eventually surface regarding the alliance with the Sinaloa Cartel. Not only will he and the PAN face the scrutiny of history, but there will also be legal and safety issues. For years retiring Mexican presidents have generally been able to take their millions and become elder statesmen. But the current situation in Mexico is different. According to Anthony Coulson, when the PRI party regains power there will be "civil war in Mexico." Even though the reconstituted Zeta Cartel seems to have all the cunning and sophistication of a blunt instrument they will make a serious run to displace the Sinaloa Cartel when Calderon leaves office. Already significant remnants of the leadership and families of the dethroned cartels are aligning with the Zetas. They have the intelligence, money, and influence to guide the Zetas. "During the coming conflict everything will be up for grabs. The battle for the Arizona, Texas, New Mexico, and California routes will be a battleground. The only thing the Mexican government will continue to control is Mexico City."[53]

To redeem himself, President Calderon faces the unenviable task of not only separating himself from Chapo Guzman, but also arresting or killing him. Although both of these tasks are easier said than done, the removal of Guzman would erase the importance and consequences of the unholy alliance. In the end, Calderon would become a hero.

There are two downsides to this scenario for Calderon. First, if and when Guzman exits the scene, the Zetas will sweep across Mexico and most likely form an alliance with the PRI. Second, Chapo Guzman knows what President Calderon is thinking and is two steps ahead of him.

A House of Cards

The situation in Mexico raises serious issues regarding the American effort to interdict and disrupt drugs coming across the border.

DEA official Anthony Coulson asserts that the key question is, "When did our government become aware of the agreement between President Calderon and Chapo Guzman?" Because more than one person has knowledge of this arrangement.[54]

An even more serious issue arises. It is at this point that the specter of the Colombia experience appears. Multiple sources indicate there is a United States connection to the relationship of the Mexican government and the Sinaloa Cartel. But perhaps this is a "Medvedev moment" and the administration will not have the flexibility to let this information out until its last term.

"What we say we are doing in Mexico is a complete charade. It's a complete denial of the truth," declares Coulson. "But what we are doing is a house of cards that will fall apart."[55]

A War Mexico Can Not Afford to Win

Over fifty thousand Mexicans have died in drug-related killings since President Calderon went to war with (certain) cartels, and the pace of death is quickening.

But in the numbers game, deaths don't count. The reality is that even if the Mexican government were free of corruption, the outcome of its "war" on the Mafiosa would be dictated by economics. A source within the Mexican government has revealed the extent of Mexico's reliance on the drug trade and remittances from illegal immigrants. At least 25 percent of Mexico's gross domestic product comes from wealth generated by the Mafiosa, while another 18 percent of the gross domestic product comes from remittances from illegal immigrants employed in the United States. Another source claims these percentages are understated.

The consequences of these two figures cannot be underestimated. It means that Mexico is fighting a war it cannot afford to win. It means that Mexico is not fighting a war against drugs, but a war to help determine who controls the drug trade.

The United States enables and helps maintain Mexico's drug economy by pursuing a de facto policy of open borders. Administration after administration has tolerated an environment where drug smuggling is allowed to flourish and human trafficking is encouraged, understandable, and inevitable. These are political choices, and law enforcement failures are the result of those agendas.[56]

Former DEA official Anthony Coulson says, "The ultimate victims of those agendas are the people that are in the throes of addiction in America. The question for the American people to answer is, has what we have allowed in Mexico exceeded and violated our values as an American society?"

And another question is, how does the American government maintain its open border policy? The federal government maintains its open border policy with a culture of lies.

Endnotes

1. Secretary of State Hillary Clinton, "Remarks on United states Foreign Policy," U.S. Department of State, September 8, 2010, http://www.state.gov/secretary/rm/2010/09/146917.htm.

2. Gary Thrasher, interview, August 7, 2010.

3. Gary Thrasher, interview.

4. Gary Thrasher, interview.

5. Gary Thrasher, interview.

6. Mexican rancher, interview, 2011.

7. Gary Thrasher, interview.

8. Bracero Program, Wikipedia, http://en.wikipedia.org/wiki/Bracero_Program.

9. Bracero Program, Wikipedia.

10. Gary Thrasher, interview.

11. Gary Thrasher, interview.

12. Gary Thrasher, interview.

13. Gary Thrasher, interview.

14. "Remarks on United States Foreign Policy."

15. Antonieta Cadiz, "México no es Colombia," *La Opinion*, September 10, 2010.

16. Juliet Paez Prada, "A talk with Colombian journalist Elizabeth Mora-Mass," *New York University*, http://www.nyu.edu/classes/keefer/ww1/paez.html.

17. Gerardo Reyes, "Los Pepes ¿Solución en México?" *El Nuevo Herald*, May 26, 2009.

18. Drug Control: Counternarcotics Efforts in Colombia Face Continuing Challenges (Testimony, 02/26/98, GAO/T-NSIAD-98-103).

19. Anthony Coulson, interview, April 26, 2012.

20. Protected source, interview, 2010.

21. Tim Golden, "Salinas Brother Is Tied by Swiss to Drug Trade," *The New York Times*, September 19, 1998.

22. Tim Golden, "Salinas Brother Is Tied by Swiss to Drug Trade."

23. Anthony Coulson, interview, April 26, 2012.

24. Anthony Coulson, interview, April 26, 2012.

25. Stanley Meisler and Jonathan Peterson, "U.S.-Mexico Drug Statement Tinged by Acrimony," *Los Angeles Times*, June 9, 1998, http://articles.latimes.com/1998/jun/09/news/mn-58123.

26. Salim Dominguez, interview, June 21, 2010.

27. Anthony Coulson, interview, April 26, 2012.

28. Anthony Coulson, interview, April 26, 2012.

29. Rod Rothrock, Cochise County Chief Deputy, interview, August 21, 2010.

30. Anthony Coulson, interview, April 26, 2012.

31. Analyst, interview, 2011.

32. Analyst, interview.

33. Gary Thrasher, interview, August 7, 2010.

34. Gary Thrasher, interview, August 7, 2010.

35. Anthony Coulson, interview, April 26, 2012.

36. Gary Thrasher, interview, August 24, 2010.

37. Gary Thrasher, interview, August 24, 2010.

38. Informant, interview, 2010.

39. Informant, interview, 2010.

40. Colonel John Gold, interview, November 23, 2010.

41. Analyst, interview, 2011.

42. "Former Agent Faces Charges in Drug Case," *The New York Times*, September 6, 2011, page A16, New York edition.

43. Anthony Coulson, interview, March 30, 2012

44. Informant, Interview, 2011.

45. Anthony Coulson, interview, March 30, 2012.

46. Anthony Coulson, interview, March 30, 2012.

47. Anthony Coulson, interview, March 30, 2012.

48. Anthony Coulson, interview, March 30, 2012.

49. Anthony Coulson, interview, March 30, 2012.

50. Anthony Coulson, interview, March 30, 2012.

51. Analyst, interview.

52. Anthony Coulson, interview, March 30, 2012.

53. Anthony Coulson, interview, March 30, 2012.

54. Anthony Coulson, interview, March 30, 2012.

55. Anthony Coulson, interview, March 30, 2012.

56. Anthony Coulson, interview, March 30, 2012.

Chapter Fifteen

A Culture of Lies

"The border is as secure now as it has ever been ... "
DHS Secretary Janet Napolitano, September 14. 2010[1]

BORDER PATROL AGENT BRIAN A. Terry died on the night of December 14, 2010. He was allegedly killed by a well-armed group of bandits. As a member of BORTAC, a highly trained tactical unit of the Border Patrol, Terry was part of a team patrolling a wild stretch of Arizona over a dozen miles north of the international border and west of Rio Rico. Before looking at Brian Terry's murder, it is important to understand the political climate that made his death possible—in fact, inevitable.

The political situation did not begin with the Obama administration. The policies, dysfunction, and processes that created a culture

CBP Commisioner Bersin. US government photo.

of lies have been cascading forward through different administrations for two decades.

The present administration has not only continued the policies of previous administrations, but also doubled down on them. Reality is no respecter of beliefs, wishes, or politics—and denial does not change onrushing reality. This administration has rolled the dice and they may lose everything.

The culture of lies that has spread through many government agencies is often manifested in what appears to be insignificant ways. Alan Bersin, retiring commissioner of the CBP (Customs and Border Protection), addressed a crowd of a thousand people during a memorial to Agent Terry on January 21, 2011, in Tucson, Arizona. Bersin promised to "restore the rule of law" to the US-Mexico border.[2]

However, only four days after the murder of Border Patrol agent Brian Terry, Secretary Napolitano visited Arizona with a different message. "Here's the message that I gave to our Border Patrol agents down there, which is that the work they are doing is producing very, very strong results," she said. "And you can see that in every metric, there is no doubt that the border, which I know very well having dealt with it since '93 when I became US attorney here, is a very different place than it was five years ago."[3]

DHS Secretary Napolitano. US government photo.

Secretary Napolitano essentially was restating what she told a Washington think tank on June 24, 2010, "The numbers tell the story, and they do not lie ... violent crime is down on the US side of the border, while seizures of illegal weapons, drugs, and cash are up."[4]

However, there is a singular problem with numbers and Homeland Security. The numbers are frequently not only false, but fall apart when confronted by the truth.

In 2010 a meeting was held at the DEA office in Tucson. Attending the meeting was United States Representative Gabriel Giffords; National Security Advisor John Brennan; Alan Bersin, the head of Customs and Border Protection; John Morton, the chief of ICE; Anthony Coulson of the DEA (in charge of drug enforcement for southern Arizona); and the head of every law enforcement agency in Southern Arizona.

The question was raised, "What percentage of the border is secure?" Almost everybody in the room offered an estimate. It was finally agreed that 51 percent of the border was secure and the number pleased most of those present.[5]

Coulson recalls seeing Representative Giffords look down at her full water glass and slipping two fingers over the mouth of the glass. She said, "Okay, you're all doing such a wonderful job here. Let me tell you something. If I cover 51 percent of this glass and tip it over, what's going to happen?" Looking at the national security advisor, the head of CBP, and the chief of ICE she concluded, "So, you have no control over the border."

Representative Giffords makes a point. US government photo.

"It was the clearest statement of the truth you would ever want to hear," observes Coulson. However, Homeland Security did not redouble their efforts to secure the border. Shortly after Giffords's incisive observation, Secretary Napolitano changed the public relations message to "the condition of the border" and not the percent of the border that is secure. Today, Napolitano speaks about the "low crime rates along the border" despite the unprecedented volume of drugs smuggled into the country often under the nose of authorities. Unfortunately, Gabriel Giffords is not available to put that deception to sleep.

The institutionalized lies and deceptions that cripple our country's response to the current border crisis began in the early 1990s.

Memories of San Diego

The crisis on the border first became apparent to the American public with the television images of hundreds of illegal immigrants crossing San Diego freeways in the early '90s. Every night Southern Californians witnessed human waves spilling into America's promised land. On average, two fatalities a day resulted from illegal immigrants being struck trying to cross freeways on foot.[6]

There were so many illegal immigrants crossing that some Americans were becoming desensitized. More than a few drivers advised each other, "If you hit someone, don't stop. It will cause you nothing but trouble."

Forensic anthropologist Dr. Madeline J. Hinkes recalls, "In those days they [illegal immigrants] used to come up along the ocean, and deaths as a result of drowning were common. Enforcement started at the ocean, which pushed crossers inland to Highway 5. To prevent the migrants from crossing Highway 5, a fence was built down the middle of the highway."[7]

According to Dr. Hinkes, who has spent much of her career identifying the remains of illegal immigrants, "There was no coherent strategy to deal with the influx." As Dr Hinkes and the San Diego Medical Examiner's Office attempted to deal with identifying victims of the chaos, citizens were growing angry. Residents saw their property overrun and vandalized on a regular basis.[8]

The politics of the left and right began a dialogue, which stretches into present day. The problem is the dialogue about "just looking for a better life; America is a land of immigrants" and periodic charges of racism obscured the true nature of what was occurring. Businesses wanted cheap labor, and government bureaucrats were happy to help. Citizens of San Diego County were witnessing the result of that cooperation.

In short, as more than one high-ranking member of the Border Patrol has observed, "The border is just about as secure as the government wants it at any particular time."

"That's the way it was when I started in San Diego in '75 and the way it was in Tucson when I retired in '03. It's still that way today," observes former deputy chief of the Tucson Sector Ed Pyeatt. He laughs when considering how the "desired level of control" is adjusted and met. "It depends on the way the strategy (by the Border Patrol) is employed."[9] And that depends on what the politicians want, which depends on political pressure from the voters and contributions from business and special interests, including the illegal immigrant lobbies.

Pyeatt can remember the early '90s when thousands were crossing in the open. It was a momentary tipping point, when political reality trumped the contributions politicians were receiving from special interests that had a stake in illegal immigration. It was obvious law and order was breaking down, and it was becoming an embarrassment for San Diego. Through the efforts of US Representative Duncan Hunter, double fences were erected.

"We're talking real fences, not this crap Tucson has," says Pyeatt. "We're talking about a fence with a road and then another fence. The fence was working so good the Border Patrol didn't want to build a third fence, but the people in town were saying, 'we want three.'" Eventually three fences were built from the water through Imperial County."[10]

Unlike Secretary Janet Napolitano's often-repeated talking point, it was not a question of an illegal immigrant "bringing a eleven-foot ladder to a ten-foot fence." Pyeatt believes that the difference between the fence in the San Diego Sector and Tucson Sector is a reflection of the representation each area has in Congress.[11]

In Pyeatt's opinion Congress has the public "hoodwinked." Senators and representatives "will say, 'I voted for an appropriation in 1986 or in 1988 or 2004 and 1,500 hundred agents were added.' They want to be perceived as being for border control, but they want the employers to know they haven't done anything substantial to add to effective control. They don't really want to do anything substantial to stop traffic coming across the border."[12]

Operation Gatekeeper

The illegal traffic crossing into San Diego in the '90s created a problem and an opportunity for politicians in Washington, D.C. As noted, the uproar from voters and US Representative Duncan Hunter resulted in a double-row (and eventually a triple-row) fence along the Southern California–Mexican border. The project was called Operation Gatekeeper—and it was a perfect political solution to a problem. It provided the appearance of doing something without actually being effective overall.

Operation Gatekeeper did provide fencing and some relief from illegal immigration to the San Diego area. However, it had no effect on the actual number of illegal immigrants or drugs coming into the United States. It could have been more aptly called "Project End Run." It just shoved the problem east.

While Operation Gatekeeper was in reality a numbers-neutral venture into immigration and drug control, it helped develop a strategy that allowed statistics to be easily manipulated, then and now. A strategy that did not go unnoticed.

On June 23, 1996, two officials of the National Border Patrol Council (the union that represents Border Patrol agents) charged that Border Patrol supervisors falsified records, altered intelligence reports, put limits on apprehensions, and conducted operations to mislead the public about Operation Gatekeeper's effectiveness.[13]

Part of the problem was the new strategy that Operation Gatekeeper employed. The strategy emphasized and measured success by deterrence instead of the number of apprehensions. Hardworking agents who measured their success by the numbers they arrested were assigned to a fairly constrained area and instructed on what traffic they could pursue and for what distance. In locations, both with and without the fence, areas were divided into grids.

This deterred illegal immigrants from crossing in areas where agents were assigned, but essentially sent increased numbers of illegal immigrants around the agents and into the United States. In an odd way, it allowed more illegal immigrants to cross, but with less ability to accurately measure their numbers.

By the same token, agents became frustrated as they witnessed illegal immigrants cross, but were not able to do anything about it if they were outside that agent's assigned grid. If misused, the new strategy could provide a robust way to control the numbers count and give the Border Patrol hierarchy a sophisticated way of lying to Congress and the public—after all, "numbers don't lie."

The Border Patrol brass could brag about decreased numbers in a particular area, but overall numbers didn't really change. There was the illusion of success without real success—something the average Border Patrol agent understood. The agents' suspicions were strengthened by the visit of a Congressional Task Force. It was charged that the delegation was intentionally deceived about the real numbers of illegal immigrants crossing the border.[14]

In response to the allegations of the National Border Patrol Council, the OIG (Office of the Inspector General) stepped in to investigate.

The OIG dismissed most of the concerns raised by the National Border Patrol Council, but confirmed many of the complaints of the

Controlling the Message

The Border Patrol leadership has a history of trying to control and shape the message that they provide to the public and Congress. In 2010, a rancher invited then-chairman of the House Committee on Homeland Security, Representative Bennie Thompson (Dem., MS) to the southeastern Arizona borderlands to witness firsthand what they were experiencing. United States Representative Gabrielle Giffords facilitated his visit and accompanied him to the border.

The Border Patrol took control of the junket. They gave Representative Thompson a canned overview of "border conditions" and "progress" at a port of entry. Afterwards, the Border Patrol caravanned Representative Thompson to the border via Geronimo Trail. Giffords and a couple members of ICE who also wished to talk to Thompson about border conditions accompanied him. Several ranchers met Thompson and attempted to provide their input.[15]

As far as the Border Patrol was concerned, however, the fact-finding mission was over and it was time to return to civilization. A rancher suggested that Representative Thompson should see more of the border firsthand. Thompson was agreeable, but the border patrol strongly resisted the idea—they wanted to keep control of the message. Representative Giffords helped a Customs agent and a rancher spirit Representative Thompson away in a car for a more intimate view of the border. They spent considerable time together without the presence of the Border Patrol escort.[16]

After his private tour, Thompson was picked up by a Customs helicopter and flown out of the area, much to the chagrin of the Border Patrol.[17]

agents, especially allegations of artificial limits on apprehensions.[18] They did this by calling limited apprehensions "benchmarks."[19]

The "benchmark" standard is still in effect today. This is extremely important, because promotions within the Border Patrol are based not on exceeding the politically set benchmarks, but by meeting them.

Ironically, despite itself, the OIG was providing one of the first indications that something was systemically wrong with the Border Patrol, specifically with its management. And, in the end, this was to be proved right.

A Strategy That's Not Working

When Ed Pyeatt was in the Tucson Sector, there were over two thousand agents. He considered the number of agents inadequate for the flood of drugs and immigrants crossing the border. "The Tucson Sector stretches from Ajo to the New Mexico state line. That's a lot of border. The number of agents was inadequate because of the length of the border, but also because the strategy employed was not working."[20]

In the early 2000s, a lot of the success of interdicting smuggling of illegal immigrants or drugs was knowledge of the terrain. "In those days it meant knowing the streets of Douglas, Lukeville, Naco, and Nogales. The smugglers were coming right through the towns because the infrastructure allowed rapid movement to Tucson and Phoenix. Infrastructure is very important to successful smuggling."[21] So the strategy was to remove the infrastructure of the border towns and the highways leading north. They decided to drive the smugglers out and around the towns. One problem that resulted was that the smugglers would go around and enter the towns from the other side.

Nonetheless, the idea was that once the smuggler was deprived of the infrastructure of the towns and highways there was much more time to catch them. The strategy of minutes, hours, and days came into play (see chapter 13). The strategy never really worked effectively in the Tucson Sector because it was not implemented correctly. Moving the illegal immigrants and smugglers to other more rural areas was supposed to reduce manpower requirements in the towns and cities.

Currently, in most ports of entry the manpower requirements for the Border Patrol are still high. For example, despite being one of the most heavily patrolled areas on the southern border, Nogales is still a major corridor for drugs moving north.

"There are more cartel people in Nogales than any other United States border town," notes a Border Patrol agent familiar with the city. He indicates that the ports of entry are used as primary conduits for high-dollar drugs and, "We actually only catch about 5 to 10 percent of the drugs." He adds, "In the fiscal year 2009 we seized 1.2 million pounds of dope in the Tucson Sector. You do the math."[22]

Some of the drugs getting through ports of entry are the result of payments made to inspectors. The drug smuggler will choose a lane at the port of entry where an inspector has been paid off to let a load through. The Border Patrol tries to combat this practice by a procedure named "Chaos." Inspectors are randomly switched to other lanes of incoming traffic. The sight of vehicles frantically trying to switch lanes to follow the bribed inspectors sometimes occurs after Operation Chaos is implemented.[23]

While most inspectors and Border Patrol agents are hardworking, dedicated, and honest, there is some corruption even in the lower ranks. A veteran investigator reports a port of entry that "has at least ten dirty employees and a dirty supervisor."[24]

Reduced Standards

Corruption is an ongoing concern relative to the agencies tasked with maintaining security along the border. Former deputy chief of the Tucson Sector Ed Pyeatt noticed that the level of corruption increased as the guidelines for new recruits were lowered.[25] Adding to the problem was the sporadic use of lie detector tests with new applicants. Many new recruits were simply not given tests.

Reduced standards can also be dangerous. Currently new recruits to the Border Patrol Academy who are fluent speakers of Spanish receive fifty-five days of training. Training includes the law, firearms, operations, and physical training. For recruits who don't speak Spanish, an additional forty-four days are added. After graduating from the Academy, agents are assigned to a field training officer for twelve weeks. Next an agent will be teamed with a journeyman for three weeks. After that they are on their own and alone. It's then they learn, "It's not the dark that'll scare you—it's what's in the dark."[26]

Agents in the past who could not master rudimentary Spanish in the field would be terminated. Presently, an agent cannot be terminated just for poor Spanish language skills.[27]

As Jim Runyon, a former instructor at the Border Patrol Academy, observed, "If you're out in the dark doing a lay-up, it's real important to be able to understand Spanish. You got to be able to understand if the group coming up on you is talking about picking cotton, or shooting any cotton-picking gringo they might run into."[28]

Just as the entry of illegal drugs through border towns has not been eliminated, the highway infrastructure is still used by smugglers. Semipermanent highway checkpoints have been established on major highways near the border in the Tucson Sector. A dozen Border Patrol agents and drug-sniffing dogs often staff these checkpoints.

However, the usefulness of these checkpoints is compromised by management policies. For example, when it is raining or windy the checkpoints are shutdown. During these shutdowns drug shipments essentially get a green light to travel north. Former DEA agent in charge of southern Arizona Anthony Coulson noted, "When the checkpoints shut down our phone taps would light up with drug smugglers being told it was clear to go north. It was like clockwork."[29]

Surprisingly, drug smugglers do not necessarily avoid the highway checkpoints even when they are open. Cochise County sheriff Larry Dever recalls a woman being stopped for a driving infraction after passing through a checkpoint. They found she was hauling a large quantity of dope in her car. When she was questioned how she got through a Border Patrol checkpoint, she laughed and said, "Those dogs are worthless. They can't smell shit." She had been through the checkpoint numerous times.[30]

A Border Patrol agent who works a checkpoint maintains, "The dogs are pretty good, but just like people they get tired." Drug scouts also notify smugglers when dogs are taking breaks, and loads are sent through. Cars and trucks are searched only if there is something suspicious. The agent told of a suspicious conversation he had with a driver pulling up in a primary checkpoint lane:

The agent asked, "What color is your car?"

The driver answered, "Ah ... ah ... red?"

The agent ordered, "Go to the secondary lane." Upon inspection the trunk was full of dope.[31]

All of which goes to show, even in the drug world there are good and bad liars. Which leads us to David Aguilar.

The Rise of David Aguilar

Perhaps the most controversial person ever to rise to power in the Border Patrol is David Aguilar. Aguilar is important because he would become the poster boy for the Border Patrol and set the tone of management within the organization. President George Bush appointed Aguilar chief, Office of the Border Patrol, in May of 2004. He became acting deputy commissioner of US Customs and Border Patrol in January 2010 and permanent deputy commissioner in April of that year. Some people consider Aguilar a political animal first and an administrator second—the ultimate yes-man.

President George Bush is greeted by chief of the Border Patrol David Aguilar during a visit to Southern Arizona.

The key to Aguilar's rise was the almost six years he spent as chief patrol agent for the Tucson Sector of the Border Patrol. Aguilar had over 2,100 agents and two hundred support personnel under his command in the Tucson Sector, where he honed his style of leadership and management.

He commanded the Tucson Sector from a raised desk, much like J. Edgar Hoover had in his FBI office. In that way, whenever anyone approached him, they were not able to look down upon him. He surrounded himself with yes-men and at the same time knew how to please his Washington superiors. It was often said the ability to please him was more important than the agent's actual performance.

To many ranchers and others in the Tucson Sector, David Aguilar had a problem. They felt he had difficulty in telling the truth. Behind his back many called him David "Agui-liar."

Cochise County sheriff Larry Dever recalls meeting with Aguilar in his office and discussing highway checkpoints. Aguilar was in the process of establishing a system of temporary checkpoints, which would be in an area for a few days and then moved to another area.

Sheriff Dever asked Aguilar if he would inform him when and where the checkpoints were set up in Cochise County so he could plan accordingly. Dever recalls, "David readily agreed and we shook hands. The next day he set up a checkpoint and didn't bother to call me. He never called me. He flat out lied to me."[32]

When the number of illegal immigrants crossing the desert in the Tucson Sector started to rise dramatically and the death toll of crossers skyrocketed, an aide approached Aguilar. The aide told him the number of bodies that had been found. According to someone present at the meeting, "Aguilar's first instinct was to urgently inquire, 'How many people know about this?'" The witness was stunned. "He appeared to be much more concerned about the political ramifications of the number than the human side."[33]

The stories about Aguilar and the Border Patrol's effort to control the message are endless. A Border Patrol agent remembers attending a public relations class in Phoenix. Classes were held periodically on how to deal with the media. The classes described what to say in response to certain questions and how to avoid saying anything that might embarrass the Border Patrol.

The Border Patrol agent described how one class ended. Aguilar had dropped by, and when the class ended all the agents rose, raised a hand, and pledged to answer, "The border is safe and secure" if asked about border conditions.[34] It was a lie of course, but the lie was policy.

A Blast from the Past

It was like San Diego all over again. In 2004, the same year Aguilar became head of the Border Patrol, a whistleblowers document appeared making serious allegations about how the Tucson Sector had been run under Aguilar. The charges were eerily similar to those made in the '90s regarding the San Diego and El Centro (located in California) Sectors.

The document was sent to the Department of Homeland Security and Office of Personnel Management Inspectors General. The same document was also carbon-copied to the chairman of the US Senate Appropriations Committee and the chairman of the US House of Representatives Appropriations Committee.

The eleven-page document read in part, "Chief David V. Aguilar's selection by Commissioner Bonner to head the Border Patrol drew what can only be described as widely felt distaste and fear for the future of the Border Patrol. Agents indicated that they had been limiting their attempts to catch illegal immigrants under direction from Chief Aguilar."[35]

It continued, "In order to elevate apprehension statistics [in comparison to getaways] in Tucson, the agents were directed to stick to limited, fixed, widely dispersed corridors, and catch only those illegal immigrants that they personally observed. All the while, the agents were aware of tremendous numbers of illegal immigrants pouring through areas between their known positions. The agents were instructed not to cut sign and track those individuals known to be entering the country; reports of "sign" of illegal immigrants that are not caught are recorded as "getaways." With no "getaways," and apprehensions limited to those who come into an agent's view, the apprehension rate of the sector appears to be nearly 100 percent."[36]

And criticism was not limited to the whistleblowers' complaints. Aguilar was so unpopular with rank and file Border Patrol agents that in 2007 the National Border Patrol Council gave him a unanimous vote of no confidence. The union council, saying the resolution reflects growing dissatisfaction with top managers over "misguided policies and politics," listed some of the "more troubling reasons" for the no-confidence vote:[37]

> » "Declaring our borders to be secure while millions of people illegally slip across them every year."
> » Perpetuating the "strategy of deterrence" despite clear and convincing evidence that it does not deter anyone from illegally crossing the border.

> » Prohibiting Border Patrol agents from enforcing immigration laws in "interior" towns and cities, including many that are only a short distance away from the border.
> » Preventing Border Patrol agents from pursuing vehicles that flee from them, even those that are carrying tons of narcotics or other dangerous contraband."

Unlike Operation Gatekeeper, there appears to have been no formal investigation of the charges made in the whistleblowers document or the vote of no confidence. Nor was Chief Aguilar's position among his supporters or superiors threatened.

On February 25, 2009, Chief Aguilar received another unanimous vote of no confidence from the representatives of the National Border Patrol Council. The vote asserted that Aguilar's agenda resulted in "bad management by SES-level managers, compromising security for trade, commerce, pro-open borders, and to protect the illegal alien agenda of corporate America which has led to diminished security at the US/Mexico borders."

It further criticized the "screw up and move up" policies of CBP. It went on to condemn Aguilar for the CBP's "lack of training coupled with late background checks."[38]

Many agents agree with the charges made in the whistleblowers document and with the complaints contained in the "votes of no confidence." In particular, a large number of veteran agents agree the statistics coming out of Homeland Security should be suspect.

The federal government may not want the states' help with illegal immigration, but they want the local authorities to cooperate with their drug enforcement. In cases where less than five hundred pounds of drugs are seized the feds turn the smugglers over to the local county attorneys for prosecution. The counties cannot afford the cost of prosecuting so many cases.[39] The result is that many drug smugglers go free, but the CBP gets to brag about drug seizures.

If at First You Don't Succeed

As of 2012 the Border Patrol frequently uses the technique of intentionally allowing the smugglers to escape and just seizing the load. This tactic allows Homeland Security to boast about drug seizures and not have to worry about arresting and processing smugglers.

A problem that encourages this technique is the increasing difficulty of bringing smugglers to justice. As soon as smugglers are confronted they drop their loads and scatter. The likelihood of convicting a drug smuggler diminishes greatly as soon as he has separated himself from the dope.

Rancher John Ladd recalls witnessing a group of smugglers seated on the ground with their shirts off. Border Patrol agents were photographing them. Ladd assumed they were photographing tattoos for identification, but was told they were trying to show the marks on their shoulders from having transported the heavy bundles of dope that were scattered around them.

An agent told Ladd that it was becoming "harder and harder" to make a case against smugglers and that even the pictures they were taking would do little good. Ladd noted a camera on a tower nearby. "Can't you get the tape from that camera?" asked Ladd. The agent told him there was almost no chance of that happening.[40]

The Border Patrol policy of allowing many smugglers to escape provides the smuggler on-the-job training and little risk. Which in the end has the effect of encouraging and increasing the amount of drugs crossing the border successfully.

Rigging the Numbers

Quite simply, the Border Patrol rigs the numbers regarding drugs or border crossers through policy, spoken and unspoken. The Border Patrol can adjust the numbers of illegal immigrant apprehensions to suit the political needs of Homeland Security. One method that is used extensively is to deploy agents in areas of sparse illegal traffic.

As mentioned in the whistleblowers' earlier accounts, it cannot be overemphasized how much the Border Patrol's policy toward getaways is used currently to manipulate numbers. Again, getaways are illegal immigrants or smugglers who were known to be in a certain area, but not apprehended. These are people detected by cameras, radar, heat sensors, motion sensors, aircraft, ground radar, observation by agents, tracks, or civilians who report them.

Border Patrol agents are *discouraged* from reporting getaways.

It makes the numbers look bad because there are *so many* of them. Reliable sources indicate that in the spring of 2011 the Ajo Border Patrol Office received a memo from DHS "not to count getaways."[41] The same memo circulated in several other offices.

Some offices were instructed that sensors and cameras be removed from some high-traffic areas, including some areas within the Tohono O'odham Nation. There is a surprisingly accurate method that can extrapolate the actual numbers of getaways from the numbers picked up by sensors or on cameras. A source inside Homeland Security relates that when getaways are counted and the actual number is extrapolated, it indicates that well over 70 percent of illegal immigrants and smugglers are crossing the border successfully—which is bad for DHS management's image and the administration's agenda.[42]

Amnesty Through Policy

David Aguilar is not the only controversial Homeland Security figure. Assistant Secretary John Morton of ICE (Immigration and Customs Enforcement) became embroiled in the controversy with Arizona's SB 1070. Morton also declared, "The best way to reduce illegal immigration is through a comprehensive federal approach."[43]

In a sense, he is another Homeland Security official who appears uncomfortable with enforcing the laws. He wants the immigration laws changed so his job description will more closely parallel his political beliefs. And one of those beliefs is amnesty for illegal immigrants.

In June of 2010, ICE assistant secretary John Morton received a unanimous vote of no confidence from all 259 ICE union officials. The Unions represent seven thousand ICE employees. Included in the letter of no confidence were the following points:[44]

"1. While ICE reports internally that more than 90 percent of ICE detainees are first encountered in jails after they are arrested by local police for criminal charges, ICE senior leadership misrepresents this information publicly in order to portray ICE detainees as being non-criminal in nature to support the Administration's position on amnesty and relaxed security at ICE detention facilities.

"2. The majority of ICE ERO Officers are prohibited from making street arrests or enforcing United States immigration laws outside of the institutional (jail) setting. This has effectively created "amnesty through policy" for anyone illegally in the United States who has not been arrested by another agency for a criminal violation.

"3. ICE Detention Reforms have transformed into a detention system aimed at providing resort like living conditions to criminal aliens. Senior ICE leadership excluded ICE officers and field managers [the technical experts on ICE detention] from the development of these reforms, and instead solicited recommendations from special interest groups ... putting detainees, ICE officers and contract guards at risk."

ICE is a perfect example of how the imposition of political agendas trumps the rule of law.

Metrics

Again and again, the political agendas of this administration and past administrations have been promoted by Homeland Security's manipulation of the numbers. Customs and Border Protection often recite "metrics" to indicate their performance, but sometimes it's difficult for the metrics to keep pace with the official line.

Many charge the reason Janet Napolitano declares that "the border is as secure as it's ever been" is because she wants to get onto the real agenda that's important to her and the administration, which is "comprehensive immigration reform."

In a 2010 hearing regarding Homeland Security threats, Representative Blake Farenthold asked Homeland Security director Napolitano, "What percentage of control do you think we have of either of our borders?"[45]

"In terms of manpower, technology, infrastructure; we have effective control of the majority of both borders," replied Napolitano. "It is a project that is never-ending ... we realize that when you are a country as large as ours—with the kind of land and borders we have—that you are never going to seal those borders."[46]

According to Customs and Border Protection (CBP) at the end of fiscal year 2010, the US government had "effective control" of about 44 percent of the southwest border and 2 percent of the four thousand-mile-long northern border.[47]

It's at this point things get tricky. The GAO (General Accounting Office) defines 873 miles of the two thousand-mile southern border under "operational control." The GAO further breaks "operational control" into two categories. Category one is "controlled." This means that illegal crossers and smugglers can be detected at and are apprehended at the immediate border. The GAO says about 129 miles of the 873 miles noted above fit into category one.[48]

According to the GAO, the rest of the 873 miles under "operational control" is defined as category two, which they describe as "managed." Managed is defined as a multitiered deployment that allows the deterrence, detection, and apprehension of illegal immigrants and smugglers at a depth of sometimes more than one hundred miles from the border.[49] This is why there are armed squads of smugglers penetrating deep within Pinal County, Arizona, and members of the major Mexican cartels in almost every city in the United States.

How this translates into "the majority of both borders" being under effective control as described by Secretary Napolitano is highly debatable.

Falsifying the Records

The situation is so fundamentally flawed that in a practical sense the government has hidden the truth about the border from itself. Records that go to Washington, D.C., are being altered and falsely executed. Often the lies become fact in order to fit political agendas. The end replaces the means.

Records can be changed by acts of omission and acts of commission. An example of altering records by omission is illustrated by a comment made by Cochise County sheriff Larry Dever. On April 1, 2011, Sheriff Dever reported that a supervisor with the Border Patrol told him that the agency's Arizona office was instructed to keep the number of "apprehensions down during specific reporting time periods."[50]

Dever also indicated that it was not the first time he had been told about the policy by agents over the last few years.[51]

"The senior supervisor agent is telling me about how their mission is now to scare people back," Dever discloses during an interview. "He said, 'I had to go back to my guys and tell them not to catch anybody, that their job is to chase people away. ... They were not to catch anyone, arrest anyone. Their job was to set up, posture to intimidate people, to get them to go back."[52] It was described as a policy to manipulate statistics.

The blowback from the Border Patrol was quick, which reminds one of the old western saying, the guilty dog barks first. Border Patrol

Chief Michael Fisher wrote a letter to Dever disputing the sheriff's claim. Fisher called the claim "100 percent false." He went on, "Your statement to the press (supported supposedly only by an anonymous tip) is an affront to the six thousand agents and officers serving Arizona."[53]

In response, Sheriff Dever phoned Chief Fisher. According to Dever what followed was "a very animated discussion." At the end of the discussion, Dever said, "Damn it, Mike, all you do with stuff like this is throw fuel on a fire that probably needs to keep smoldering, but it doesn't need to blow up into a big forest fire. And that's what he did."[54]

Chief of the Border Patrol Michael Fisher. US government photo.

According to Dever, Fisher said, "Well, what do I need to do?" Dever answered, "You need to bring your butt down here with your supervisors and go into a room and they can throw all the darts they want to at me. I want to explain to them how this thing evolved.

"I don't get up in the morning and try to figure out how I can poke the Border Patrol every day," observes Dever.

Fisher flew in from Washington and brought some Tucson Sector supervisors to the sheriff's office in Bisbee. "They were kind of back on their heels and trying to lay the whole thing off on some misunderstood policies," says the sheriff.

"In a way what I said was a small thing, but it exposed a deeper insight to what they are or are not doing. Because of my comment I learned a lot more from agents coming forward and telling what they are really doing," Dever notes.[55]

TBS

Dever's initial comment that caused the furor with the head of the Border Patrol related to a policy called TBS (Turned Back South). It's one of the ways Homeland Security and the Border Patrol management manipulates the statistics. The way TBS works in reality is demonstrated by the checkpoint operated by the Border Patrol on Interstate 19 north of Nogales.[56]

Normally there will be several agents assigned to the checkpoint as backup. When, for example, illegal immigrants are transported north on the Interstate, it is a common practice to have them unload before they reach the checkpoint and to walk around it. The vehicles proceed through the checkpoint and will pick the illegal immigrants up at some prearranged point. It's the job of the backup agents to watch for this activity and to arrest the illegal immigrants as they make a wide berth around the checkpoint.

If the backup agents encounter a group they estimate (for example) at a hundred illegal immigrants, the agents might stop half a dozen while the rest scatter. The agents report they apprehended six illegal immigrants, and classify the others as TBS, even though they regroup, continue north, and catch their rides to the American dream. Traditionally the estimated ninety-four that continued north would have been classified as getaways, but as noted previously, reporting getaways is highly discouraged by the Border Patrol hierarchy.[57] In today's world they are simply classified as TBS.

A more insidious and potentially more dangerous form of information manipulation is the overt falsifying of records. This is best illustrated by looking at the National Guard deployment along the border. The most recent presence of the Guard was to a large degree necessitated by the political pressure generated by a concerned public after the murder of rancher Rob Krentz.

For the record, the deployment has not been very helpful. According to many Border Patrol agents, the Guard units often have poor equipment as well as poor attitudes. One agent observed, "During the day some Guard units spend ten hours with ancient binoculars. One pair was so bad they had to look through only one side. They have some equipment as good as ours, but it isn't doing much good."[58]

Another agent offers, "At border stations the National Guard personnel may watch monitors, see movement on a sensor screen, and report it as a moving head when it's a rabbit. They can't tell a cow from a person."[59]

Despite being trained and retrained, results don't improve much, another agent notes. "There are some good guys, but it depends on their work ethic. They aren't getting paid much. Other fellows just sit and watch screens and bullshit, while we're filling out logs, watching sensors, calling in locations from screens. It's frustrating. We can hardly get the phone answered sometimes. They're kind of slugs."[60]

But when apprehensions are brought up, the truth not only gets buried—records are sometimes physically manipulated. When an agent makes an apprehension he fills out an 826 Form in the field that reports the number of people he apprehended and/or contraband. It also lists who assisted in the apprehension (another agent, ICE, BORTAC, a K-9 unit, National Guard.) The agent signs the form and is responsible for the validity of the information he has supplied. The 826 goes to the station with the prisoners and is entered into the E3 system.

Somewhere between leaving the agent's hand in the field, going through the E3 system at the station, and arriving in Washington, D.C., the reports are often altered. Despite having made no discernible contribution, many reports will include "National Guard" as assisting in the apprehensions. "Hell, I was fifty miles away from the closest National Guard unit during an apprehension and they got credit for an assist. They didn't have anything to do with it," says an agent.[61]

The effect of the record falsification is to provide a metric that proves the value of the few National Guard troops deployed and blunts the idea that another fifteen thousand trained Border Patrol agents are needed.

It has come to light that many agents were originally required to make the false entries, but complained to their union. The union stepped in and agents no longer had to falsify the reports. Supervisors then falsified the reports.[62]

In addition to records being purposefully falsified, agents are sometimes told that what they witness in the field is false and not to be spoken about. In March of 2011, Alan Bersin, then commissioner of US Customs and Border Protection, visited Arizona. In one instance, he was given a briefing by ICE personnel that included videos taken by hidden cameras (including some from volunteer groups), agents' observations, civilians' written statements, and sensor data.[63]

Each time shortcomings regarding border security were addressed, Bersin would interrupt and say, "We have the border under control." After being told this four or five times, it was apparent to the presenters that Bersin had no interest in the very real problems that ICE was facing on the border.[64]

In December 2011, Alan Bersin stepped down as commissioner of US Customs and Border Protection. His replacement was none other than David Aguilar, who had been serving as deputy US commissioner of the US Customs and Border Protection since April 4, 2010.

The culture of lies is not confined to the Border Patrol or Customs or Homeland Security. It is everywhere, including the Department of Justice.

Eric Holder Analyzes the Numbers

In the hands of the Homeland Security or the Department of Justice, statistics can become meaningless. This is illustrated by an interchange between Attorney General Eric Holder and United States Representative Jason Chaffetz (Rep., Utah) on May 3, 2011, during a House judiciary hearing.[65]

Chaffetz related how he had just visited the border and was told that the United States only has 15 percent of it under effective control. "I was shocked. I went for hours along the border and there was nothing more than a barbed wire fence cut in many places and never even saw a Border Patrol agent. What in your opinion do we have to do to secure the border? Because it's not happening," asked Chaffetz.[66]

Attorney General Holder, sticking to Janet Napolitano's statements, declared, "Well, I think, you know, the situation along the border is better now than it probably ever has been."

"How do you come to that conclusion?" asked Representative Chaffetz.

Without hesitation Attorney General Holder offered, "You base it on the number of people we stopped, the number of drugs we recover, the number of guns …"

Representative Chaffetz interrupted, "So if the number of apprehensions go up is it better, or if the number of apprehensions go down is it better?"

Attorney General Holder replied, "Well, I mean it usually … it depends, you know it's a whole bunch of things. It's certainly a function of our, uh, the number of people we're trying to get in. It's also a function of our—how effective our enforcement efforts are. Which is not to say there are issues still problems along the border and I think we have to do all we can to secure our border, and I think that one of the ways we do that is to really look comprehensively at this whole immigration question."[67]

The Utah representative remained focused. "No doubt, we got to fix legal immigration and do a lot of other things. But, the statistic of apprehensions—if it goes up are we doing a better job of securing the border or if apprehensions go down are we doing a better job of securing the border?"

"That's a difficult one to answer," the attorney general replied.

Representative Chaffetz said, "I know. That's why I asked you."

The attorney general took another run at the question. "You can say that if we are apprehending more people, we're stopping more people coming through—on the other hand getting fewer people, it is entirely possible that our enforcement efforts are working and fewer people are trying to get in. It's a difficult question to answer."[68]

To be fair, Holder's last statement is not far off—both could be true. However, that's why accurate numbers of illegal immigrants and smugglers crossing the border is critical. Today's numbers are fluid, situational, and manipulated. It is simply statistically impossible to draw meaningful conclusions from false data. One wag in Homeland Security, when asked about this, smiled and asked, "When was the last time Eric Holder visited the border?"

A Lie Gone Mad

Politics is the art of moving an agenda forward. If the political agenda is in harmony with reality, it can be beneficial. If it is in conflict with reality, the consequences can be disastrous. The real art of politics is to realize the difference. All of which leads to the doorstep of the ATF (the Bureau of Alcohol, Tobacco, Firearms and Explosives.)

The ATF claims that 90 percent of the guns reaching the cartels in Mexico come from "straw buyers" who purchase the weapons from gun shops on the US side of the border. The guns are then smuggled into Mexico and into the hands of the cartels.

In an April 16, 2009, joint news conference in Mexico City with President Felipe Calderon, President Obama declared, "This war is being waged with guns purchased not here but in the United States. More than 90 percent of the guns recovered in Mexico come from the United States. Many from gun shops that line our shared border."[69]

Myth Busters

The private security analysis organization Stratfor is the latest to debunk that claim. They report that the bogus number was reached by selectively using numbers from a 2009 GAO report on arms trafficking to Mexico. The GAO reported that in 2008 approximately thirty thousand weapons were confiscated from criminals by Mexican authorities.[70]

According to Stratfor, information regarding only 7,200 (24 percent) weapons was presented to the ATF to be checked by E-Trace. Of the 7,200 guns submitted, only four thousand could be traced by the ATF. Finally, of the four thousand guns that could be traced, results indicated that 3,840 (87 percent) came from the United States.[71] It is from this self-serving math that the "90 percent myth" was created.

In the real world, the data means the confiscated guns positively traced back to the United States amount to less than 12 percent of the total number of guns seized by the Mexican government in 2008.[72]

A contractor that worked undercover for two decades with government agencies combating international arms trafficking scoffs at the government's "90 percent myth." He is one of the world's leading authorities on the subject, having worked in the Middle East, Africa, Asia, Mexico and South America. He indicates the Mexican Army supplies a large number of the weapons finding their way into the hands of the cartels. Others come through Central America, Cuba, Venezuela, West Africa and China.[73]

While the number of weapons supplied to the cartels from the United States only amounts to 12 percent of the total, a large number of those weapons (numbering in the thousands) were smuggled into Mexico with the consent and knowledge of the ATF, an agency within the Department of Justice.

An Indictment of Failure

And yet the myth continues. On April 26, 2012, the ATF announced that the Mexican government had seized over sixty-eight thousand guns from the United States since 2007.[74] The question arises, if this number is true, why was the ATF wasting huge amounts of its resources arming drug cartels through Fast and Furious instead of busting the incredible number of straw buyers that must be scurrying around border gun shops? Are there large numbers of huge gun trafficking organizations flying under the radar that are so difficult to find that the ATF had to create one? What was and is the ATF's agenda?

Whatever the purpose, promoting the "90 percent myth" would result in the murder of hundreds of people and Border Patrol agent Brian Terry.

Endnotes

1. Gary Martin, "DHS chief: SW border is largely controlled," *Arizona Daily Star*, September 14, 2010, http://azstarnet.com/news/local/border/article_4954de05-e810-54b1-b1fa-ec225519ba44.html.

2. Alan Bersin, memorial to Agent Brian Terry, Tucson, Arizona, January 21, 2011.

3. Daniel Gonzalez and Dan Nowicki, "Janet Napolitano confirms bandit gang killed border agent," *Arizona Republic*, December 18, 2010.

4. Ceci Connolly, "Obama administration announces new border security measures," *Washington Post*, June 24, 2010, http://www.washingtonpost.com/wp-dyn/content/article/2010/06/ 23/AR2010062305358.html.

5. Anthony Coulson, interview, April 26, 2012.

6. Madeleine J. Hinkes, "Migrant Deaths Along the California-Mexico Border: An Anthropological Perspective," *Journal of Forensic Medicine* Vol. 53, No. 1 (January 2008).

7. Dr. Madeleine J. Hinkes, interview, December 4, 2010.

8. Hinkes, "Migrant Deaths."

9. Ed Pyeatt, interview, May 8, 2010.

10. Ed Pyeatt, interview.

11. Ed Pyeatt, interview.

12. Ed Pyeatt, interview.

13. USDOJ/OIG Special Report, "Operation Gatekeeper: An Investigation into Allegations of Fraud and Misconduct," July 1998, http://www.justice.gov/oig/special/9807/exec.htm.

14. USDOJ/OIG Special Report, "Operation Gatekeeper."

15. Border Patrol agent, interview, 2010.

16. Border Patrol agent, interview.

17. Border Patrol agent, interview.

18. USDOJ/OIG Special Report, "Operation Gatekeeper."

19. USDOJ/OIG Special Report, "Operation Gatekeeper."

20. Ed Pyeatt, interview.

21. Ed Pyeatt, interview.

22. Border Patrol agent, interview, 2011.

23. Border Patrol agent, interview, 2010.

24. Protected source, interview, November 20, 2011.

25. Ed Pyeatt, interview.

26. Instructor, Border Patrol Academy, interview, 2011.

27. Instructor, Border Patrol Academy, interview.

28. Jim Runyon, interview, February 1, 2011.

29. Anthony Coulson, interview, March 18, 2012.

30. Sheriff Larry Dever, interview, October 14, 2010.

31. Border Patrol agent, protected source, 2010.

32. Sheriff Larry Dever, interview, October 14, 2010.

33. Protected source, interview, 2011.

34. Border Patrol agent, interview, 2010.

35. Whistleblowers document, "To the Department of Homeland Security and Office of Personnel Management Inspectors General," 2004.

36. Whistleblowers document, "To the Department of Homeland Security."

37. Vote of No Confidence, National Border Patrol Council, February 28, 2007, http://www.nbpc2554.org/docs/No%20Confidence%20 Vote%20-%20Press%20Release%20(04-23-07)%20Letterhead. pdf.

38. Vote of No Confidence, National Border Patrol Council, February 28, 2007.

39. Sherriff Larry Dever, interview, October 14, 2010.

40. John Ladd, interview, March 7, 2012.

41. Homeland Security employee, interview, 2011.

42. Homeland Security employee, interview.

43. *Chicago Tribune*, May 19, 2010.

44. *Vote of No Confidence*, National Immigration and Customs Enforcement Council, June 11, 2010.

45. Janet Napolitano, Testimony before House Homeland Security Committee, February 9, 2010, Cspan 3.

46. Janet Napolitano, Testimony before House Homeland Security Committee, February 9, 2010, Cspan 3.

47. Edwin Mora, "Border Patrol Data Contradicts Napolitano's Testimony That U.S. Has 'Effective Control of the Great Majority' of Both Northern and Southern Borders," Wednesday, February 09,

2011, http://cnsnews.com/news/article/border-patrol-data-contra-dicts-napolitanos-testimony-us-has-effective-control-great.

48. "Preliminary Observations on Border Control Measures for the Southwest Border," GAO, GAO-11-374T, February 15, 2011, http://www.gao.gov/products/GAO-11-374T.

49. "Preliminary Observations on Border Control Measures for the Southwest Border."

50. Jana Winter, "Exclusive: Federal Agents Told to Reduce Border arrests, Arizona Sheriff Says," FoxNews.com, April 1, 2011, http://www.foxnews.com/us/2011/04/01/exclusive-federal-agents-told-reduce-border-arrests-arizona-sheriff-says/.

51. Jana Winter, "Exclusive."

52. Jana Winter, "Exclusive."

53. Michael Fisher, letter to Sheriff Larry Dever, April 4, 2011.

54. Sheriff Larry Dever, interview, April 23, 2011.

55. Sheriff Larry Dever, interview, April 23, 2011.

56. Border Patrol agent, interview, 2011.

57. Zack Taylor, interview April 28, 2011.

58. Border Patrol agent, interview, 2011.

59. Border Patrol agent, interview, 2011.

60. Border Patrol agent, interview, 2011.

61. Border Patrol agent, interview, 2011.

62. Interview, official of National Border Patrol Council, Local 2544, April 11, 2012.

63. Protected source, 2011.

64. Protected source, 2011.

65. House Judiciary Hearing, May 3, 2011, http://www.c-spanvideo.org/program/299299-1

66. House Judiciary Hearing, May 3, 2011.

67. House Judiciary Hearing, May 3, 2011.

68. House Judiciary Hearing, May 3, 2011.

69. President Obama and President Calderon, joint press conference, Mexico City, White House, Office of the Press Secretary, April 16, 2009, http://www.whitehouse.gov/the-press-office/joint-press-con-ference-with-president-barack-obama-and-president-felipe-calde-ron-me.

70. "Mexico's Gun Supply and the 90 Percent Myth" is republished with permission of STRATFOR, http://www.stratfor.com/weekly/20110209-mexicos-gun-supply-and-90-percent-myth.

71. "Mexico's Gun Supply and the 90 Percent Myth."

72. "Mexico's Gun Supply and the 90 Percent Myth."

73. United States contractor, interviews, 2010, 2011.

74. "ATF says Mexican officials seized 68,000 guns from the US since 2007," *Arizona Daily Star*, April 27, 2012, http://azstarnet.com/news/local/border/atf-says-mexican-officials-seized-guns-from-us-since/article_05d16eba-3039-5fda-b64b-ee093ff422d8.html.

Chapter Sixteen

Dying with Honor

"Brian Terry died with honor, but for no reason ..."
Anonymous Border Patrol agent

AT THE UNIVERSITY OF Texas El Paso, Homeland Security secretary Janet Napolitano declared, "Violent crimes in Southwest border counties have dropped by more than 30 percent and are currently among the lowest in the nation per capita."[1] David Lowell, a rancher in Santa Cruz County, Arizona, doesn't necessarily agree. The rancher is quick to announce that there were close to a dozen shooting incidents in rural Santa Cruz County in the last year and a half that he knows of. It was on his ranch that BORTAC (the Border Patrol's tactical unit) agent Brian Terry was murdered on the night of December 14, 2010.

In response to Napolitano's "borders never so secure" and "low crime rate" statements, rancher Lowell is very direct. Lowell notes, "She automatically lies unless the situation doesn't allow a lie and then she might be induced to tell the truth."[2]

A More Civilized Time

Like most veteran ranchers on the border, Lowell remembers when crossing the border was "no big deal." Most crossers were vaqueros or farm workers looking for work. There was little question of migrating permanently to the United States. "There weren't many of them. There were no documents and no bad feelings," notes Lowell. "You'd get used to seeing the same people. They'd come and a few months later go home. In the '70s, there wasn't a penalty for hiring them. I stopped hiring in the '80s when it became illegal for employers."[3]

David Lowell ranches an area of fifty square miles in some of the most rugged areas in Arizona. His Atascoso Ranch stretches from west of Rio Rico south to Pena Blanca Lake and east toward

Nogales. The southernmost boundary of the ranch is five miles from the Arizona/Mexico border. It is wild country and until the late '90s mostly peaceful. Money, drugs, and illegal immigrants changed everything.

"It was about ten years ago things started to turn bad," he says. "Organized groups of illegal immigrants started to cross in big numbers. Wholesale dumping of trash would stretch in ribbons across my ranch." He pauses and continues, "Pine Canyon is one of the most beautiful places on my ranch. It has ponderosa pines ... now it's littered with trash. It's a drug way station."[4] Worse, unlike ten years ago, the area is now dangerous—very dangerous.

"There are scouts on my ranch. They are semipermanent. They're in high places with binoculars keeping a watch on the Border Patrol and people from different cartels.[5]

"There will be groups of twenty mules, each with a sixty- or seventy-pound bundle of dope crossing my ranch. Usually there'll be an armed man ahead of the mules with a cell phone and another armed guy behind them."[6] This has changed since the influx of bandits who try to steal loads from other cartels. There now are more armed men accompanying each load.

Dangerous Country

Lowell recounts the growth of violence in the area. "It was late afternoon [on December 29, 2009]. Two Border Patrol agents were on ATVs (all-terrain vehicles) in Ramanote Canyon when they were fired upon." One or two cartel members shot at the agents from a concealed position. One agent was shot in the ankle. The agents took cover and called for help. A Border Patrol helicopter responded and flew over only to be shot at. It was after dark when a mounted unit of the Border Patrol reached the area.[7]

A Border Patrol agent relates another version of this story. He indicates that the helicopter might have not been fired upon, but was making up the story as an excuse not to land. At that time there were apparently restrictions where helicopters were allowed to land in the Peck Canyon area. The reasons for the restrictions are cloudy, but were either related to the possibility of the area becoming a wildlife refuge or because of danger from ground fire.

"There have been at least ten other shooting incidents I recall in the last eighteen months. It was about six months ago I began to notice a lot of shootings were clustered in an area about a mile in diameter—where Ramanote Canyon meets Peck Canyon," observes Lowell.[8] It is the same area where BORTAC agent Brian Terry would be murdered.

"There have been various people wounded or shot at in the area. There have been a couple of bodies found that we never heard any more about. It was about two years ago one of our cowboys found a human head, which was pretty close to the area where Agent Terry was shot. When the sheriff's deputies came to pick up the head they made a careful search around the area for a body to go with it and our cowboy also looked and found nothing."

"Nothing much was heard about it. There's been a concerted effort by the government to sweep these violent incidents under the rug," says Lowell.[9]

One of the shooting incidents at the junction of Ramanote Canyon and Peck Canyon involved a group of illegal immigrants "that claimed they were just walking into the country, but they were more likely drug mules heading back to the border. They were shot at and ran down the canyon and one of them stumbled over a body."[10] To the west of the area where the body was discovered, game and fish officials were shot at and two archers held up at gunpoint, robbed, and stripped.

"There was another body near Pena Blanca Lake and another northwest of where the BORTAC agent was killed," continues Lowell. The drug smugglers use the area because of the rough terrain, canyons, and mountains. "The Forest Service would never admit this publically but they told me on their maps they counted something like eighty-seven drug trails through that general area (the Atascoso Mountains, Ramanote Canyon and Peck Canyon—all of which cross the land Lowell ranches.)[11]

As recently as two years ago, much of the border area south of the Atascoso ranch was separated from Mexico with a barbed wire fence. The border is remote and some areas are in effect no-man's land. A former Border Patrol agent and a retired Forest Service employee hiked into an isolated location in the Pajarito Mountain Wilderness

Area (just north of the border) because they had heard rumors about a rape tree. After a five-mile walk they found it.[12]

Despite the level of drug traffic, Lowell is very supportive of the Border Patrol. "We view them as comrades. We are very glad to see them on our ranch. They're responsive. We're both on the same side of the fence trying to stop illegal activity."[13]

Candid Camera

The Border Patrol has placed thousands of sensors along trails and the far-flung areas of the border. In addition, they have also placed dozens of concealed video cameras that are activated by motion. Some of these cameras have excellent resolution. They are useful in determining traffic patterns, determining usage, and identifying people crossing the borderlands from Mexico.[14] As noted previously, it has been reported that some cameras have been removed from high traffic areas.[15]

Nonetheless, in November and December of 2010, Border Patrol video cameras in the remote country of Santa Cruz County, Arizona, were recording not only how porous the border was, but the particular routes that armed smugglers and illegal immigrants followed deep into the United States.

Among those observed by the video cameras was one group of six to eight armed men who regularly made trips north across the border. The men were armed with AK-47s. The Border Patrol not only saw them entering the United States but exiting. Periodically these men were recorded in the Pajarito Mountain Wilderness, Ramanote Canyon, and Peck Canyon (see map). The video was so good many of the faces were recognizable.[16] The Border Patrol surmised they were "escorts" for drug smugglers.

As explained earlier, the area from Rio Rico west to Arivaca and south to the border is extremely dangerous. While the Border Patrol attempts to police the area they are not trained to meet large groups of armed men. This task often falls to the tactical units of the Border Patrol. BORTAC is officially described as "the global special response team for the Department of Homeland Security's (DHS) Bureau of Customs and Border Protection (CBP). Its mission is to respond to terrorist threats of all types anywhere in the world in order to protect our nation's homeland."[17]

There are many BORTAC units in Arizona, New Mexico, and Texas. One unit was stationed in Naco, Arizona, and consisted of a pool of thirteen men. On the night of December 14, 2010, a four-man team was deployed to an area in Santa Cruz County, Arizona, where Ramanote Canyon meets Peck Canyon. The team consisted of detailer BORTAC Agent Gabriel Fragoza (from the Blythe Station/ Yuma Sector), BORTAC agent Timothy Keller (from the Calexico Station/El Centro Sector), Agent William Castano (who also served as a medic), and BORTAC agent Brian Terry.[18]

Laying Up

It had been unseasonably cold in Arizona that month. Forty-year-old agent Brian Terry intended to go home to Michigan soon to spend Christmas with his father, mother, stepmother, sisters, and brothers for the first time in years. He had already mailed his Christmas presents.

Two weeks earlier, he had phoned his stepmother, Carolyn Terry, after leaving a lay-up in the same area of Peck Canyon. "He called on his way home [to Sierra Vista] and said he was 'frozen to death' because it got down to seventeen degrees in the mountains. He said it was cold, cold, cold," relates Carolyn Terry.[19]

"He told me I can't tell anybody, but they had been out looking for dirty agents," says Carolyn. "He went out the next week in the same area and said his team caught two illegals."

An individual close to Agent Terry discloses that he had been writing letters to his superiors critical of how certain policies were handicapping the Border Patrol's efforts.[20] Whether the letters involved information regarding dirty agents or Border Patrol policy is not known.

The report of the letters gain further credibility because of a conversation Brian had with his father during the summer. Brian expressed to his father that he was "disappointed with things that were going on with the Border Patrol."[21]

His father asked, "You're not going to quit are you?"

Brian replied, "No."

"What's going on?"

Brian answered, "I can't talk about it."

Brian Terry (left) and his father Kent Terry.
Photo courtesy of Kent and Carolyn Terry.

Whatever Brian's concerns, he and his unit were presumably deployed the night of December 14 because a "group had been detected coming across the border and moving north into the Pajarito Mountain Wilderness area."[22] This "group" was not identified as bandits.

Despite this, the Border Patrol would later assert that Agent Terry and the other members of the team were assigned to "intercept bandits." This is a truly odd assertion since "intercepting bandits" is outside the legal jurisdiction of the Border Patrol.[23]

By 10:30 PM Terry and three other BORTAC agents were in place and laying up on a ridge at the junction of Ramanote Canyon and Peck Canyon. Below them to the south, they could observe two trails that ran toward them. It was a clear night, and it would be several hours before the moon set.

Ramanote and Peck Canyon area (South is to the left).
Photo by William Daniel.

To the agents' left (bottom of photo), Peck Canyon led toward Rio Rico. Behind Terry (to the north and northeast), trails spread out toward Interstate 19. One agent watched toward the south with thermal binoculars.[24] The problem was, as the four BORTAC agents focused their attention to the south, death was hurtling at them from the northeast.

A group of perhaps two dozen smugglers had allegedly unloaded a ton of dope in a grove of trees by Interstate 19 and were moving quickly through a canyon that would lead toward the southwest and Cummings Mesa—the ridge above the junction point of Ramanote Canyon and Peck Canyon. Moving along a canyon ridge ahead of the mules was their escort, six to eight men armed with AK-47s and other weapons. There was a report of over "thirty unidentified persons" moving between Interstate 19 and Peck Canyon.[25] It is unclear why the message did not get to Brian Terry and his team.

The Murder

It is not known whether or not the BORTAC unit heard their footsteps or voices first, but they were faced in the wrong direction. The armed men who had been on point for the retreating smugglers had reached the mesa. The radio report from that night states, "At approximately 11:10 PM, a group of approximately five individuals approached their position, coming from the east."[26]

Taken by surprise, the BORTAC agents let them pass—at least most of them. Five or six of the armed escort passed the agents and started down the trail from the mesa into the junction of Ramanote and Peck Canyon. The four BORTAC agents rose and confronted the men. The agents yelled out "Policia ... Policia."[27] The escort continued to move away, except for at least one man still closing in on the agents from the rear.

According to the incident report, "BORTAC Agent Gabriel Fragoza deployed two rounds from a less-than-lethal device [bean bags from a shotgun]." Immediately, fire was returned by several of the men in the drug escort. Agent Terry was slightly behind his fellow agents and leaning forward.

Terry was shot and fell to the ground. Unknown to the other agents a round from an assault weapon had ripped into Terry's lower back, about twenty-nine inches down from the right shoulder.[28] The shooter had been the escort still coming up on the BORTAC agents from the rear. The shooter dropped the weapon and ran north.

With Terry on the ground Agent Fragoza "discharged an unknown number of rounds from his service-issued sidearm." Agent Timothy Keller "also discharged an unknown number of rounds from his service-issued M-4 rifle."[29] One of the escorts in front of them was shot, and the others scattered into the night.

It was over in seconds. BORTAC agent Brian Terry called out after the shooting, "I can't feel my legs." Agent William "Willie" Castano went to Terry, who soon lost consciousness. The agent reports that Terry died soon after being shot.[30] Five feet behind Agent Terry was the AK-47 that killed him.[31]

The escorts who escaped to the north blended in with the drug mules, all of whom were without bundles and could pass as simple illegal immigrants.

Crime Scene Investigation

While Brian Terry lay mortally wounded, Kevin Jones of the Border Patrol Tucson Investigations Branch was notified of the shooting. Thirty minutes after the shooting, the Border Patrol's "Critical Incident Team" was en route.[32] Their mission would be to ensure the crime scene was not disturbed and to begin gathering preliminary information, but not to conduct interviews or touch evidence.

The scene around Peck Canyon was chaotic. A command post had been established, the hunt for suspects was being organized, and assets, medical and otherwise, were pouring into the area. Border Patrol agent Brian Terry was reported unresponsive and without a pulse at 11:40 PM.[33]

The Critical Incident Team arrived and began securing the actual crime scene. They located shell casings and three weapons, and tried to preserve tracks. The FBI arrived on the scene within an hour of the shooting. They took charge of the crime scene and of the investigation. Several members of the Critical Incident Team showed the FBI where weapons and shell casings were located. The FBI took pictures of the crime scene, interviewed agents, and removed three weapons. Shortly thereafter, a man by the name of Manuel Osorio-Arellanes of Choix, Sinaloa, Mexico was taken into custody. The suspect was wounded.[34]

Brian Terry was pronounced dead at 1:06 AM, December 15, 2011.[35] His body remained at the scene until the FBI released it. At 1:35 AM it was reported that four suspects were in custody, and the FBI indicated that they were looking for one more person.

The FBI transported the guns, two AK-47s, and reportedly an SKS assault rifle to their lab where they would conduct ballistic tests. When the dust settled, there was one dead border patrol agent, one shot-up suspect, and four additional suspects in custody.[36] The Border Patrol was left searching for one more suspect, and the family of Brian Terry would be left searching for answers.

Happy Holidays

On the morning of December 15 the Border Patrol came to the house of Brian Terry's younger sister, Kelly Willis. "Brian had her down as next of kin in case anything happened to him," relates his stepmother Carolyn Terry. "Kelly called me at 7 AM and told me that Brian had been shot. The Border Patrol never called me. I called information and got the number for the Naco [Arizona] station. It was about 9 AM that morning when I called and got to talk to a chaplain down there. We talked for a while. I was told Brian was shot with an AK-47 in the back. I asked the chaplain if his vest would repel the bullet. He said Brian had a seventy-pound vest that could stop a AK-47 bullet."[37]

After Carolyn's conversation with the chaplain, communication with the Border Patrol was meager. Everybody was upset that the Border Patrol never even contacted Brian's dad."[38]

"The first one that called us was Napolitano the day before the funeral. She didn't care about Brian. Everything she said was just political. It was so useless I can't even remember what she said," Carolyn says.[39]

Brian Terry's father told Secretary Napolitano, "You got to wake your man up in the White House." Napolitano responded, "He's done more in the last two years than any other president."[40]

The family's other major exchange with the administration occurred at the funeral home during the visitation. "We were led into a room and told President Obama was going to talk to the family. We sat there for thirty minutes and finally left the room. Then three hours later they came rushing up to us and told the family to go back to the room because he was on the phone."

A disappointed Carolyn Terry continues, "I guess it took them that long to get his little message written down so he could read it to us. Then he couldn't even read it right. He fumbled it up. At the end President Obama said, 'Michelle and I hope you have a happy holiday.'" The family couldn't ask him anything. Carolyn muses, "He actually said that. 'Michelle and I hope you have a happy holiday.'"[41]

THE WHITE HOUSE
WASHINGTON

December 21, 2010

Dear Mr. Terry:

Michelle and I send our heartfelt condolences over the loss of your son, Brian A. Terry. There are no words to express the sadness of the loss of a loved one.

Your son served his country admirably as a Marine, police officer, and a Border Patrol agent. While his family, friends, and colleagues grieve his passing, we are grateful for his selfless service and many contributions to our Nation. We are inspired by his patriotism, his commitment to public service, and the high esteem with which he was held by all who had the pleasure to know him.

While words cannot ease your loss, please know that Brian's service and sacrifice in the line of duty made this country more safe and secure. Michelle and I join you and your extended family in remembering Brian, and we will keep you and your family in our thoughts and prayers.

Sincerely,

Note from President Obama given to Kent Terry.
Photo courtesy of Kent and Carolyn Terry.

"Some of the guys that Brian was working with that day he was shot came to the funeral home at the end of the visitation.[42]

"One of them said he was ten feet away from Brian and he was the first one to get to him. He said Brian yelled, 'I'm hit' and he said he ran to him. He said he had a peaceful look on his face," relates Carolyn.[43]

"I asked, 'Do you think he was gone then?' He answered, 'yes.'"[44]

"There were twelve or fifteen of them, all BORTAC. They went to the back of the funeral home and took a lot of pictures of themselves with Brian's dad. Brian had talked so much about his dad. They wanted to meet his dad."[45]

"I remember one of the agents. His name was John, and he was off that day [December 14]. He said he got the call and was told Brian was shot. He cried all the way into the station." Another agent assured Carolyn Terry that they had the weapon that killed her stepson.[46]

The funeral for forty-year-old Brian Terry was held Wednesday, December 22, 2010, at Detroit's Greater Grace Temple. Hundreds packed the church to remember Terry.[47] In attendance was Homeland Security secretary Janet Napolitano. She declared, "We resolve, I resolve, to pursue swift justice for those responsible for his death, and we resolve, I resolve, to do everything in our power to protect those who put their lives on the line every day for our nation's safety and security."[48]

A Man of Honor

A friend read a passage at the funueral that Brian Terry had written. "If today is the day, so be it. If you seek to do battle with me this day, you will receive the best that I am capable of giving. You may kill me, but I'm willing to die if necessary. I do not fear death for I have been close enough to it on enough occasions that it no longer concerns me. What I do fear is the loss of my honor and would rather die fighting than have it said that I was without courage."[49]

Photo Courtesy of Kent and Carolyn Terry.

At the time of Brian Terry's death, he was wearing bands on each wrist referencing, "Honoring the Fallen."[50] And now, Brian Terry was among those he honored.

After the funeral the Terry family received almost no information concerning the shooting or the investigation. Finally, Kelly, Brian's sister, was contacted and told that when the family came out for a memorial that was to be held in Brian's honor in Tucson, they would have some information they could share.[51]

Who is in Charge?

In Tucson there was also a lack of news about the slaying. The FBI would respond to questions by insisting that it was an ongoing investigation and they couldn't comment. The Border Patrol would refer questions to the FBI. Presumably, the US attorney for Arizona, Dennis Burke (former chief of staff to then Arizona governor Janet Napolitano from 2003 to 2008), could have given some information, but he wasn't talking, which is not to indicate that nothing was happening. A lot of people were positioning themselves.

Going practically unnoticed, one day after the murder of Brian Terry, a man identified as Jamie Avila was arrested in Phoenix on suspicion of smuggling guns across the Arizona border into Mexico to the cartels. Unknown to almost everyone, the arrest was an immediate result of the murder of Brian Terry. The ATF was beginning to scramble to protect itself from a major blunder.

Two days after the shooting, on December 16, John Evans was promoted to chief attorney of the US attorney's Criminal Section in Tucson. In that position he would be the direct supervisor of the prosecutor assigned to the Brian Terry case. John Evans had a reputation as a very "hands-on guy."[52]

At the same time, the US Attorney's Office for Arizona assigned veteran prosecutor Jesse Figueroa to the Brian Terry case. In addition, Tim Jefferson, a "victims advocate" at the US Attorney's Office was assigned to the case. At times, Jefferson would appear more as an advocate for the Department of Justice than the Terry family.[53]

At this point the FBI could not have released information if it had wanted to. The US Attorney's Office was calling the shots—sort of. The actual line of command in this case is very short. It looks something like this:

> US Attorney (prosecutor) assigned the shooting case > John Evans > Dennis Burke > Lanny Breuer > Eric Holder

Putting the Lid On

Two days later, on December 17, Homeland Security Secretary Janet Napolitano arrived in Arizona "to visit with border patrol officials."[54] Secretary Napolitano was expected to get a firsthand report on the progress of the investigation of the murder of Agent Terry, but that was not the entire purpose of her visit. It appeared to some she wanted to put the lid on information coming out of the Border Patrol, because there had been "serious snafus." Agents supposedly were told not to talk to anyone about the Brian Terry murder. Some agents wondered if they could even talk to their spouses about it.[55]

The first indication of trouble ahead in the Brian Terry case emerged December 16, the same day the three non-injured suspects (all non-US citizens) in the Terry shooting were brought before a judge for their initial appearance, as well as another man found in the Peck Canyon area the next day. For some reason, their names were not released.

The wounded suspect captured after the Terry murder, Manuel Arellanes, aka Manuel Arellanes Osorio, was sitting in a hospital room giving an interview. Arellanes, thirty-four, a Mexican national, had been convicted in Maricopa Superior Court in 2006 for aggravated assault on a police officer.

Arellanes's alleged story was, "We found the guns on their way south. We didn't want to leave them for someone to get hurt." He asserted all of his group had found AK-47s." Arellanes went on to say they "heard gunshots aimed towards them and shot back in defense. When they heard somebody speaking in English and identifying themselves as the Border Patrol they stopped shooting."

Despite a scarcity of suspects, David Gonzales, US Marshal for Arizona, remained optimistic, declaring, "I'm sure that in the next week or two there will be indictments coming down in connection with the shooting."[56]

In reality, it appeared more likely the Brian Terry murder case was going to follow the same fate as the case involving rancher Rob Krentz earlier in the year. There was a report that the shooter of Brian Terry had crossed into Mexico near Sasabe shortly after the murder.[57] The family of Brian Terry was still looking for answers.

You Need to Settle Down

A memorial service for Agent Brian Terry was planned for Tucson on January 21, 2011. The service would be an opportunity for his fellow agents, law enforcement personal, and citizens to honor his sacrifice.

The Border Patrol also had told Carolyn Terry that they might be able to provide the family with more information regarding his death. She was told they would be able to fly over the Peck Canyon area where Brian was shot. The family wanted facts. "They hadn't told us anything."[58] It was a sad occasion, but the family was hopeful of getting more information.

They had heard a lot of rumors about "friendly fire" or a "dirty agent." They had also heard that Brian had been killed with a gun bought in the United States. Carolyn said, "I just wanted to know what happened to Brian."[59]

Carolyn Terry and family members arrived in Tucson for the memorial honoring Brian on the afternoon of January 20. The Border Patrol took them to the hotel. It was only a twenty-minute drive, but it would set the tone for the rest of the weekend. The Border Patrol driver, a chaplain, informed Carolyn "there wouldn't be time" to helicopter over the location in Peck Canyon where Brian was shot.[60]

They reached the hotel, were shown to their rooms, and in a short time informed they would be able to meet with officials and hear what was happening with the case. They were led into a room at the hotel with a large, long table.

Present were a couple of men from the FBI, Jesse Figueroa (an assistant US attorney), Tim Jefferson (a DOJ victims advocate), a high-ranking person from DHS, and representatives from the Border Patrol. "There were a total of twelve of them," recalls Carolyn. There were also eight Border Patrol chaplains and four or five public relations people. The chaplains and public relations people stepped outside and the meeting commenced.[61]

The meeting started and a Border Patrol representative announced that Brian had not been killed by friendly fire. It was also stated they had retrieved a bullet from Brian's body and it was a .30 caliber that matched the ballistics of a weapon they had retrieved. At the same time an FBI or Border Patrol official mentioned that three weapons had been recovered at the scene of the shooting.[62] It was the last of any meaningful information that came from the meeting.

Carolyn wanted to put a rumor to sleep. She asked, "Was Brian shot by a dirty agent?"

They told the family, "Well, we can't discuss that. It might hurt the case." It was a phrase used frequently during the meeting.

Carolyn Terry and Brian's brother Kent Terry Jr. continued asking questions. At one point one of the government representatives said to Carolyn, "You read the newspapers too much and are on the Internet too much." She responded angrily, "I don't have a newspaper delivered to my house. I work full-time and my husband is handicapped—I don't have time for the paper or the Internet."[63]

"I think they thought we were just going to sit and listen, not ask questions." Kent and Carolyn asked them about inconsistencies. Were there five or eight bandits? Were there five or six BORTAC Agents? (She would later discover from a friend Brian worked with that there were only four agents.) Kent Terry Jr. became so upset with the government's lack of responsiveness, he walked out of the meeting. He told them, "You people asked us to come to meet with you and then you take up our time and don't answer any of our questions."[64]

Carolyn asked if Brian was shot with a weapon bought in the United States. One of the government representatives answered, "We don't make AK-47s in the United States." An offended Carolyn Terry responded, "I didn't say they were made here. I asked if they were bought here." At that point she left the meeting.

The chaplain who met Carolyn at the airport and drove her to the hotel asked, "What's going on in there?" She answered, "Nothing. That's the problem. Nothing is going on in there." A man from the meeting came over and told Carolyn, "You need to settle down."[65]

The Border Patrol has a reputation for controlling and managing events, whether it involves a congressperson or a victim's family. In contrast, the Border Patrol Union is very independent and looks after the interests of its members and not the agenda of the Border Patrol. Local 2544 of the National Border Patrol Council reached out to the Terry family with an offer to share any information they had regarding Brian's death. It was an offer the family was eager to accept.

However, Brian's sister Kelly Willis was told a meeting with representatives of the Border Patrol Council was not on the agenda and wouldn't fit the schedule. Some family members were informed that the Union just wanted to present them with a plaque and there wasn't time. The Border Patrol contacted the Union, requesting they not meet with the family.[66]

It was Saturday night and there was nothing scheduled. At 7 PM, the family members met with representatives of the National Border Patrol Council. In that single meeting they were given more information than they had received from the Border Patrol hierarchy in weeks. The family was told they were free to do with the information what they wanted. They could keep it to themselves or share it.[67]

Never Take a Knife to a Gunfight

There was a growing feeling among some observers that the Border Patrol and Homeland Security were covering up information. There had been three major screwups. One of the most significant involves the Border Patrol's rules of engagement. It is something President Obama understands, even if the DHS couldn't grasp it. As President Obama advises, "You never take a knife to a gunfight."

Areas of Santa Cruz County, Pinal County, and Cochise County Arizona are extremely dangerous. There are groups of very well armed, determined, ruthless, intelligent, resourceful, and sometimes desperate men who are intent on smuggling drugs across the border to meet the habit of America's junkies.

However, the BORTAC units are apparently either restricted by the Border Patrol's rules of engagement to use nonlethal rounds when first encountering men armed with AK-47s, or they are poorly trained about the consequences of that use. It may be politically correct, but as illustrated on December 14, 2010, nonlethal force creates a situation where an agent can be killed.

The Border Patrol flip-flopped on this several times, before CBP Director Bersin said it was the agents' choice as to whether or not to use "nonlethal' bean bag rounds. If this is true, it showed poor judgment by Border Patrol managers. Whatever the story, the curriculum surrounding the use of nonlethal force at the Border Patrol changed as a result of the incident.

Another mistake made the night of December 14 was that a BORTAC agent fired first. The man who fired the rounds simply "screwed up." The area is full of "rip crews" that steal loads of dope or rob illegal immigrants. It is typical for a rip crew to announce itself as "Policia."

It is not typical for BORTAC or Border Patrol agents to fire first. In the case in question, the smugglers (from the agents' point of view) were moving away from them. The perceived threat was appearing to diminish. Smugglers understand a genuine Border Patrol agent can't fire upon them unless there is an actual threat of deadly force present.[68] The smugglers apparently made the split-second assumption that they were being attacked by a rip crew.

A third mistake was underestimating the threat facing the agents, which is the result of the political environment. The BORTAC team was sent into an area where there could be more than two dozen smugglers. Are four men enough to meet the threat? A veteran Border Patrol agent related that if he and a couple of other agents were to run into eight men armed with AK-47s crossing the border, he'd "get the hell out of there."[69]

Finally, everyone concerned was not aware that there was a "stone-cold killer" among the smugglers.

To the Terry family, the death of Brian was a tragedy. But for the rest of the country the shooting was about to become a national scandal.

Endnotes

1. Homeland Security, "Remarks on Border Security at the University of Texas at El Paso," news release, January 31, 2011, http://www.dhs.gov/ynews/speeches/sp_1296491064429.html.

2. David Lowell, interview, February 5, 2011.

3. David Lowell, interview.

4. Pine Canyon is located one half mile west and slightly north of where Agent Terry was slain.

5. David Lowell, interview.

6. David Lowell, interview.

7. David Lowell, interview.

8. David Lowell, interview.

9. David Lowell, interview.

10. David Lowell, interview.

11. David Lowell, interview.

12. Border Patrol agent, interview, 2011.

13. David Lowell, interview.

14. Border Patrol agent, interview, 2011.

15. Security analyst, interview, 2011.

16. Security analyst, interview, 2011.

17. http://bortac.com.

18. BORTAC Shooting Incident (11 TCANGL 121570000077), and United States of America v. Manuel Osorio Arellanes, aka Manual Arellanes, aka "Paye" et.al. CR-11-0150-TUC-DCB-JCG, United States District Court, District of Arizona.

19. Carolyn Terry, 1nterview, January 13, 2011.

20. Border Patrol agent, interview, 2011.

21. Carolyn Terry, interview, February 3, 2012.

22. Security analysts, interview, 2011.

23. Security analysts, interview.

24. Brady McCombs "Records show agents fired beanbags in fatal border gunfight," *Arizona Daily Star*, March 3, 2011, http://azstarnet. com/news/local/crime/records-show-agents-fired-beanbags-in-fatal-border-gunfight/article_681d29cf-845a-5aea-9f34-3837d70b8a31. html.

25. Border Patrol agent, protected source, 2010.

26. BORTAC Shooting Incident (11 TCANGL 121570000077).

27. Border Patrol agent present at scene on December 14, 2010.

28. Brian Terry, ML 10-02444, autopsy report, Santa Cruz County, Arizona, December 15, 2010.

29. BORTAC Shooting Incident (11 TCANGL 121570000077)

30. BORTAC Shooting Incident (11 TCANGL 121570000077)

31. Carolyn Terry, interview, February 22, 2011.

32. BORTAC Shooting Incident (11 TCANGL 121570000077)

33. BORTAC Shooting Incident (11 TCANGL 121570000077)

34. BORTAC Shooting Incident (11 TCANGL 121570000077)

35. BORTAC Shooting Incident (11 TCANGL 121570000077)

36. BORTAC Shooting Incident (11 TCANGL 121570000077)

37. Carolyn Terry, interview, January 13, 2011.

38. Carolyn Terry, interview, January 13, 2011.

39. Carolyn Terry, interview, January 13, 2011.

40. "DHS boss Napolitano addresses criticisms from Terry family," KGUN9, December 22, 2010.

41. Carolyn Terry, interview, January 13, 2011.

42. Carolyn Terry, interview, January 13, 2011.

43. Carolyn Terry, interview, January 13, 2011.

44. Carolyn Terry, interview, January 13, 2011.

45. Carolyn Terry, interview, January 13, 2011.

46. Carolyn Terry, interview, January 13, 2011.

47. Robin Schwartz, "Hundreds Attend Funeral Service for Border Patrol Agent Brian Terry," myFOXDetroit.com, December 22, 2010, http://www.myfoxdetroit.com/dpp/news/local/ hundreds-attend-funeral-service-for-border-patrol-agent-brian-terry-20101222-wpms.

48. "Napolitano at Funeral of BP Agent," KGUN News, December 22, 2010.

49. "Hundreds Attend Funeral Service for Border Patrol Agent Brian Terry," myFOXDetroit.com, December 22, 2010, http://www.myfoxdetroit.com/dpp/news/local/hundreds-attend-funeral-service-for-border-patrol-agent-brian-terry-20101222-wpms.

50. Brian Terry, ML 10-02444, autopsy report.

51. Carolyn Terry, interview, January 13, 2011.

52. Intelligence analyst (ret.), interview, 2011.

53. Carolyn Terry, interview, January 13, 2011.

54. Brian McCombs, "Napolitano in Tucson today to visit with Border Patrol officials," *Arizona Daily Star*, December 17, 2010, http://azstarnet.com/news/local/article_5668f178-0a09-11e0-8c25-001cc4c03286.html.

55. Border Patrol agent, interview, December 2010.

56. Dennis Wagner, "Arizona border shooting: Still no charges in agent's killing," *Arizona Republic*, December 30, 2010.

57. Supervisor Border Patrol (ret.), interview, 2010.

58. Carolyn Terry, interview, January 13, 2011.

59. Carolyn Terry, interview, January 13, 2011.

60. Carolyn Terry, interview, February 15, 2011.

61. Carolyn Terry, interview, February 15, 2011.

62. Carolyn Terry, interview, February 15, 2011.

63. Carolyn Terry, interview, February 15, 2011.

64. Carolyn Terry, interview, February 15, 2011.

65. Carolyn Terry, interview, February 15, 2011.

66. Carolyn Terry, interview, February 15, 2011.

67. Carolyn Terry, interview, February 15, 2011.

68. Border Patrol agent, interview, February 15, 2011.

69. Border Patrol agent, interview.

Chapter Seventeen

A Criminal Organization

"In six hours we'll have these guns on the other side of the border."
Tucson ATF agent to confidential informant

SATURDAY, JANUARY 16, 2010, was a beautiful day in Glendale, Arizona. A man pulled up in front of the Lone Wolf Trading Company and sat for a moment. A few minutes later the same man, Jaime Avila, Jr., walked out of the gun store with three AK-47-type firearms.[1] He had paid cash and had an Arizona driver's license. The serial numbers had been entered into eTrace, a system used by the ATF to keep track of guns in case they are stolen or used in crimes.[2] There didn't appear to be anything unusual. The man put the AK-47s in his vehicle and exited onto Peoria. He'd be back.

In fact, Jamie Avila, Jr., reportedly had been a steady customer of the Lone Wolf Trading Company. He is said to have started buying guns in October 2009.[3] On November 25, 2009, records show Avila had purchased five Herstal 57 caliber semiautomatic pistols.[4] Apparently he liked the pistols so well he returned on January 11, 2010, and bought three more Herstal pistols.[5] Each time he paid cash. Avila, Jr., is reported to have also visited other gun shops.

While Jamie Avila, Jr., appeared to be just another gun aficionado to the casual observer, he was being watched closely by the ATF. Three days after the January 16, 2010 purchase of the three AK-47s, the ATF entered his name into the Suspect Person Database.[6] The ATF database keeps track of gun purchase totals by suspects. Monthly reports were delivered to an ATF Intelligence Group supervisor and the ATF Field Intelligence support team member in Phoenix.

A task force inside the Phoenix ATF called Group VII was watching Jamie Avila, Jr., and twenty or thirty other individuals. It was pursuing a sting operation with the code name Fast and Furious.

Its goal was to allow "straw buyers" (Jaime Avila, Jr. in this case) to purchase weapons that would be transferred to "prohibited" persons. The guns would intentionally be permitted to cross into Mexico. The weapons then would supposedly lead to higher-ups in the cartels.

While selected gun dealers cooperated with the ATF in this effort, at least one gun dealer wanted to stop participating in sales like those to Avila, Jr., as early as October 2009.[7] But the ATF operation was not going to stop because of reluctant gun dealers or other government agencies. Fast and Furious supervisor David Voth responded, 'If it helps put you at ease, we are continually monitoring the suspects using a variety of techniques which I cannot go into detail."[8] The gun dealer was not told the guns would cross the border.

In reality, not only did the ATF encourage gun dealers to sell weapons to straw buyers, but they also protected the straw buyers and their confederates from being busted. In this case, Jaime Avila, Jr., was allegedly pulled over by CBP (Customs Border Protection) officials during the spring or summer of 2010 in southwest New Mexico, near the Mexican border. It is reported that Avila had two AK-47s and thirty other weapons in the vehicle.[9]

According to a reliable source, the CBP officials contacted the ATF about the weapons in the vehicle. They were supposedly told by the ATF or a United States attorney to "allow Avila to proceed without seizing the weapons."[10] The ATF rationalized that by letting the guns reach Mexico they might lead to the imagined leader(s) of the gun smuggling organizations. Instead of arresting one or two straw buyers on a hit-or-miss basis, they would crack a big case and be able to extradite a big shot from Mexico. But at least two of the weapons ended up at the murder scene of BORTAC agent Brian Terry.

Group VII's operation Fast and Furious will give eternal credence to some ATF agents' observation that "The ATF can't even do the wrong thing right." The template for disaster originated in Tucson in 2006.

Operation Wide Receiver

In 2006, a Tucson gun dealer by the name of Mike Detty was in Phoenix at a gun show. Detty, a former Marine, is a well-known writer. His expertise is weapons. His articles appear in popular gun magazines and law enforcement publications. He has held a FFL (federal firearms license) for years and works out of gun shows and his home. Detty's ambition growing up was to work in federal law enforcement. He graduated from the University of Arizona, and was looking forward to a career in law enforcement. However, that ambition was short-circuited when he had to take a medical discharge from the Marines.

At the Phoenix gun show, "There were some kids [twenty-two to twenty-four years old] buying AR-15s. They bought six AR15s on a Saturday." The next day they came back and wanted to buy more AR-15s. "I told them I was out, but I'd have twenty of them for the show in Tucson the next week," recalls Detty. One of the young men said, "I'll take them all."[11]

"It was very suspicious—they didn't ask for a discount or anything. So, Monday morning I relayed the information to the Tucson ATF office and they asked me to come down and talk to them."[12] It was during that meeting that Detty signed an official Confidential Informant Agreement with the ATF.

Over a six-month period the young men would buy weapons from Detty and drive them to a confederate in San Diego, who would transport them across the border. The buyers became lazy and decided they would ship the guns to San Diego via UPS. Unfortunately for the buyers, they chose a UPS store run by a retired Secret Service agent. The retired Secret Service agent opened one of the boxes thinking it might be drugs. He notified the Phoenix ATF office of the gun shipment (which they knew about), and they notified the San Diego ATF office.[13]

According to Detty, "The case could have easily gone on, but the special agent in charge (SAIC) of the California area didn't want the shipment to go through."[14] After that, the buyers disappeared off of Detty's radar until about a year later, when one of the men named Carlos showed up in Tucson.

Carlos appeared with someone who had "legitimate" cartel connections in Caborca, Sonora. At the meeting that night, the man with the presumed cartel connections bought six guns. Detty asked if the guns were going south. The man replied without hesitation,

"Yeah, they're going south. Everything is going to Mexico."[15] Operation Wide Receiver was off and running.

The cartel buyer had a "cousin" who every couple of weeks would have a big barbeque in central Tucson. "The barbeques would attract some not-so-nice people—not the cream of society," relates Detty. She (the cousin) would tell the Mexican Nationals, "Hey, you guys need guns? We got a guy, but the only thing is I get a hundred dollars for every gun you buy as a finder fee."[16] It was through this connection that operation Wide Receiver grew and grew.

The Tucson ATF office was being stretched thin. Detty recalls being in the ATF office in Tucson when agents would come in complaining that a buyer was taking too long to get across the border. In one instance an agent said, "Hey, Detty, the next time we have to follow your guys all night, I'm just going to shoot those bastards."[17] To get help with surveillance, the Tucson office hired off-duty Tucson Police Department officers.

After seven months, some of the Tucson ATF agents thought they had more than enough evidence for a case. They wanted to shut Operation Wide Receiver down. The ATF special agent in charge of operations in Tucson at that time, Chuck Higman, reportedly told Detty, "Look, we're going to have to cut these guys back because we are getting way too much political pressure about the number of guns [going south]."[18]

Apparently some of that pressure was coming from the ATF Supervisor in charge of the Tucson Office. It is reported that he was doing battle with the head of the ATF in Arizona and New Mexico—a man out of the Phoenix Office named William Newell.[19]

According to some sources, the Phoenix office insisted the ATF was doing nothing illegal because the ATF didn't physically take the weapons across the border, they just watched. Whatever the rationale, it is reported that Newell overruled the Tucson ATF supervisor.[20]

"Days later they said go ahead and sell the guns," recalls Detty. "To them it's all about the numbers. I guess they just never thought any of those guns would come back here and kill anybody."[21]

The Tucson supervisor persisted and requested the case be closed. The Phoenix ATF office and presumably the agent in charge, William

Newell, overruled this request. According to Mike Detty, no gun went across the border without Newell's permission.[22]

Finally, the ATF office in Tucson took action to slow the process down. "It got so crazy that toward the end of this investigation, they [the ATF in Tucson] said, 'Too many guns are going south, there's too many people getting involved; it's getting too complicated.'"[23]

The Tucson office decided they would at least shut down all the peripheral players. For example, an important buyer drove a truck full of weapons to the border with a minor player in a vehicle behind him. The minor player was stopped for a secondary inspection and busted, while the major player was waved through.

"It scared the shit out of the guy [the major buyer] ... for all intents and purposes that day my sales to these people stopped," Detty says. He thought it might take a while for the ATF and US attorney to get "their ducks in a row and start making arrests."[24] It didn't happen.

Six months later, the case was passed to a US assistant attorney out of Washington, D.C., by the name of Laura Gwinn. Gwinn specializes in RICO cases and has prosecuted MS-13 gangs in the United States.

Nearly three years elapsed between stopping the half load of guns going into Mexico and any arrests. Finally, in November of 2010 six people were arrested in connection with the case in which Mike Detty had invested so much time and exposed himself to so much risk as a private citizen. The number of people charged fell about forty short of what Detty and the Tucson ATF agents expected. Surprisingly, the defendants were charged only with violations of falsifying the 4473 forms they filled out when buying the weapons.[25]

The defendants were not charged with the more serious crime of conspiring to illegally buy guns. They were not charged with conspiring to transport "weapons of war" to Mexico. They were not charged with illegally exporting "weapons of war" to Mexico. There were two reasons the government didn't make more serious charges.

First, by the very nature of the ATF operation, there were serious legal questions that could be raised if certain charges were made. This was not insurmountable if everybody stuck to his or her stories.

Mike Detty was becoming the second problem. The government

had underestimated him. Detty was a non-ATF expert in the agency's operation. He had cooperated with the Tucson ATF in other gun-smuggling cases. In total, Mike Detty sold five hundred weapons to straw buyers. He estimates that over 90 percent of the guns went into Mexico.[26]

In October of 2009 US Assistant Attorney Laura Gwinn started to look at the Operation Wide Receiver case. She asked Detty, "Do you have any notes on the case?" He replied that he had kept notes since he became a confidential informant with the ATF. In fact he had a six hundred-page journal recording his experiences and inter-changes with both the smugglers and the ATF. He also related that he had recordings and videos. Gwinn requested to see the material.[27]

Detty meet with Gwinn. On her cart there were twenty binders and boxes of files. Gwinn said, "Well, there's the result of your work." The informant handed over his journal and left, feeling he had done a good job and there would be a strong case made against the gun smugglers.[28] He was in for a surprise. A week later he was essentially persona non grata with the ATF.

He was being shunned because of his journal. Not only did he know too much, he had written it down and recorded it. He called the special agent in charge for the ATF in Arizona, William Newell, and asked what was happening—was it his journal? According to Detty, Newell had read the journal but denied it had any effect on how he was being treated. Looking back Detty observes, "There might have been some embarrassing material in the journal."[29]

The issue was, if Detty's journal showed up in discovery, not only might the defendants walk, but ATF might also be open to criminal charges of their own.

A Lesson Not Learned

Mike Detty was disappointed and disillusioned with his experiences as a confidential informant for the ATF. He wanted to help his country and bought the ATF story that they were after the big time players in Mexico. In fact, of all the cases he was involved with, only about two dozen people were charged with any crimes.

Of those, they were mostly charged with violations of fraudulent statements on the 4473 forms. Most of those convicted got sentences of fifty or fifty-two months. In one case, the smugglers (one nick-named Rambo) were former friends who had attended Mesa High School together. One generation removed from Mexico they had contacts.[30] The ATF gave them the illusion of making easy money selling guns in Mexico.

After Detty's exile from the ATF, US Attorney Laura Gwinn called to warn him that the way one of the indictments was written, it was obvious he was the confidential informant.[31] The ATF had discussed with Detty early on that they would help him with the witness protection program if the need developed.

"But the ATF really doesn't make promises of any kind. They only suggest," notes Detty. There was no protection. There were no cartel leaders brought down or even implicated.

But there was the murder of Brian Terry. When Detty learned it was an ATF-condoned weapon that was found by the body of the murdered agent, he frantically called one of the few ATF agents still talking to him. "Was it one of my guns?" he asked. He was told no.[32] The gun was from another operation called Fast and Furious.

"There are some hardworking guys out there and some people just along for the ride. Sadly to say, the leadership is what is really screwed up with the ATF," Detty says. "This guy Newell up in Phoenix—I swear I'd punch him in the nose if I ever got the opportunity. The guy is just an out-and-out liar. He's one of these guys that had political ambitions about becoming director of the ATF."[33]

Detty learned one last lesson from his association with the ATF. He learned that the ATF had learned nothing. Essentially, the ATF had accomplished nothing of significance while running Operation Wide Receiver except help arm the cartels in Mexico. Yet, he was told the ATF used Operation Wide Receiver as a model for other operations—including Operation Fast and Furious.[34]

The Road to Hell

The road to hell may be paved with good intentions, but in the case of Fast and Furious it was guided by politics and ambition. Oddly, both Wide Receiver and Fast and Furious had their beginnings with the major government agency reorganization that occurred in Washington, D.C., after 9/11 and a man named Bill Newell.

As officials scrambled to determine which agencies would be restructured or merged, it was immediately apparent the Bureau of Alcohol, Tobacco, and Firearms was considered the "bastard child of the Treasury." It was like the INS was to the Department of Justice. There was talk that the ATF should "disappear." It was suggested the FBI should absorb the ATF. However, the FBI resisted the "opportunity." The FBI noted that the ATF was a regulatory agency and the FBI's job was investigating—not regulating. In reality, nobody wanted to take on the ATF.

In 2002 President George W. Bush signed the Homeland Security Act, and not only was the Department of Homeland Security created, but the ATF was also rechristened the Bureau of Alcohol, Tobacco, Firearms, and Explosives (while retaining the abbreviation ATF) and given to the Department of Justice to oversee.

In the wake of the ATF's near death experience, Bill Newell (a GS-15 in the ATF) and middle managers in the agency decided they had to do something to put the ATF on the map. Newell's position in the agency was curious, but powerful.

Because the ATF has had six acting directors since 2002, considerable power had been inherited and concentrated in the hands of special agents in charge (SAIC) who ran the regional offices. Rising above all others in this regard was Bill Newell. He filled the leadership vacuum and in a practical sense acted as the de facto director of the ATF.[35] According to one insider, "Bill Newell was larger than life and became the spokesman for the ATF." Another acquaintance of Newell felt that "His ambition far exceeded his capabilities."

For better or worse, it appeared that Newell and other middle managers were setting policy and programs within the ATF. The result was a pilot program created in late 2004 and tested the next year in El Paso, called Operation Gunrunner. The mission was based on the premise that straw buyers were purchasing guns for others to transport across the border to drug cartels. The focus was on arresting straw buyers.[36]

Newell was sent west to take charge of the Phoenix office of the ATF around 2006. By that time many people were calling him "the voice of the ATF." And the voice of the ATF was selling Operation Gunrunner.

He briefed then Arizona governor Janet Napolitano on Operation Gunrunner and won her over immediately. An enthusiastic Napolitano said, "We've got to brief Bill Richardson (then governor of New Mexico) on this and maybe we can get Arnold (Schwarzenegger, then governor of California) on board." As one observer notes, "By the time Napolitano becomes secretary of Homeland Security she is already in Newell's pocket."

Operation Gunrunner was changing. Newell is said to have led the charge to expand and change Project Gunrunner, which helps explain the Wide Receiver operation in Tucson. During the Wide Receiver time period the ATF provided Mexico a way to trace weapons captured at the sites of crimes. The problem was that the tracking system didn't work very well.[37]

Wide Receiver and other Tucson-based gunwalking operations demonstrated the shortcomings of not only this tracking system, but perhaps also of including Mexican authorities in gunwalking operations at all. One thing is for sure: the ATF learned that in order to trace weapons recovered at crime scenes in Mexico, the ATF had better run the system.

More importantly, the ATF was changing the targets of Operation Gunrunner. No longer were they interested in straw buyers. Gunrunner was evolving into a program that allegedly would use straw buyers to target cartel "kingpins" in Mexico by letting guns walk.

Turf Wars

As Operation Gunrunner was evolving, the ATF was encountering some blowback with its Wide Receiver program—and it was coming from ICE (Immigration and Customs Enforcement). The ATF had the authority to regulate gun purchases, but no authority to allow and essentially facilitate guns walking south. ICE had the legal responsibility to regulate everything that crosses the border. And the news of what was happening in Tucson was getting around.

A few ICE agents on the ground in Tucson and along the border had become aware that the ATF was letting guns cross into Mexico. They were upset because it not only violated the law, but also because it could ultimately get people killed, including American law enforcement personnel. Higher up the ICE food chain, the concerns were different. The ATF was intruding on ICE's turf. At the very least there were ICE managers who thought they should be involved in one way or another.

Throughout 2008 tensions grew between ICE and the ATF as Bill Newell and others began to develop the new program called Fast and Furious. The divide between the two agencies came into the open when an ASAIC (an assistant special agent in charge) from ICE in Phoenix, confronted George Gillett, an ASAIC from the ATF Phoenix office." ICE wanted to be involved with Operation Gunrunner. These discussions occurred several more times.

The ATF pushed ahead. In October 2008, key ATF field personnel as well as supervisors assembled in Washington, D.C. ATF personnel assigned to Mexico also attended the meeting. It is reported that during this gathering the policy of allowing guns to "walk" was announced.[38]

A Bad Idea Whose Time Has Come

A new administration took office in January of 2009 as Fast and Furious was moving toward implementation. With the new administration Janet Napolitano became the head of the Department of Homeland Security. And because of Napolitano, the star of another key player in what would become the Fast and Furious debacle was on the rise. His name was Dennis Burke.

US Attorney Dennis Burke was a close confidant of Janet Napolitano. Department of Justice Photo.

Dennis Burke had served as chief of staff to Arizona governor Janet Napolitano from 2003 to 2008. After the 2008 election Burke was a member of President Obama's transition team and became a senior advisor to Department of Homeland Security secretary Janet Napolitano. In September 2009 Burke became the United States attorney for the District of Arizona. He would return to Phoenix and would soon be allied with Bill Newell.

One of the problems the ATF had faced with Wide Receiver was that many people within ICE indicated that it was illegal to knowingly permit guns to walk across the border. Indeed, ICE had interdicted a couple of loads.[39] Technically, every weapon transported out of the country needs an export license. ICE was a potential problem for Fast and Furious.

Through the summer of 2009 the ATF supposedly continued to seek ways to bypass ICE when Fast and Furious was started. The ATF attempted to obtain export license information directly from the State Department. The State Department told ATF they needed to obtain the information from Homeland Security (ICE). The ATF then approached the FBI to obtain export license information. The FBI explained they needed to go to their local ICE office.[40]

It was clear that some in the ATF had concerns about the legal issues involved in allowing guns to cross into Mexico. Nonetheless, Fast and Furious was launched in October of 2009. Jaime Avila and Uriel Patino began purchasing guns in Arizona gun shops. Gun shops which were encouraged by the ATF to sell the weapons. Weapons the ATF not only watched move south, but often facilitated by preventing interdiction.

OCDETF

To gain support, funding, and perhaps legal and political cover for Fast and Furious, in December of 2009 the ATF approached the local Organized Crime Drug Enforcement Task Force. Supervisory agents attended the meeting from ICE, the FBI, the DEA, and the US Marshal's Service. In addition the United States Attorney's Office for Arizona was represented, as well as all local law enforcement authorities that might be affected by the ATF request.

The ATF made a formal presentation to OCDETF for Fast and Furious and requested it become an "OCDETF Investigation."[41] Such presentations are often general in nature and it is not clear if the concept of gunwalking was discussed. According to insiders, the names of the ATF's straw buyers Avila and Patino were mentioned, but not the names of any drug kingpins that were going to be targeted. This omission in the presentation was because the ATF had no idea who they allegedly were going after.

In order for a case to become an "OCDETF case," there must be unanimous agreement and each participant must literally sign off on the case. At least one participant in the late 2009 meeting objected, presumably ICE. The details of this objection are unknown, but the ATF persisted behind the scenes.

Mutts or Zeta Sicarios?

During the period after the ATF presentation was sidelined by OCDEFT, the FBI realized that the straw buyers mentioned by the ATF were on active wiretaps the agency was using. "These guys, Patino and Avila were mutts as far as the FBI and DEA case," notes someone high in the DOJ. Another source reports, "They were nothing, but that's what the ATF was working."

Contrary to the current spin, the DEA and FBI tried to help the ATF. The FBI in El Paso turned over their line sheets (summaries of the content of tapped phone conversations) to the ATF and included some additional information. What the FBI gave to the ATF was in fact a link between Patino and Avila to two extremely dangerous and important members of the ultraviolent Zeta cartel. These two men were sicarios (assassins) who operated in El Paso, Las Cruces, and Ciudad Juarez. The Sicarios at this point were targets of a joint DEA/FBI case—they were not informants.

The DEA and the FBI were essentially giving the ATF "access to these folks." Both the FBI and the DEA have excellent documentation about ATF's reply to this offer. Despite DEA and FBI encouragement, the ATF said, "We are not interested."[42]

While the ATF apparently wasn't interested in pursuing the connection between their two straw buyers and the Zeta sicarios, they reportedly told OCDETF that the Sicarios were targets of their investigation.

In January 2010 there was a surprising reversal by OCDETF. Fast and Furious became an "OCDETF Investigation." And ICE was on board. A person in the inner circle of ICE said, "We're going to be all in. We're working this. This is our priority case."

Whatever brought ICE and the ATF together is unclear. One result was, an agent from ICE was imbedded with the ATF. After Fast and Furious blew up, the agent's importance was routinely minimized. However, he is a key to the Fast and Furious scandal. He was to Fast and Furious what Mike Detty was to Wide Receiver. With an almost obsessive compulsive flair, the embedded agent sent extensive, detailed, and daily reports of what was happening to ICE headquarters in Washington.

An individual high in the Department of Justice who has reviewed these reports says, "Included are emails, notes, and volumes of additional information." The DOJ is holding over thirteen thousand pages of documents which detail the activities of the ATF and ICE, as well as the response of the FBI and DEA to the ATF's lack of interest in the Sicarios. All of which leads to the cover up of Fast and Furious.

Cover Up

The cover-up started almost immediately after Brian Terry's murder. Phones started ringing December 15, 2010. Life had just gone to hell for numerous ATF agents, supervisors, managers and ATF acting director Kenneth Melson. An insider says, "There was a very high pucker factor at the ATF that day."

The guns found at the scene of the murder were being traced. Twenty-one hours after the shooting, an ATF intelligence expert emailed top ATF officials that she had successfully traced two of the guns found at the murder scene. They were AK-47s that were part of the Fast and Furious operation. She added she was "now researching the trace status of firearms recovered earlier today by the FBI."[43]

To the relief of the ATF the third gun was not part of Fast and Furious and disappeared from their radar screen. But had evidence disappeared from the crime scene? The third gun went missing, and Brian Terry's stepmother, Carolyn Terry, was one of the few to notice.[44]

Several hours after the shooting, ATF agents had boots on the ground at the Peck Canyon murder scene.[45] The ATF was especially concerned because one of "their" AK-47s had been found directly behind slain BORTAC Agent Terry. Messages were going out from Homeland Security to CBP (Custom and Border Protection) supervisors not to talk to anyone about the murder of Brian Terry.

To stay in front of the story and its apparent complicity in allowing the murder weapon that killed Brian Terry to walk to Mexico, the ATF conferred with the U.S Attorney's Office for the State of Arizona. The US Attorney's Office approved the immediate arrest of Jaime Avila, Jr.—the man who had allegedly bought the two AK-47s the Border Patrol recovered at the scene of Agent Brian Terry's murder.

It was like Operation Casablanca all over again. The ATF and US Attorney dispatched law enforcement officers to pick up anyone involved with their gunrunning scheme. Avila and almost all of his gunrunning associates were arrested because of the ATF's fear of the ramifications that might result from Brian Terry's murder.

The irony is the case against Avila, Jr., had been made the very first time he bought a weapon intended to walk.[46] However, the "bigger fish" scenario of Fast and Furious had provided Avila with a free "get out of jail card" for a year and a sizable income. Worse, the scenario had killed Brian Terry.

On January 25, 2011, the ATF announced, "Beginning earlier this morning, a multi-agency law enforcement task force rounded up and arrested twenty defendants named in the fifty-three-count Avila indictment, which was unsealed today. (Among those arrested was Uriel Patino, a roommate of Jaime Avila, Jr.) More than one hundred officers were involved in the operation."[47]

Despite the looming scandal, US Attorney for Arizona Dennis Burke remained on message. In a TV interview Burke indicated Americans buying guns for the cartels "don't seem to care at all that these guns are being shipped down to Mexico with the purpose of being used by Mexican drug cartels."[48]

William Newell, special agent in charge of the ATF Phoenix Field Division, asserted in an amazing example of moral self-incrimination, straw purchasers "that knowingly falsify ATF firearms forms in order to supply Mexican drug cartels with firearms have as much blood on their hands as the criminals that use them."[49]

Newell was asked if his agency would ever knowingly allow weapons to cross into Mexico. He denied it with a simple, "Hell no!"[50]

Endnotes

1. United States of America v. Jaime Avila, Jr., Indictment, Case 2:11-cr-00126-JAT, Jan 19, 2011.

2. Bureau of Alcohol, Tobacco, and Firearms, National Tracing Center, "Multiple Sale Summary," January 19, 2010.

3. Senator Charles Grassley, letter to Attorney General Eric Holder, February 9, 2011.

4. Senator Charles Grassley, letter to Attorney General Eric Holder.

5. Senator Charles Grassley, letter to Attorney General Eric Holder.

6. Senator Charles Grassley, letter to Attorney General Eric Holder.

7. Senator Charles Grassley, letter to Attorney General Eric Holder

8. ATF Group VII Supervisor David Voth, e-mail message to Cooperating FFL, April 13, 2010.

9. Senator Charles Grassley, letter to CBP Commissioner Alan Bersin, March 26, 2011.

10. Senator Charles Grassley, letter to CBP Commissioner Alan Bersin.

11. Mike Detty, interview, April 22, 2011.

12. Mike Detty, interview, April 22, 2011.

13. Mike Detty, interview, April 22, 2011.

14. Mike Detty, interview, April 22, 2011.

15. Mike Detty, interview, April 22, 2011.

16. Mike Detty, interview, April 22, 2011.

17. Mike Detty, interview, April 23, 2011.

18. Mike Detty, interview, April 22, 2011.

19. ICE employee, interview, August, 2011.

20. ICE employee, interview, August, 2011.

21. Mike Detty, interview, April 22, 2011.

22. Mike Detty, interview, April 22, 2011.

23. Mike Detty, interview, April 22, 2011.

24. Mike Detty, interview, April 22, 2011.

25. Mike Detty, interview, April 22, 2011.

26. Mike Detty, interview, April 23, 2011.

27. Mike Detty, interview, April 23, 2011.

28. Mike Detty, interview, April 23, 2011.

29. Mike Detty, interview, April 23, 2011.

30. Mike Detty, interview, April 23, 2011.

31. Mike Detty, interview, April 22, 2011.

32. Mike Detty, interview, April 22, 2011.

33. Mike Detty, interview, April 22, 2011.

34. Mike Detty, interview, April 22, 2011.

35. Former official, Department of Justice, interview, 2012.

36. Working draft report, *Review of ATF's Project Gunrunner*, September

2010, U.S. Department of Justice, Office of the Inspector General, http://www.justice.gov/oig/reports/ATF/e1101.pdf.

37. Former official, Department of Justice, interview.

38. Protected source, interview, 2011.

39. Protected source, interview, 2011.

40. Protected source, interview, 2011.

41. Former official, Department of Justice, interview.

42. Former official, Department of Justice, interview.

43. "Exclusive: Third Gun Linked to 'Fast and Furious' Identified at Border Agent's Murder Scene," *FOX News*, September 9, 2011, http://www.foxnews.com/politics/2011/09/09/exclusive-third-gun-linked-to-fast-and-furious-identified-at-border-agents/.

44. Carolyn Terry, interview, May 4, 2011.

45. Protected source, interview, 2011.

46. Seth Nadel, interview, March 6, 2011.

47. Office of the United States Attorney, Dennis K. Burke, District of Arizona, "Grand Juries Indict 34 Suspects in Drug and Firearms Trafficking Organization," news release, January 25, 2011, http://www.justice.gov/usao/az/press_releases/2011/PR_01252011_Press%20 Conference.pdf.

48. "Over 200 rifles intercepted in latest gun running ring bust," February 17, 2011, azfamily.com.

49. Dennis Burke, press conference, January 25, 2011.

50. William Newell, press conference, January 25, 2011.

Chapter Eighteen

La ATFamilia

"Don't participate in any illegal activities unless under my direction."
Warning to potential informant Manuel Celia-Acosta by
lead Fast and Furious investigator Hope MacCallister[1]

PERHAPS HOPE MACCALLISTER'S WARNING to would-be informant Manuel Celia-Acosta should have been addressed to members of the ATF. Despite Bill Newell's denial, the ATF was in deep trouble. A source high in the DOJ notes that when the thirteen thousand pages of documents mentioned in the previous chapter are released, "People in the ATF are going to jail."[2] Other officials say the umbrella of criminal complicity could include individuals in ICE.

In the weeks following the murder of Border Patrol agent Brian Terry, the ATF scrambled to cover their tracks. In March of 2011 the ATF went back to the DEA and FBI, indicating "they were now interested in adding the two Sicarios to their case." They were told by the FBI it was too late—the two men were now informants.

The ATF responded by trying to implicate the DEA and FBI in some kind of wrongdoing. The ATF charged they had never been informed that their "targets" were informants for the DEA and FBI. Of course, the ATF had been invited to join the investigation in January of 2010 and weren't interested.

An observer familiar with the affair commented, "They never wanted kingpins. They had the straw purchasers and that was their golden goose. If they had kept working those small purchasers they could have kept their thing going and going and going, which is what they wanted to do.

"If the ATF had hooked their case with Patino and Avila to the

Zeta Sicarios targets that were being investigated by the FBI in early 2010 they would have lost control. The El Paso FBI and DEA would have been calling the shots. They [the ATF] had no intention of bringing an indictment or closing a case."

Fingerprints in All the Wrong Places

In an attempt to further spread the blame and deflect criticism, the ATF pointed to ICE's involvement with Fast and Furious. In particular, the ATF claimed an ICE agent was embedded with them in Phoenix. There was validity to this charge, and the director of ICE, John Morton, knew it.

The problem was ICE in Phoenix, had not only involved the agency with Fast and Furious, but had made it the number one priority.

Senator Charles Grassley of Iowa made an inquiry early in 2011 regarding ICE's possible involvement with Fast and Furious. Essentially, ICE indicated to Senator Grassley that their involvement was minor, and consisted of a single agent who acted as nothing more than an observer.

However, in reality ICE was operating in a "circle the wagons" mode. The second week of March 2011 a verbal communication came from the headquarters of ICE. The message regarding Fast and Furious was, "Conversations and meetings information should not be memorialized in memos."[3] It was not the first such message after the murder of Brian Terry and it would certainly not be the last.

What was going on behind the scenes at ICE was serious. A very angry John Morton called the agent in charge of the Phoenix ICE office, and asked about the degree of ICE's involvement with

Director of ICE John Morton looks for fingerprints. US government photo.

Fast and Furious. Reportedly, Morton was assured, "We don't have our fingerprints on this."

Without hesitation Morton responded, "Wait a minute. Explain to me how we don't have any fingerprints on this but you're sending reports up here every day and I'm getting a report on this investigation every week?" Insiders explain the agent in charge of the Phoenix office volunteered to look into the matter, but Morton had completely lost trust in him. The bottom line is that Morton summoned the agent in charge to Washington and sent his own independent team to Arizona for a full report on ICE and its connection to Fast and Furious.

Director Morton has had the results of his investigation sitting in his office for over a year. He knows exactly what ICE's exposure was with Fast and Furious. And yet despite having the real story, ICE is sticking to the original spin that ICE had only embedded an inexperienced agent to act as an observer inside the ATF.

Another law enforcement official who has seen internal ICE documents concludes, "ICE is also responsible for the ATF's 'gunwalking.' They knew what was happening and they should have stopped it."

Whatever ICE's motivation, it appears many were drawn into the gunwalking scheme out of ambition. Newell had contacts at the White House, and had a fan running Homeland Security. On top of it all US Attorney Dennis Burke had the ear of Secretary Napolitano. They were close personal friends. "Their relationship is more like brother and sister. They were joined at the hip," comments a person familiar with them. For some, getting on the Fast and Furious bandwagon was just a good political move.

Stop the Bleeding

More than a few high-ranking personnel within the FBI and DEA want the administration to release the documentation that is available and get the debacle of Fast and Furious behind them. Among these individuals are persons who have read and reviewed many of the thousands of documents the DOJ is withholding from Congress. The ATF and ICE would take the brunt of the blowback, but it would stop the bleeding. Those same personnel believe that there is no way it will happen until after the 2012 presidential election.

An insider observes, "The problem is the ATF wasn't really wanting to catch kingpins. And if you accept that proposition, the question is why was the ATF permitting guns to walk?" The answer to that question is politically explosive and involves the Second Amendment.

Another significant concern is not only that some people in the ATF and ICE could end up in jail, but persons higher up in the administration might have to face obstruction of justice and perjury issues.

No One Is Above the Law

"The ATF was the largest single supplier of illegally exported weapons from the United States to the Mexican cartels, " says Senior Special Agent Seth Nadel (Ret). Seth Nadel is an expert on gunrunning and the law.

Nadel spent twenty-seven years with Customs. He served seventeen years on the Mexican border. Most of that was in the San Diego area, but the last year was in Arizona. Nadel was also involved in investigating international arms dealing. He helped prevent Iranians from buying parts to F16s and a foreign security agency from purchasing a Hawk missile system in the United States.[4]

During his career he arrested nearly a thousand people for illegal import or export of weapons and only one was found not guilty.[5] He looks not only at the legal issues regarding Operation Fast and Furious, but also considers the strategy itself—namely, intentionally allowing guns to be smuggled into Mexico.

"I will say unequivocally that there is no law enforcement purpose served by letting guns go to Mexico. There are no charges to be made—nothing. There is nothing to be gained." Nadel adds, "According to the statute, the case is made on the fact that they [the straw buyers and smugglers] attempted to violate United States Neutrality Law.[6]

"Occasionally, we would follow narcotics to arrest people in the United States. But the odds of following anything in Mexico are almost impossible. They would have to tell the Mexican police what they wanted to do and get permission from the Mexican government to conduct surveillance in Mexico, which isn't going to happen."[7]

According to Nadel, even if Mexico granted permission to run an operation in their country (like tracking guns to cartel kingpins), the corruption throughout the Mexican government would doom the effort. As soon as one Mexican law enforcement or military person knew about the operation, everyone would know what was going on—including the cartels. Plus, the ATF would only have a supporting role in Mexico. ATF personnel in Mexico cannot even carry weapons.

Despite this, Nadel thinks at the very least, the people running Fast and Furious had "an obligation to inform the Mexican government that they were allowing thousands of guns to be illegally transported into their country."[8]

A Dangerous Ruse

"Fast and Furious was nothing but a ruse," Nadel says. "How are you going to build a conspiracy in Mexico and build charges against people in Mexico—Mexican citizens—without surveillance, without phone records, without typical investigative techniques? You simply are not."[9]

Nadel views the theory behind the ATF's program as dangerously flawed. "It was like saying we're going to let more cocaine get out on the street so we can get more people involved in the business and arrest more people. That's not stopping the supply of cocaine. Except here, they're killing the guys that I used to work with."[10]

Nadel refers to the February 15, 2011, case where two unarmed ICE agents, Jaime Zapata and Victor Avila, were run off the road while driving from Mexico City to Monterrey, Mexico. Avila was seriously wounded, and Zapata was killed. Zapata was murdered with a handgun purchased in north Texas.[11]

Nadel believes it is important to understand the culture and thinking inside the ATF. "They always believe a case with ten guns is more important than a case with one gun. I have personally called ATF when I had a person that was a convicted felon in possession of a sawed-off shotgun. That's two felonies right there. They wouldn't come down, because it was only one gun."[12]

Exporting Guns—Legally

"I arrested a lot of people for exporting arms, ammunition, and implements of war without benefit of a State Department license," says Seth Nadel. "To export weapons to a foreign country a State Department license is needed." (Which is why the ATF looked into the requirements to obtain gun export licenses in 2009.)

Nadel rattles off the requirements to legally transfer a weapon to another country from the United States. "In order to export firearms or ammunition, you have to register with the State Department as an exporter. Then you have to obtain a license for a specific export. Getting a license requires that you get something called an end-user certificate, which is issued by a government entity in the country of destination."

He continues, "The end-user certificate declares that importing the weapon does not violate any laws within the country (for example, Mexico). Then you submit all the documentation about the guns—how many, what kind, and what caliber—to the State Department, to get an export license for that shipment and that shipment only."[13] Nadel notes that the end-user certificate in this case would have to have been approved by the Mexican Department of Defense. "But in this case of Fast and Furious the Mexican government had no idea the guns were even headed their way."

Nadel believes the ATF was allowing the guns to walk into Mexico for several reasons. "President Obama and Secretary of State Clinton keep repeating that 90 percent of the guns [supplied to cartels] traced came from the United States. By letting 2,500 guns go to Mexico, then the number of guns that can be traced go up."[14]

He thinks that if it had not been for the Agent Brian Terry shooting, the ATF would have held back and then made a flurry of arrests just before budget hearings. "For example, Waco was timed to occur just before their budget hearings. One of the things that helps them increase their budget is 'junk on the bunk.'"[15] If the ATF brings a lot of seized guns before Congress it helps them increase their budget—the same goes for arrests. "Look what we've done. Just think what we could do with a bigger budget."

A Smuggling Stimulus Program

Jamie Avila operated from October 2009 to early 2011 before being arrested. An irritated Nadel asks, "Why? I arrested people with one gun. The United States attorney prosecuted them and the court sentenced them. One of the ways Customs tried to make smuggling more expensive and difficult was by prosecuting guys at the lower end of the spectrum. One gun can bring ten years in prison and a $10,000 fine.[16]

"If you keep arresting the mules here—the guys that are buying one gun here or one gun there, the cost of business goes up. The mules demand more money per gun or they won't do it at all. But if you let them get away with it, all you do is provide more guns [to the cartels] that will kill more law enforcement officers on both sides of the border."[17]

In effect, by letting guns walk, the business of gun smuggling was artificially stimulated by ATF policies (and Fast and Furious) beyond normal levels.

The profitability and apparent lack of risk of the illegal gun smuggling business encouraged others to participate. This phenomenon was obvious with the earlier Tucson cases such as Operation Wide Receiver.

In exchange for permitting smugglers to supply thousands of guns to the cartels since 2006, the ATF did not bust any cartel kingpin in Mexico but it did succeed in contributing to the murder of an untold number of innocent people—including women and children.

According to one high-ranking Mexican lawmaker, because of Fast and Furious, "We have 150 cases of injuries and homicides with arms that were smuggled and passed illegally into our country."[18] (The president of the Lower Chambers of Deputies pondered, "What happens the next time if they need to introduce assassins ..." The irony of this statement is it may be true.)[19]

Nobody Is Above the Law

Did the ATF and personnel in the ATF conspire to violate the United States Neutrality Act? Nadel answers, "Oh yes. They were conspiring. An aggressive US attorney that really wanted to go after them could charge those agents and supervisors that allowed guns to go to Mexico as knowing coconspirators in exporting firearms from the United States. They had a legal obligation to stop them. They did not do so. The ATF could be viewed as having conspired, confederated, and agreed with persons wishing to export firearms from the United States without a license from the secretary of state."[20]

In addition, the ATF knowingly allowed crimes to be committed. Nadel elaborates, "The technical term for what they did according to federal statute is called misprision of a felony. This means you have knowledge of a felony and fail to report it to an appropriate authority. Somebody might say they [the ATF] are the appropriate authority. No. They would need the agreement of the US attorney in each of the districts where it was allowed to happen."[21]

According to Nadel, in this case it appears the ATF has a partial "get out of jail free card." It is reported that the ATF and Fast and Furious had supervision by the US attorney for Arizona in Phoenix.[22] If the ATF informed the US attorney of each incident of guns going into Mexico or had a blanket acknowledgement by the US attorney for all guns being allowed to cross into Mexico, the criteria to satisfy an accusation of "misprision of a felony" fall short. But then a larger issue appears. Can a US attorney grant permission to anyone or any agency to break laws?

The ATF and Foreign Policy

By their actions with Fast and Furious, the ATF was assuming a foreign policy role that is reserved to the secretary of state and the president of the United States. According to Nadel, the ATF in reality had decided by their actions, "They were going to assist a revolution in Mexico, but it was not a revolution by the people, it was a revolution by the cartels."[23]

They had determined they were not going to let one or two guns go to Mexico, but thousands of guns. Nadel points out that the ATF's action was taken, "knowing the cartels were actually challenging the government of Mexico (as noted by secretary of State Clinton.) The action was taken with the knowledge the cartels run large portions of Mexico. By arming the most powerful cartels the world has known, the ATF was in fact making a foreign policy decision that would help destabilize the government of Mexico."[24]

Who Is Responsible?

Not only did the ATF actions threaten the stability of the Mexican government, but the current administration. How the situation plays out depends on how well the administration can maintain the cover-up. If they do as poorly as Nixon they are doomed.

The heart of the cover-up is to hide who was ultimately responsible for Fast and Furious. ATF whistleblower senior agent John Dodson has said that the gunwalking strategy was approved all the way up to the Justice Department.[25] President Obama denied that US Attorney General Eric Holder approved the policy of allowing guns to walk to Mexico. But does the denial make sense?

The attorney general certainly had knowledge of Operation Gunrunner. He refers to it in a speech made in Cuernavaca, Mexico, April 2, 2009. During the Arms Trafficking Conference he indicates the importance of Operation Gunrunner and a strategy or attack "that focuses on the leadership and assets of the cartel." Again, by 2009 Operation Gunrunner has mutated from a program that focused on arresting straw buyers of guns in the United States to one that lets guns walk across the border without arresting straw buyers.

Further, according to Darren Gil, the head of the ATF in Mexico, Assistant Attorney General of the United States Lanny Breuer had full knowledge about Fast and Furious in the summer of 2010.[26] Unknown to Gil, there was a request for a wiretap regarding Fast and Furious that was submitted by the Phoenix ATF Office to the DOJ and signed by Breuer in March of 2010.

Is it believable that Assistant Attorney General of the United States Breuer's report from his Mexico City meeting in the summer of 2010 didn't cross his boss's desk? Whatever the truth, Attorney General Holder testified before Congress that he became aware of Fast and Furious weeks after the murder of Brian Terry. There is considerable evidence this is not accurate.

An editorial in the Mexican publication *La Jornada* made a very important point. It stated, "It seems unlikely that the attorney general of the neighboring country, Eric Holder, had not been aware of the participation of three police and security agencies of such importance to the US government and therefore, the allegations in his favor made by President Barack Obama seem not very plausible. If Fast and Furious was a government decision, it would be extremely serious for the White House to hide it. On the other hand, if the highest echelons of US public power had no idea of these illegal activities, that ignorance would suggest an egregious lack of control in Washington's actions against drug trafficking."[27]

Apologies and Questions

Whatever the truth, the family of Brian Terry lives with the consequences. They grieve for him and are angered by an apparently insensitive, tone-deaf, and uncaring government. The family is looking at legal remedies for the government's actions. The have retained legal representation to investigate the government's actions.[28] The Terry family wants to know the truth about what happened to Brian and why it happened. They also want the government to admit their wrongdoing. And while the administration doesn't offer an apology, several ATF agents do.

According to a CBS interview, when ATF senior agent Brian Dodson heard one of the Fast and Furious guns was used to kill BORTAC Agent Brian Terry, he was "crushed." Dodson said he "hoped speaking out helps the Terry family." He said, "First of all, I'd tell them that I'm sorry. Second of all, I'd tell them I've done everything that I can for them to get the truth."[29]

A few days after Dodson's testimony before congress he phoned Carolyn and Kent Terry to apologize for the part he played in Fast and Furious. Carolyn Terry said, "He was very emotional. He was really struggling. He kept apologizing for what he had done. I told him several times he was not responsible for Brian's murder. I felt so sorry for him and thanked him for telling what was going on. His call meant a lot to us." Shortly thereafter, they received a call from another whistleblower and an email from a third, apologizing for their actions in Fast and Furious.[30]

However, there is something that is more important than an apology. An answer to the question, "Is our government above law?"

Endnotes

1. Report of Investigation, Bureau of Alcohol, Tobacco, Firearms and Explosives, U.S. Department of Justice, No. 785115-10-0004, Report 292.

2. Former official, Department of Justice, interview, 2012.

3. Protected Source, 2011.

4. Seth Nadel, interview, March 5, 2011.

5. Seth Nadel, interview, March 5, 2011.

6. Seth Nadel, interview, March 5, 2011.

7. Seth Nadel, interview, March 5, 2011.

8. Seth Nadel, interview, March 5, 2011.

9. Seth Nadel, interview, March 5, 2011.

10. Seth Nadel, interview, March 5, 2011.

11. Kelly Holt, "Gun connected to ICE agent Zapata's death traced to Texas," The New American, March 1, 2011, http://www.thenewamerican.com/usnews/crime/item/7435-gun-connected-to-ice-agent-zapatas-death-traced-to-texas.

12. Seth Nadel, interview, March 6, 2011.

13. Seth Nadel, interview, March 6, 2011.

14. Seth Nadel, interview, March 13, 2011.

15. Seth Nadel, interview, March 13, 2011.

16. Seth Nadel, interview, March 6, 2011.

17. Seth Nadel, interview, March 6, 2011.

18. Kim Murphy and Ken Ellingwood, "Mexico lawmakers demand answers about guns smuggled under ATF's watch" *Los Angeles Times*, March 10, 2011, http://articles.latimes.com/2011/mar/ 10/nation/ la-na-mexico-guns-20110311-1,

19. Contractor, interview, 2011.

20. Seth Nadel, interview, March 6, 2011.

21. Seth Nadel, interview, March 13, 2011.

22. Seth Nadel, interview, March 13, 2011.

23. Intelligence officer, interview, 2011.

24. Seth Nadel, interview, March 13, 2011.

25. Sharyl Attkisson, "Agent: I was ordered to let U.S. into Mexico," *CBS News*, March 3, 2011, http://www.cbsnews.com/2100-18563_162-20039031.html.

26. Sharyl Attkisson, "ATF gunwalking: Who knew, and how high up?" *CBS News*, March 25, 2011, http://www.cbsnews.com/8301-31727_162-20047027-10391695.html.

27. "Washington: aliado no confiable," *La Jornada Editorial*, July 7, 2011, http://www.jornada. unam.mx/2011/07/07/edito.

28. Brady McCombs, "Family of slain agent weighing legal action," *Arizona Daily Star*, June 23, 2011, http://azstarnet.com/news/local/ border/article_8963cb97-43b2-5b3a-835f-f97dc75c732d.html.

29. Sharyl Attkisson, "Agent: I was order to let U.S. into Mexico."

30. Carolyn Terry, Interview, September 7, 2011.

Chapter Nineteen

Who Watches the Watchmen?

"Oh no, it's not the ATF's responsibility to know where the guns went."

Quote attributed to US attorney for
Arizona Dennis Burke by Carolyn Terry[1]

ALL OF THE NARRATIVES in this book lead to some final questions. Among them, will Brian Terry's murder be more than another tragic border story? Will the pain of the Terry family be more than another forgotten sacrifice? Indeed, the death of Brian Terry is the story of the thousands of American and Mexican victims of open borders and the isolated pain their loved ones endure.

"We take it day by day," explains Brian Terry's stepmother, Carolyn Terry. "It's really hard, because Brian would call his dad every day. When he went out and when he came back." Carolyn related what they had done since the memorial service she attended in Tucson for Brian on Memorial Day, 2011. Because of an illness, Brian's father, Kent Terry, had not been able to travel to the memorial for his son, but Kent's health improved, and he and Carolyn flew to Tucson in April, 2011. There were things they had to do and had to see. They were grateful to the Border Patrol for having kept Brian's locker just the way it was on the last day he had used it.[2]

Since Brian's estate was in probate, they went through a few legal steps and got the documentation they needed to enter their son's home in Sierra Vista. Kent and Carolyn Terry picked up the key from the Tucson Sector Border Patrol Headquarters.

Upon entering Brian's home, they had a surprise. All the drawers had been rifled, DVDs and CDs dumped on the floor, and the contents of a chest gone through. Even more surprising, a computer that had been moved to the bedroom after Brian's murder was sitting on a table in his office—plugged in. Apparently, the single item stolen was a badge belonging to Brian. There were no signs of forced entry.[3]

As Carolyn and Kent left the house, they wondered what the intruder was looking for and if they had found it. She thought about the critical letters that Brian had written to his superiors. Kent and Terry returned the key to the Border Patrol and told them what had happened. They were told, "We'll look into it." Before returning home they had dinner with two of Brian's teammates.[4]

An Unwelcome Guest

Carolyn pauses and thinks. She explains that in mid-February they received a phone call from the United States attorney for the State of Arizona, Dennis Burke. Burke wanted to visit them in a week. So the last week of February, US Attorney Dennis Burke and DOJ Victims Advocate Tim Jefferson were sitting in the Terrys' Michigan home. The story about Brian Terry's death was changing. "In response to everything we had heard in Tucson, Burke said, 'No, it's not like that.'"[5]

The conversation turned to the guns found at the scene of the murder. The public was being told was there were only two guns found the night of the shooting. It was not what Carolyn had been told. (In fact, court records only identify two possible murder weapons.)[6]

"The FBI told us at the meeting in Tucson that they had the gun that shot Brian," relates Carolyn Terry. "We were also told there was a third gun." Burke reportedly told the Terrys on this visit, "We don't have the gun and we will never have the gun."[7] Carolyn thought, "How can you be so sure?"

The story about Brian's location when he was murdered had also changed. The report that Brian and the other three BORTAC agents were on a ridge had been altered. Carolyn was told, "Brian was down on the dry creek bed with one other agent by the water tower when he got shot."

Carolyn later checked the dry creek bed narrative out with one of Brian's team members in Tucson. "I don't want to upset you, but was Brian in the dry creek bed by a water tank when he was killed?" The agent, who was the first to reach Brian after he was shot, said, "What water tank? No, we were all up on the ridge." She had asked him before, but after US Attorney Dennis Burke's assertion, she wanted to hear it again.

The teammate said, "There was a dry creek bed like a horseshoe around us." He told Carolyn and Kent their son was shot when he was repositioning himself. Carolyn Terry also remembers being told in Tucson that the gun that killed Brian was found five feet behind him. The bullet was also recovered, and it matched the ballistics of the gun.[8]

It brings to mind a veteran Border Patrol agent's admonition. "The final story about how the shooting took place will bear little resemblance to what actually happened."

The information the Terrys gleaned from the February meeting with Burke at their home was minimal and according to Carolyn was mostly the result of them asking questions. The meeting lasted an hour and a half and consisted largely of Burke talking about himself, like how he attended Notre Dame.

One statement Carolyn Terry made did not go over well: "The ATF is responsible for all those guns that were sold and where they went." Burke allegedly responded, "Oh no, it's not the ATF's responsibility to know where the guns went."[9]

Carolyn Terry thinks that Burke made the trip to Michigan because the family might bring legal action against the ATF, DOJ, or people within those organizations. "He really stressed that the ATF was not responsible for any of the guns that were sold through the gun stores." she adds, "You'd have to be a dummy to believe that." After leaving Carolyn and Kent's home, Burke visited Brian's mother, two sisters, and brother.[10]

The appropriateness of Dennis Burke's visit to the Terry family was questionable. Carolyn knew he was involved in Fast and Furious. (Note: A "Briefing Paper" authored by the Phoenix Group VII [Gunrunner/Strike Force] and dated January 8, 2010, clearly states that Bill Newell (Phoenix special agent in charge) and the US attorney for Arizona, Dennis Burke, "repeatedly met regarding the ongoing status of this investigation and both are in full agreement with the current investigative strategy."][11]

In other words, Carolyn and Kent Terry were sitting across from a man that had signed off on a program that very likely contributed to the death of their son. In fact, because of his approval of the operation there are those who might charge Burke played a role in supplying the murderer of Brian Terry with the murder weapon. But then, as Burke allegedly insisted, "We don't have the gun and we will never have the gun."[12]

An Indictment

On May 6, 2011, the phone rang in Carolyn Terry's living room. She answered, and a voice said, "This is ABC News." They wanted to know Carolyn and Kent's reaction to the indictment of Manuel Osorio-Arellanes for second-degree murder of their son. A shocked Carolyn Terry burst into tears. "I couldn't even talk. I was crying because it hurt so bad that they [ATF] were treating us like that."[13]

The man from ABC News said, "You didn't know about this?"

Carolyn composed herself and answered, "No."

He responded, "I don't know why you are out of the loop like this."

The day before, she had tried to call Tim Jefferson, the DOJ victims advocate on the case, to ask him a question, "but as usual he was nonresponsive."[14]

Carolyn also observed that US Attorney Dennis Burke made a trip to Michigan when his own interests appeared to be at stake, but wouldn't lift the phone to tell the family of the indictment.[15]

The press release from the US Attorney's Office included a statement from US Attorney Dennis Burke. "Today's indictment is an important step in this case, but it is only a first step to serving justice on behalf of Agent Brian Terry, his family, and the other agents who were with Terry and their families." Burke added, "His family deserves to see justice served, and everybody involved in this investigation is deeply committed to making that happen."[16]

Heavenly News

On August 30, 2011, Carolyn Terry received information from an aide to the House Committee on Oversight and Government reform. She was told Kenneth Melson had resigned as ATF director (he was assigned to Office of Legal Policy within the DOJ), and US Attorney Emory Hurley (a key player in Fast and Furious) was removed from

Patrolling

Manuel Osorio-Arellanes was shot and arrested the night of December 14, 2010, at the location in Peck Canyon where Brian Terry was murdered. The indictment against Osorio-Arellanes is informative because it reflects on the prosecution's intent and reasoning. For the public, the idea of a charge of second-degree murder seems like a good deal, but it may not turn out that way for the Terry family.

Osorio-Arellanes could have been charged with first-degree murder, but was not. Since three coconspirators are in Mexico, there is a remote chance the Mexican government might eventually find them and extradite them back to the Unites States. Mexico doesn't permit capital punishment. This means that if there were any possibility of the three men being executed in the United States, Mexico would not extradite.

This led to the odd phrasing in the indictment regarding what the armed group of Mexicans were doing the night they murdered BORTAC agent Brian Terry. The indictment reads, "Manuel Osorio-Arellanes ... and others traveled together to the area of Mesquite Seep; and ... were patrolling the area in single file ..."[17]

Patrolling? In his thirty years of law enforcement, Billy Breen (retired Department of Public Safety detective lieutenant) has never heard of a group "patrolling." Breen asserts the US attorney was trying to avoid using the words "robbers" or "drug escorts."[18]

"If they had been described as a rip crew (which they were originally), according to statute they would have to have been charged with first-degree murder. If they had been characterized as a drug escort, it would have been an admission that the ATF, and by association the US Attorney's Office, had supplied weapons to a Mexican cartel," says Breen. Hence, the defendants were "patrolling" on American territory.[19]

the criminal division of the US Attorney's Phoenix office. The best news according to Carolyn Terry was that US Attorney Dennis Burke had resigned. Carolyn said, "Hearing about Burke's resignation was like heaven to us.[20] We were told the murder case against Manuel Osorio-Arellanes was going to be transferred from Phoenix to a prosecutor in San Diego."

A week later the Terry murder case was transferred to the US attorney for the Southern District of California, Laura Duffy.

In Late October, two men from the Inspector General's Office who were investigating Fast and Furious for the DOJ visited Carolyn and Kent Terry. Carolyn told the investigators about their suspicions regarding Brian's murder, including that when their son's computer was finally turned over to their lawyer, the hard drive had been removed.[21]

According to Carolyn, "They listened politely, but said, 'You've told us a lot of interesting information but we are really concerned about what Dennis Burke told you.'" It was obvious to Carolyn and Kent they had Burke in their crosshairs. One item that piqued their interest was when Carolyn related the interchange she had with Burke about the "third gun" found at the shooting scene.[22]

One of the investigators asked where they heard about a third gun. Carolyn indicated the family had heard about it frequently, including from the head of the Border Patrol. Carolyn noted that after Dennis Burke visited the Terrys there was no more talk about a third gun from anyone.

Also present at the meeting was the Terrys' attorney. The attorney asked when the investigators expected the inspector general's report would be released. The investigators answered, "In a couple of months."[23] The investigators spent a little over an hour and then left to question other family members about Dennis Burke's activities when he was in Michigan.

In November US Attorney Laura Duffy visited Carolyn and Kent Terry. Duffy is best known for her prosecution of members of the Arellano-Felix drug cartel. Assistant US Attorney David Leshner, the head attorney for the criminal investigation, and Assistant US Attorney Timothy Coughlin, the attorney for the Fast and Furious investigation, accompanied Duffy. Duffy and Coughlin said little and it was up to Leshner to do the talking.[24]

Leshner set up a projector and showed slides that had been taken recently at the sight where Brian was murdered. He did most of the talking. Over thirty people from the DOJ had returned to the murder scene looking for the smallest traces of evidence. As the Terrys watched the slides, they wanted to know precisely where their son was murdered. Leshner indicated a general area shown in one of slides.

What intrigued Carolyn was that Dennis Burke's version of the shooting had changed. Former US Attorney Burke had reportedly said the four BORTAC agents were in a wash when the shooting started. Duffy's group had now placed the Border Patrol agents back up on a ridge above the wash.[25]

The trio was at the Terrys' house almost three hours, but Kent and Carolyn Terry felt they didn't learn much. No new information was offered on Manuel Osorio-Arellanes, the man charged with second-degree murder for his participation in Brian Terry's murder. The Terrys were especially interested in learning if there was any progress in catching the person who actually shot their son. There was no indication of any progress.

Crime and Semi-Punishment

According to an insider who has seen all the evidence, the government has a very weak case.[26] Since the Border Patrol fired first (albeit with beanbags), Manuel Osorio-Arellanes could stage a very strong self-defense argument. In reality, Manuel Osorio-Arellanes and the government will most likely agree on a plea bargain. Some observers predict Manuel Osorio-Arellanes will spend less time in jail than anyone expects.

Which means if any persons named in the indictment do end up being extradited, they too will not be in jail long. For the government, it is a win-win situation. A plea agreement would make them look like they did their job, plus there will be no messy testimony in court regarding how the Phoenix ATF and the Department of Justice enabled the gun trade between straw purchasers and the cartels and contributed to the death of Brian Terry.

However, the bottom line for the government may not be how much time Manuel Osorio-Arellanes spends in jail, but whether members of the ATF, ICE, and Eric Holder's Department of Justice will be joining him.

We Are Looking at You!

On May 3, 2011, three days before the indictment against Manuel Osorio-Arellanes was unsealed, Eric Holder sat before the House Judiciary Committee. While it's likely Osorio- Arellanes

Attorney General Eric Holder.
Department of Justice Photo.

isn't going to fry, United States Attorney General Eric Holder was in the hot seat. Eric Holder was testifying in front of the House Judiciary Committee, and it was United States Representative Darrell Issa's (Rep., CA) turn to question him.

Issa asked, "When did you first know about the program officially called Fast and Furious?"[27]

"I am not sure about the date, but I probably heard about Fast and Furious over the last few weeks," Holder answered.

(Holder's response could very well be perjury. Senator Charles Grassley (Rep., IA.) stated in a Chicago radio interview, "But I'm kind of flabbergasted by him saying to the House that he really didn't know about this until just lately because on January 31, I personally handed him a letter so that he would know about my investigation and know about this gunrunner situation, but they don't seem to be willing to own up to it."][28]

"The president said on March 22, you didn't authorize it," noted Issa. "Did the deputy attorney general authorize it?"

Holder answered, "My guess is no. I think Mr. Cole was not in the department at the time that operation started."

"But he's been aware of it much longer," said Issa.

"Much longer?" asked Holder.

"Yes, since you have only been aware of it a few weeks. How about the head of the Criminal Division, Lanny Breuer? Did he authorize it?"

(Breuer approved an authorization for a wiretap application concerning Fast and Furious on March 10, 2010.)[29]

Holder answered, "I'm not sure whether Mr. Breuer authorized it. You have to understand the way in which the Department operates. Although there are ... there are operations, this one has gotten a great deal of publicity—"

An angry Darrell Issa interrupted, "Yeah, there are two dead Americans because of this failed and reckless program. I would say it hasn't gotten enough attention, has it, Mr. Attorney General?"

The attorney general looked for protection and responded, "Not neces ... I mean there's an investigation that is underway." He added, "We have cases that will go to trial in June of this year ..."

The two men sparred back and forth and then things heated up.

"Mr. Attorney General, isn't it true that those cases that will go to trial in June are just a bunch of meth addicts that did the buying? You do not have what the program was supposed to produce. You do not have the kingpins; you don't have the places where they went. What you have are people you already had on videotape many months before indictments were brought. Isn't this true?" asked Issa.

"There are cases that are important that we are trying to bring, that we want to try successfully, and they are part of a scheme. They are part of a scheme ..." Holder answered.

Issa read a note from James Cole, an assistant attorney general, that said in part, "If we have knowledge of guns about to cross the border, we must take immediate action to stop the firearms from crossing the border." Issa paused and asked, "That's your policy today?"

"That is our policy. That is certainly the policy I've tried to impose—"

Issa interrupted. "Isn't Fast and Furious inconsistent with that policy?"

"Well, that's one of the questions we will have to see. Whether or not Fast and Furious was conducted in a way which was consistent with what Jim wrote there and what I've said today."

The congressman announced, "We are not looking at the straw buyers. Mr. Attorney General, we are looking at you. We are looking at you and your key people who knew or should have known about this and whether or not your judgment was consistent with good practices. Or if the Justice Department is basically guilty of allowing weapons to kill Americans and Mexicans."

Holder was not happy. "I take great exception to what you said," he responded. "The notion that somehow or other this Justice Department is responsible for those deaths you mentioned—that assertion is offensive."

Issa retorted, "What if it's accurate, Mr. Attorney General?"

Later, in a curiously timed statement to reporters, Attorney General Holder again asserted that neither he nor senior members of the DOJ approved of Fast and Furious. "The notion that somehow or other that this thing reaches into the upper levels of the Justice Department is something that, at this point, I don't think is supported by the facts."[30]

The Scandal of the Missing Gun

The murder of Brian Terry resulted in three cover-ups. The first concerned the flawed rules of engagement the night of the shooting that lead to a Border Patrol agent in Peck Canyon firing two beanbag rounds against cartel members armed with AK-47s.

Second was the frantic scramble of the ATF and ICE to cover up their Fast and Furious operation, which helped thousands of guns cross into Mexico and arm the cartels. It was such an obviously enormous blunder that the third event almost went unnoticed.

There had been considerable talk about the third gun recovered at the murder scene where Brian Terry was shot. Brian's BORTAC team members spoke about it at his funeral, and officials talked about it, as did members of the Border Patrol union. It is clear the SKS assault rifle allegedly recovered was not a Fast and Furious weapon. Apparently a third gun from the murder scene was traced.[31]

There is evidence the gun was bought from a Texas gun store and may have been linked to a government informant. An informant characterized as a "stone-cold-killer."[32]

It is further charged that the "Stone-Cold-Killer was given $70,000 of seed money. Apparently this money was supposed to be given to Uriel Patino (the roommate of Jaime Avila, who bought the AK-47s found at the Brian Terry murder scene) to finance the purchase of weapons. The day Avila purchased the infamous two AK-47s, Patino was waiting for him in his car.[33]

If neither of the AK-47s found at the Peck Canyon murder scene are responsible for the murder of Brian Terry (and the ATF claims they are not the murder weapons), then it may well be that the informant's SKS assault rifle was the weapon that killed Brian Terry.

It presents the possibility that the killer of Brian Terry may have been a paid government informant. This gives some credence to an early rumor that Brian was shot by so-called "unfriendly friendly fire." It is also interesting to note that there is a widespread belief among many in the Border Patrol that a dirty agent killed Brian Terry.[34] This may just be an unbelievable, ridiculous rumor. However, with Fast and Furious, unbelievable, ridiculous rumors keep coming true.

The Importance of the Brian Terry Murder

There has been a trail of evidence that something is structurally, fundamentally wrong as regards the open border and the government's actions related to it. The stories of ranchers, the death of rancher Rob Krentz, the statements of law enforcement personnel, and even the testimony of cartel people give validity to this premise. Behind the policy of open borders is something profoundly dangerous.

The murder of Brian Terry exposed an incredible and complex web of government malfeasance. Wrongdoing, which was previously displayed in such small bits and pieces, could no longer be ignored. The events surrounding the murder were simply so extreme no agenda could hide it. In one event the government was exposed as an agenda-driven political machine and the bureaucrats were along for the ride.

The circumstances and cover-ups resulting from Brian Terry's murder were so outrageous, some people stepped forward, including the ATF whistleblowers, Senator Grassley, and United States Representative Issa. And foremost among these has been Carolyn Terry and her unrelenting quest to find out the truth behind the murder of her stepson.

The End Justifies the Means

According to many, the ATF was willing to break the law in order to attain an end. The ringleaders of Fast and Furious claimed they were after the cartel kingpins of gunrunning. Others charge that the ATF may have been trying to curry favor with an administration intent on pursuing stricter gun control laws.

It simply doesn't matter which of these agendas were true. The issue is that a human life, be it Brian Terry's or a Mexican citizen's, is far more important than agendas.

The specter of a government providing seed money to an operation such as Fast and Furious is deeply troubling. The idea a paid informant may have killed Brian Terry or paid for the weapons is a national scandal.

The more pressing issue is that the government actions described in this book are not aberrations. Rather they are the result of a government that is ready to regulate everyone else, but not itself. For example, there is a strong case to be made that the only people who need more stringent gun control laws are those employed within the ATF.

The Keystone

The open border is a political choice that results from catering to special interest groups. It is the keystone that locks many issues together, among them drugs, immigration, gunrunning, money laundering, sanctuary cities, and terrorism. Without open borders all of the connected issues would shrink to much more manageable proportions. It is why many people advocate that the border must be secured before the other issues *can* be solved.

It is important to remember that the result of a policy or activity is usually reflective of intent. The result should be judged and not the rhetoric. For example:

1. The border is open and unsecured because the government and some politicians want it that way.
2. A result of an open border is that there is an almost unlimited supply of drugs coming into America.
3. A result of an open border is that we are vulnerable to terrorists crossing the border.
4. Politicians sometimes profit from failure. The failure to secure the border is an example. Big money can be made off failure. A case in point is the high-tech fence that was finally put to death by Secretary Napolitano. On its long trip to the dustbin of history, hundreds of millions of dollars were spent (some say plundered). Of special interest is the theory that is not without some validity, that the high-tech fence was sabotaged.

The items above are generally related to corruption of one form or another. And this is all leading to the process that made the death of Brian Terry inevitable. The last letter in the Greek alphabet, omega, best describes it.

Omega

It is common for persons with boots on the ground to think of confrontations or conflicts as straight-line encounters. For example, Brian Terry and his team were sent into the Peck Canyon area supposedly to block and stop a load of drugs that had crossed earlier that evening into the United States. It was apparently a simple straight-line event—block, stop, and arrest.

However, Brian Terry died because he and his team were actually involved in an omega- shaped event. Imagine Terry and his team at the opening of an omega shape.

An Omega symbol

They are facing out, expecting to encounter the bad guys coming from the south. But they are doomed, because behind them are the events that will in fact dictate the outcome of the night's encounter.

Along the legs of the omega behind them are the bad decisions that would kill Brian Terry:

1. The team is equipped with beanbag rounds. In one of the most dangerous areas of the United States the unit is supplied with nonlethal rounds that, if fired first, might cause a deadly response. Their superiors should never have permitted the unit to take nonlethal rounds into that area.
2. Their unit is equipped with two shotguns, one rifle, and four pistols. They have been ordered into an area where they will be outgunned.
3. There have been no plans made for emergency evacuations in case of a violent encounter and injuries.

4. The decision has been made to insert a four-man team, when it is known that a drug escort squad with up to eight men armed with AK-47s crossed the border south of them earlier and may be encountered.

5. The operation was given thumbs-up by a supervisor who was not familiar with the situation—or worse, was aware of the danger.

6. Air reconnaissance is not coordinated with the BORTAC team, although an air unit sees thirty to forty persons in the area behind and to the east of the team's location.

7. The guns the Mexican escort unit is armed with were supplied with the help of the ATF and the United States Attorney's Office for Arizona.

8. A paid government informant may have paid for the weapon that will kill Brian Terry.

9. A stone-cold-killer informant may be among the smugglers Brian Terry will encounter in Peck Canyon.

10. In reality, there is little commitment by superiors to a successful outcome, despite Brian and his team being very motivated.

Illustrating the other leg of the omega shape perfectly, the armed (courtesy of Fast and Furious) Mexican squad comes up on the BORTAC unit out of the east and from behind. A beanbag (changed to two in a later FBI report) round is fired and a firefight erupts. Brian Terry is shot from behind.

Most encounters involved with government corruption or the cartels are omega events, not straight-line engagements. (Chapo Guzman's turning Juarez into a killing field is an omega event.)

An omega event can be either tactical or strategic in nature. Typically an individual positioned in front of the legs of an omega-shaped event assumes they are involved in a straight-line encounter. (Hence, Guzman's motivation for turning Juarez into a killing zone is assumed to be for control of a drug corridor, when his objectives are much more complex.)

The contractor who explained this process maintains that not knowing the difference between a straight-line encounter and an omega encounter is like playing a football game without a playbook. Omega events can occur with something as simple as a phone call, or as complex as Operation Fast and Furious.

That's what happened to Brian Terry on December 14, 2010.

Endnotes

1. Carolyn Terry, interview, May 4, 2011.

2. Carolyn Terry, interview, May 4, 2011.

3. Carolyn Terry, interview, May 4, 2011.

4. Carolyn Terry, interview, May 4, 2011.

5. Carolyn Terry, interview, May 4, 2011.

6. "Exclusive: Third Gun Linked to 'Fast and Furious' Identified at Border Agent's Murder Scene," *FOX News*, September 9, 2011, http://www.foxnews.com/politics/2011/09/09/exclusive-third-gun-linked-to-fast-and-furious-identified-at-border-agents/.

7. Carolyn Terry, interview, May 4, 2011.

8. Carolyn Terry, interview, May 6, 2011.

9. Carolyn Terry, interview, May 6, 2011.

10. Carolyn Terry, interview, May 6, 2011.

11. Briefing Paper, Phoenix Field Division, Phoenix Group VII (Gunrunner/Strike force), January 8, 2010.

12. Carolyn Terry, interview, May 4, 2011.

13. Carolyn Terry, interview, May 6, 2011.

14. Carolyn Terry, interview, May 6, 2011.

15. Carolyn Terry, interview, May 6, 2011.

16. "Manuel Osorio-Arellanes Charged for the Murder of Border Patrol Agent Brian Terry in Arizona," news release, United States Attorney's Office, District of Arizona, May 6, 2011, http://www.justice.

gov/usao/az/press _releases/2011/PR_05062011_Osorio_Arellanes.
html.

17. United States of America v. Manuel Osorio Arellanes, aka Manual
Arellanes, aka "Paye." et.al. CR-11-0150-TUC-DCB-JCG, United
States District Court, District of Arizona.

18. Bill Breen, interview, May 9, 2011.

19. Bill Breen, interview, May 9, 2011.

20. Carolyn Terry, interview, February 3, 2012.

21. Carolyn Terry, interview, February 3, 2012.

22. Carolyn Terry, interview, February 3, 2012.

23. Carolyn Terry, interview, February 3, 2012.

24. Carolyn Terry, interview, February 3, 2012.

25. Protected Source, 2011.

26. House Judiciary Hearing, May 3, 2011.

27. Senator Charles Grassley, interview by Don Wade & Roma, WLS
Radio, May 5, 2011.

28. Authorization for Interception Order Application, Memorandum,
U.S. Department of Justice, March 10, 2010.

29. Jeremy Pelofsky, "Attorney General Eric Holder seeks distance
from gun sting," Reuters, September 7, 2011, http://www.
reuters.com/article/2011/09/07/us-usa-mexico-guns-idUS-
TRE7867LD20110907.

30. "Exclusive: Third Gun Linked to 'Fast and Furious.'"

31. "Exclusive: Third Gun Linked to 'Fast and Furious.'"

32. "Exclusive: Third Gun Linked to 'Fast and Furious.'"

33. Border Patrol manager, 2011.

Chapter Twenty

Agendas and Border Security

"Maybe they'll need a moat. Maybe they want alligators in the moat!"

President Barack Obama, 2011

ON MAY 10TH, 2011 President Obama and Homeland Security Secretary Janet Napolitano traveled to El Paso to promote his comprehensive immigration reform agenda. An agenda that apparently is a litmus test that all of his appointees must learn to repeat in their sleep before being appointed. Usually, whenever a border security issue stumps an administration official they fall back to the tried and tested immigration reform speech—which is meaningless, but distracts the listener from the life-and-death issue of border security.

It disguises the fact that this administration is not any more interested in securing the border than were previous administrations. This was reinforced in El Paso when President Obama wheeled out some of Janet Napolitano's "goalpost" rhetoric.

President Obama lamented, "But even though we've answered these concerns, I suspect there are still going to be some who are trying to move the goalposts on us one more time. You know, they said we needed to triple the border patrol. Well, now they're going to say we need to quadruple the border patrol. Or they'll want a higher fence."[1]

It was the president's next lines that said it all. President Obama joked, "Maybe they'll need a moat. Maybe they want alligators in the moat!"[2]

To millions of Americans border security is not a joke. To Americans that are victimized, injured, or have had relatives and loved ones killed because of open borders, President Obama's comment is at best insensitive. To Sue Krentz a moat and an alligator is no joke—her husband Rob Krentz is still dead, killed by a drug smuggler and an open border.

To the family of BORTAC agent Brian Terry, the comment is cruel and uncaring. Brian Terry was killed by a "patrolling" squad of Mexican drug escorts armed with AK-47s that had crossed an open border and had penetrated deep into America. Open borders are no joke to the families of the dead. The joke apparently confirmed a theme running through most of the interviews that make up this volume: Most politicians simply don't care.

Evidently from the president's lofty perch the present level of border security is OK for average Americans. If it is truly so great then perhaps it would be a satisfactory standard of security for American airports. The GAO in a 2011 report indicated that the Border Patrol had achieved "varying degrees of operational control for 873 of the nearly 2,000 southwest border miles."[3] This means 44 percent of the southern border is under some degree of "operational control." Would it be satisfactory from a security point of view if only 44 percent of the airports were regulating who was getting on planes and what they were carrying?

And more to the point, would the president like a 44 percent "operational control" standard for security used at the White House? What 44 percent of the grounds would he like fenced? What 44 percent of the grounds would he like "secured?" Perhaps he would feel more secure for himself and his family if he put Secretary Napolitano in charge. Perhaps at some point the president would call for a quadrupling of his guard to secure the White House grounds and some politician could ridicule him while pandering to their base.

The El Paso appearance of President Obama was a revelatory performance. In that moment the president defined why the border is not secure. He has no commitment to secure it. It's nowhere on his agenda. But again, he is not unique. Few presidents before him have cared about securing the border either.

The bottom line is, an American citizen has as much right to be secure in their ranch house on Geronimo Trail as the president does in the White House on Pennsylvania Avenue.

The Politics of Failure

Operating between the corruption, greed, and narcissism of two governments, cartels are allowed to run wild and have their way with the citizens of the United States and Mexico. Both the American and Mexican governments appear blind to their primary responsibility, the protection of the needs and rights of their own citizens.

It is crucial to understand that failure within the government has become institutionalized. It is as if the federal government has immunized itself against success. This also has been a theme throughout this book—the federal government and most politicians have a vested interest in failure and how to pitch the failure to gain more power and money. Failures make it appear as if the government is the only hope to undo insolvable problems, which ironically it either has created or perpetuates. The border is not an exception to the rule. There is simply too much money, power, and potential power at stake for many politicians to want to do differently.

However, in addition to millions of citizens, there are thousands of state and local law enforcement personnel and federal employees who truly would like to see our disastrous border policy reversed. Some of these people have had intimate contact with the border; they have put their lives on the line and continue to do so every day and night.

The failure of America's war on drugs or its attempt to secure the border is not the fault of the vast majority of hardworking Border Patrol agents, DEA agents, ICE agents, FBI agents, or even ATF agents. They do the best they can, but they are handcuffed by political agendas. And the benchmarks set by these political agendas determine whether individuals have a future within those organizations. Promotions are not based on achieving law enforcement goals, but political nonperformance criteria. It is simply a political system that thrives on failure and the public's capitulation of its ideals to that failure.

Avoiding Failure

It is sometimes claimed by politicians that some issues are too complex to solve. For example, the border is too long to secure. But not everyone believes failure and capitulation is the only outcome of complexity.

In August of 1990, former secretary of the Treasury and former secretary of state George Shultz was retired and writing his memoirs. He also was on the board of directors for Chevron and a close friend of the chairmen of the board of the oil giant. Shultz had agreed to attend a management development course that was being conducted at the Tiburon Lodge for twelve Chevron managers from around the world.

One of the participants asked Shultz how he "could possibly keep track of all the things in the world from a management standpoint, a leadership standpoint, and a political standpoint?" The manager went on to note, "It's difficult to coordinate all the things we need to do, let alone tackle huge problems."

Shultz answered, "That's an important question and I use a fairly simple methodology." The former secretary of state explained, "You start off with no more than three things around a particular subject that need to be accomplished." These are overall, guiding principles regarding a subject.

He continued, "All the things that seem to come up and appear to be confusing are put up against the three guiding principles you have established. If they don't fit or contribute, you toss them out." Many of the attendees were having some difficulty understanding how Shultz's methodology worked in the real world. Then the phone rang. It was President George H. W. Bush. Saddam Hussein had invaded Kuwait. The president wanted advice.

Shultz left and talked to the president for an hour. When he came back, everyone wanted to know what they had talked about. Shultz responded, "George just wanted to know what I thought and to discuss the matter [of the invasion]." He paused and added, "It's a good way to explain what I was trying to tell you before.

"I told him that there were three things that he needed to consider in this situation. First of all, Saddam Hussein cannot be allowed to succeed. The invasion of Kuwait cannot stand. Second, Saddam must be punished for even trying something like this. Third, whatever results from this situation cannot interfere with the progress we have made in the world. The fall of the Berlin Wall and the dissolution of the Soviet Empire and the good things that are happening in the world because of it."

Shultz continued, "Those are the three things. Everything else does not count."

Shultz observed there was always a temptation to compromise those principles or to add guidelines, to go to four, five, or six. "You must have three core principles when dealing with a huge issue or you get bogged down and confused with your primary goal, and you will fail. You must establish higher-level principals when talking about enormous issues."

While this approach is not new, what is extremely important is the way Secretary of State Shultz implemented it. He did not deviate from the three basic principles that were established as guidelines and he pursued them with an uncommon tenacity. The approach outlined by Shultz rarely failed because of this.

A Framework for America

The failure of American border policy and its effect on our country can be "fixed" using George Shultz's methodology. For example, the guiding principles to take into consideration when addressing the open border disaster are:

1. The law must be obeyed and enforced. There are too many unintended consequences that arise from disobeying a law that isn't politically correct or that a strong lobby has come out against. If you can't change the law, obey and enforce the existing law without exception.

2. The dignity of all people must be respected, and everyone must be treated with compassion. A lack of respect for the law by the federal government, opportunistic politicians, drug smugglers, and illegal immigrants has created an environment where the dignity of all people suffers. United States citizens are not treated with dignity, nor are the illegal immigrants. There is little dignity in situations where people are actively involved in human trafficking, drug smuggling, identity theft, etc.

3. The economic and physical security of individual American citizens and the United States as a whole must be protected.

It will be noted that for none of the guiding principles is there a political question. It is hard to argue that enforcing laws, respecting the dignity of people and treating them with compassion, or protecting our national security are political issues.

Any agendas, suggested solutions, or political questions need to be judged against the three principles outlined above. If they conflict with any of the three guidelines, they are irrelevant to the overarching problem of fixing our shattered border policy. This includes the debates over the legalization of drugs, comprehensive immigration reform, ethnic studies, and sanctuary cities. If any of these matters aren't complementary to the three principles, they should be discarded.

The three principles work in both a macro and micro way. For example, do the current rules of engagement of BORTAC units meet the standard set by the three principles? Does the Border Patrol's falsification of reports measure up to the above guidelines? Does the action that the ATF took in supplying thousands of guns to killers in Mexico meet the standards set by the three principles? Obviously, if the standards set by George Shultz's framework had been in place, there would have never been a program called Fast and Furious, and Border Patrol agent Brian Terry might be alive.

The power of Shultz's methodology is that it strips away the roadblocks to addressing nonpolitical issues that have been politicized in order to prevent concrete solutions. In short, it provides a methodology that would permit us to secure the border without fear or favor and with compassion.

Unfortunately, the Shultz methodology requires men and women of good will who actually want to secure our border. And that depends on who can you trust.

Endnotes

1. "Texas Attorney General: Pres. Obama 'Demagoguing' the Border Security-Illegal Immigration Issue," *On the Record with Greta Van Susteren*, May 10, 2011.

2. "Texas Attorney General: Pres. Obama 'Demagoguing.'"

3. GAO Report, *Preliminary Observations on Border Control Measures for the Southwest Border*, February 15, 2011.

Chapter Twenty-One

A Broken Trust

"I'm not a politician ... I'll tell you that you are absolutely correct. We have not made a dent in the criminal organizations coming across the border with drugs."

Quote attributed to Richard Barlow,
Border Patrol Chief of the Tucson Sector, 2012.

THE SOLUTION PROPOSED IN the preceding chapter rests on an underlying premise. Namely, that people of good will can work together to secure the border. The problem is that in the year 2012, most of those who possess the influence to secure the border have personal agendas that prevent them from doing so.

The border situation has evolved during the last two decades, but one truth remains—the border to all intents and purposes is still open. Illegal immigration ebbs and flows. Today it is suppressed not by Homeland Security (as if it ever was), but by a depressed American economy. In many ways the flood of illegal immigrants disguised and distracted from two fundamentally more serious border problems. Those issues are drug smuggling and the threat of terrorism.

A final look at the border explains the current situation. It illustrates the intent, motives, and pettiness of the federal government. It demonstrates where we are today. It begins with a dead calf and rancher Ed Ashurst.

Asking Little, Getting Less

In the process of helping the Border Patrol, ranchers put up with a lot. As mentioned earlier, Ed Ashurst ranches the Mallet spread. It is located in Cochise County, some twenty miles north of the border. Ashurst has permitted Border Patrol access to the ranch like many other border ranchers. He has allowed the placement of an observation post on the property. He has supplied information and helped the Border Patrol find border crossers and smugglers.

Ashurst asks little in return for his help. He asks the Border Patrol not to lock him out of his pastures, to stay on the ranch roads, and minimize damage to his pastures—in short, to respect his livelihood. All too often, his wishes are overlooked.

Ashurst and many other ranchers are repeatedly "accidentally" locked out of their pastures by the dual use of Border Patrol locks.[1] This is of particular annoyance to Ashurst. It is a situation caused because there is little cooperation between the Border Patrol camp four miles north of him and the Border Patrol Stations at Lordsburg and Douglas. Agents are constantly locking each other out as well as Ashurst.[2]

From the point of view of many ranchers, some Border Patrol agents appear to have little respect for ranchers and how hard it is to make a living from the land. This impression often results not because of the agents, but because of Border Patrol leadership and their lack of effort to resolve issues before they become serious.

Lock Out

In August of 2011 a Border Patrol agent speeding on one of the Mallet Ranch roads hit and killed a calf. The agent tried to do the right thing and notified Ashurst. Together they filled out a report and submitted it to the Border Patrol for compensation in the amount of $750. Two Border Patrol supervisors helped and also signed the request. Ashurst waited as the request for payment went through the bureaucracy.[3] By January of 2012 there was still no payment.

In February the Border Patrol again "accidentally" locked him out of areas of the Mallet Ranch. In the first week of February, Ashurst was informed the claim for the calf would not be paid. The reason given was, "There is no evidence of negligence by the Border Patrol." It was the straw that broke the camel's back. Ashurst collected the Border Patrol locks that were on the ranch gates. He called the Border Patrol and told them to "Come and get your locks."[4]

Three Border Patrol agents came to the ranch to discuss the situation. Among those was a Border Community Liaison (BCL) officer. Ashurst told them that they would be allowed access to the ranch if they promised to keep their ATVs away, stay on the roads with their vehicles, and pay for the calf.[5]

Ashurst explained to the agents, "You will not come on this property until you have paid for the calf. We do not have a relationship. There's no trust between us and I am tired of being lied to. If the Border Patrol pays for the calf perhaps we can start a dialogue."

The BCL officer asked if Ashurst attended rancher/Border Patrol meetings. Ashurst replied, "I used to, but got tired of nothing ever being done."

The BCL officer sarcastically said, "Well with the million dollar personality you got, no telling how much good you could do." The man tossed the locks down and the meeting ended.[6]

Ashurst attached the locks to a fence by the ranch headquarters for the Border Patrol to pick up. The next day the BCL officer sent an insulting email about Ashurst to a neighbor of the rancher.[7] Ashurst reflects, "I couldn't believe how petty and nonprofessional the guy was."

An Act of Congress

Things were going from bad to worse. An executive with the Arizona Cattle Growers Association learned that the Border Patrol was drafting a letter in their legal department to send to Ashurst.[8] It was rumored to include a threat of prosecution and state that according to statutory authority, Border Patrol agents may access private lands for the purpose of patrolling within twenty-five miles from the international border. The Arizona Cattle Growers advised authorities that it would be a big mistake to send the letter. The Border Patrol was facing an open split with the ranchers.

Cooler heads at the Border Patrol decided it might be best to have a meeting between area ranchers and patrol officials. An emergency meeting was set up in fewer than four days. On February 24, 2012, a dozen or more ranchers met with fifteen or more Border Patrol officials at the Tucson Sector Border Patrol Headquarters on the Davis-Monthan Air Force Base.[9]

Security was heavy. The ranchers drove their pickups through gates covered with barbed wire and parked. Ashurst was pulling a cattle trailer and parked in a grassy area. After parking they walked down a long path bordered on both sides by high fences and entered a waiting area. They were then permitted into a conference room. No one offered them coffee or water. More than one rancher felt it was a very intimidating reception.

The Border Patrol representatives entered the conference room in their dress uniforms and armed—all spit and polish. The ranchers who had taken time off from work were dressed in jeans and boots.[10] Among those present for the Border Patrol were:

> » Richard Barlow, Tucson Sector Chief
> » Lloyd Easterling, ACPA
> » Carol Blessey, OCC (office of Chief Counsel)
> » Elaine O'Hara, OCC
> » Michael Hyatt, Agent in Charge—Sonoita
> » Humberto De la Cruz, Agent in Charge—Naco
> » Craig Weinbrenner, Agent in Charge—Willcox
> » Leslie Lawson, Agent in Charge—Nogales
> » Jose Montano, Acting Agent in Charge—Douglas

As a veteran observer of the Border Patrol has noted, one of the Border Patrol hierarchy's prime concerns is their image. For whatever reason, no reporters were allowed into the meeting.

Ashurst sat at a large square conference table with the Border Patrol officials. Behind the rancher sat some of his neighbors.[11] The meeting began with a lengthy statement from the legal counsel representing the Border Patrol, Carol Blessey.

Blessey stated the legal position of the Border Patrol in regards to the nonpayment of Ashurst's claim for the calf killed by an agent. According to the legal department in Indianapolis there could be no payment because negligence could not be proved.[12] Discontent grew among the ranchers present. There was some uncomfortable laughter and muttered comments. The lawyer repeatedly indicated that there was no way to interpret the law that would permit the Border Patrol to pay for the calf.

Sensing the growing division between the Border Patrol and ranchers, Tucson Sector Chief Richard Barlow looked for compromise. Barlow stated he had read the law and in his opinion he could authorize payment to Ashurst. The lawyer said that was not true.

According to the lawyer it was a question of negligence. Unless negligence could be proven on the part of the Border Patrol there could be no payment. There were more murmurs among the ranchers. A rancher wondered aloud if the calf was negligent for allowing itself to be struck by the Border Patrol vehicle.

Barlow asked, "Is there any way Mr. Ashurst can be paid?" The lawyer responded the law would have to be changed and that would "literally take an act of Congress."[13]

The lawyer attempted to express sympathy for Ashurst's plight and added that she would like to pay for the rancher's "pet cow" but legally couldn't.[14] At this point one rancher thought to himself that the lawyer should be tossed out a window, but considered it a waste of time since they were on the first floor. Another rancher volunteered that his family had ranched for four generations and neither they nor a hired hand had ever run over a cow.

Rancher Larry Dempster observed the proceedings and reflected, "She doesn't have any idea how silly she sounds to a bunch of hard-working ranchers."[15]

A Question of Trust

Tucson Sector Chief Barlow knew this was about more than a calf. The Border Patrol officials listened as ranchers took the floor and spoke.

Ashurst spoke forcefully about his years of experience and difficulties with smugglers, cross border criminals, illegal immigrants, and an ineffective Border Patrol that was of little help. He spoke of agents who moved from one area to another and never were anywhere long enough to learn where smugglers came through or where illegal immigrants laid up.

"I thought long and hard before locking the Border Patrol out," noted Ashurst. "But after thinking about it, I concluded that I wasn't giving anything up. In fact, this way you don't hurt my livelihood."

He observed, "Every rancher in this room knows more about the border than any of you in uniform. You would think we'd be the best friends you got, instead all you've done is made us hate you.[16]

"You like to look busy, but you accomplish nothing except make sure the numbers are skewed to the advantage of the politicians."

Ashurst continued, "I've been down Black Draw three times and never saw a Border Patrol agent. I've been on the border and could see fifteen miles, but I never saw a single Border Patrol agent. Yet, you are all over the ranch [twenty miles north of the border].[17]

Pointing to each of the Border Patrol officials at the table Ashurst added, "You guys may be able to force your way back on the ranch, but I'll treat you like a skunk in a chicken house. We have no relationship with you guys and it's not our fault. You've broken the trust and it's up to you to fix it." Ashurst then took a copy of the critical email sent to a neighbor by the BCL officer and gave it to Sector Chief Barlow. "Keep this guy away from me."[18]

Another rancher said he was rescinding his permission for the Border Patrol to have its camp on his ranch. He put the contract on the conference table and pronounced it "null and void." He then left, declaring he had to get back to work.

Rancher John Ladd, whose ranch stretches for ten and a half miles along the border, observed that all of the Border Patrol personnel present were being well paid, but the meeting was costing ranchers. He also recalled when David Aguilar (now replacing Alan Bersin as commissioner of Customs and Border Protection) was Tucson Sector chief. "He's a politician. He's the problem with the Border Patrol and he wrote the manual for the Border Patrol [tactics]."[19]

Veteran rancher Ruth Evelyn Cowan spoke. Cowan, a charismatic force, minced no words. "Well, here we are again. We stated a lot of this stuff in the early '90s and it's a lot of the same faces from the ranchers' side, but it's the same bullshit from the Border Patrol."[20] Cowan does not allow the Border Patrol on her property.

The Truth

Tucson Sector Chief Barlow was candid. "This is very clear to me. We have done a very poor job. The trust is broken and it's not your fault. It's ours. And I'm not asking you to trust us again. We'll have to earn it. I will see that it is done." He turned to his station chiefs. "I'm going to hold each one of you responsible for relations with ranchers and landowners. You are responsible for fixing this. We broke it."[21]

Ashurst noted, "There's more dope and more criminals coming across the border than ever before and it's more dangerous than ever.

I've talked to an intelligence agent who said it was going to get considerably worse before it gets better."[22]

Chief Barlow responded, "You know there aren't as many people coming across the border looking for jobs. That's pretty well dried up. Today it is about smuggling."

Looking at Ashurst he added, "I'm not a politician. I am not going to give you political talk. I'll tell you that you are absolutely correct. We have not made a dent in the criminal organizations coming across the border with drugs."

Actions and Words

In the week following the meeting at the Tucson Border Patrol Sector Headquarters there were several developments. First, a letter was sent indicating "new evidence" had been uncovered and the calf killed on the Mallet ranch would be paid for. The bureaucracy had found a way through the legal morass. Either that or, as rancher Dempster commented, "I guess Congress acted quickly."[23]

More importantly, however, smugglers were having fewer problems bringing drugs across the border than the border patrol was having with Ashurst's claim. During the same week at least two heavy loads of dope came over one of the most "secure" ranches on the border during daylight hours—the ranch of John Ladd.

Ladd provides the Border Patrol access to more than nine thousand acres of his ranch land along the international border. He can see the Naco Border Patrol Station from his ranch headquarters. There are over 250 sensors on the ranch. In addition, there are cameras on eighty-five-foot tall towers and four miles of lights stretching beside the border fence. He notes dryly that the lights are not a big help except to the smugglers. "They help the smugglers see what they're doing at night and tend to blind the infrared cameras."[24]

One of the loads that crossed the Ladd ranch within the week after the big meeting at the Tucson Sector Headquarters was spotted by an off-duty Border Patrol agent just before dark. It consisted of a couple of trucks. The agent called the Naco Station for help, but no one responded. The load of dope got away.

In the second instance a Border Patrol agent from the horse patrol found a gate that had been removed from one of Ladd's fences, and the tracks of two or three pickups that had passed through headed toward a highway. The agent notified Ladd.

Ladd responded and quickly found where and how the load had crossed the border. A cartel road crew had cut a section of the large mesh border fence, sent three trucks across a vehicle barrier using a ramp, covered the tracks around the entry point, and replaced the fence. In addition the crew cut mesquite trees and filled gullies on Ladd's property to level the makeshift road.[25]

Cartel road crews fill ruts to maintain their smuggling route across the Ladd ranch. This "road" is used regularly to transport trucks of dope north. Photo coutesy of John Ladd.

These experiences are not unusual according to Ladd. "They could shut this down by moving most of the agents to the border and putting them within eyesight of each other, but they don't want to. It would cause incidents and would be bad PR. They don't want to stop the drugs—it's deliberate. It's politics."[26]

Money and Politics

Cochise County sheriff Larry Dever sent an invitation to the Republican candidates running for the 2012 presidential nomination to come to Arizona to learn about the border situation. He recommended that the candidates not talk to politicians. He said, "If you want to know what's happening on the border, talk to ranchers. It's the only way you will really understand what's going on." None took him up on his offer.[27]

John Ladd lays out the fundamental reason the border is not closed: "Drug smuggling is such a huge business, and people that are involved in it even locally have such a big economic and political stake in it, they turn a blind eye."[28]

Few politicians in the last twenty years have wanted to be involved with the border—either Republicans and Democrats. The open borders, illegal immigration, and illegal drug trafficking have such enormous political and economic constituencies that it is political quicksand to address the issues.

Politics is the major reason that the Border Patrol, the DOJ, and Homeland Security are so incredibly successful in their inability to stop drugs and secure the border. They are essential political organizations operating as pseudo-governmental organizations. They are but reflections of their political leadership, which gives credence to the old proverb, "A fish rots from the head down." In the end, this explains why there could be a program as murderous as Fast and Furious.

Again, the open border is essentially a political issue. Critics suggest it is impossible to completely secure the border, but the truth is it's *never* been seriously attempted by our government. Critics believed slavery couldn't be abolished, the Nazis couldn't be defeated, segregation couldn't be overcome and we couldn't go to the moon. But the fundamental event that met those challenges was the political decision to do it. The border can be closed anytime politicians decide it should be closed.

John Ladd remembers when he first met Senator John McCain. "It was after McCain had his cancer surgery. I was showing him around the border. We rode together in a van. He is one of the most personable people I ever met. He has a great sense of humor."

They had a picnic lunch on the ranch. "He made some promises about the border, the Border Patrol, and agreed with me about David Aguilar."

"I saw him a couple of times after that and I said, 'Nothing has changed about the border.' McCain responded, 'Give me some time.'"

Ladd continues, "The last time I saw McCain, was when he was

Senator John McCain. US government photo.

running for president. I told him, 'You know, it's been three years since I met you and nothing has changed on the border. I don't understand with your clout in Washington why nothing has changed.'"

According to Ladd, McCain respond, "Are you a fucking idiot or what?"

Ladd wasn't offended because he knew McCain cussed like a sailor. The rancher answered, "Well, I'm not an idiot."

McCain said, "For Christ sake John, I'm running for president. I can't do anything on the border."[29]

And McCain was probably right, though he still tries. On May 4, 2011 an angry McCain questioned DHS Secretary Napolitano during a Senate hearing. "There's between 100 and 200 spotters sitting on mountains in southern Arizona, inside the borders of the Untied States of America, spotting for drug cartels who then get the drugs up to Phoenix." McCain added, "We're supposed to believe that the administration is serious about securing our borders? Well, I don't think so."

With stunning chutzpah Napolitano denied there were drug spotters sitting on the mountains in Arizona. Her reasoning was she asked the Border Patrol, "Where are the spotters that I keep hearing about? And the answer that I receive is that there are a couple of hundred tops from which a spotter could act, but there are not 200 drug spotters." And so the culture of lies and denial continues.

The moral of the story is, the more the border changes the more it stays the same. In March of 2012 Ed Ashurst had another calf run over by the Border Patrol. The ever-curious Ashurst also bought his own infrared camera and set it up on the north boundary of the Mallet ranch near the Border Patrol camp. On its first night of operation it captured images of smugglers carrying a load of dope north.[30] In late May of 2012 drugs continued to pour across the ranch of John Ladd.

It's 2012, and despite statements from Washington to the contrary, the drugs, criminals, and terrorists continue to come north. But then again, it's an election year and people are running for president.

Endnotes

1. Ed Ashurst, interview, March 3, 2012.

2. Ed Ashurst, interview, March 3, 2012.

3. Ed Ashurst, interview, March 3, 2012.

4. Ed Ashurst, interview, March 3, 2012.

5. Ed Ashurst, interview, March 3, 2012.

6. Ed Ashurst, interview, March 3, 2012.

7. Ed Ashurst, interview, March 3, 2012.

8. John Ladd, interview, March 7, 2012.

9. Larry Dempster, interview, February 24, 2012.

10. Larry Dempster, interview.

11. Larry Dempster, interview.

12. Larry Dempster, interview.

13. Larry Dempster, interview.

14. Ed Ashurst, interview, March 3, 2012.

15. Larry Dempster, interview.

16. Ed Ashurst, interview, March 3, 2012.

17. Ed Ashurst, interview, March 3, 2012.

18. Ed Ashurst, interview, March 3, 2012.

19. John Ladd, interview, March 7, 2012.

20. John Ladd, interview.

21. Larry Dempster, interview.

22. Ed Ashurst, interview, March 3, 2012.

23. Larry Dempster, interview.

24. John Ladd, interview.

25. John Ladd, interview.

26. John Ladd, interview.

27. Sheriff Larry Dever, interview, March 18, 2012

28. John Ladd, interview.

29. John Ladd, interview.

CPSIA information can be obtained at www.ICGtesting.com
Printed in the USA
BVOW021727180712

295469BV00002B/1/P